THE MINNESOTA

LIBRARY

ON AMERICAN WRITERS

LEONARD UNGER

AND GEORGE T. WRIGHT,

EDITORS

THE SEVEN *essays which appear in this book were first published separately in the series of University of Minnesota Pamphlets on American Writers and, together with the other pamphlets in the series, are intended as introductions to authors who have helped to shape American culture over the years of our colonial and national existence. The editors of the pamphlet series have been Richard Foster, William Van O'Connor, Allen Tate, Leonard Unger, Robert Penn Warren, and George T. Wright. Many pamphlets, in addition to the seven represented here, are available from the University of Minnesota Press.*

SEVEN AMERICAN STYLISTS

from Poe to Mailer: An Introduction

Edited by GEORGE T. WRIGHT

UNIVERSITY OF MINNESOTA

PRESS • MINNEAPOLIS

Library of Congress Catalog Card Number: 72-95441

ISBN 0-8166-0677-3

Permission to quote excerpts from *Poems* by George
Santayana (copyright 1923) was granted by the publisher, Charles Scribner's Sons. Permission to quote lines
from "To an Old Philosopher in Rome" was granted
by Alfred A. Knopf, Inc., and Faber & Faber, publishers of *The Collected Poems of Wallace Stevens* (copyright 1954). Excerpts from *Selected Poems, 1923–1943*
(copyright 1944) by Robert Penn Warren are reprinted
by permission of the William Morris Agency, Inc. Excerpts from *Brother to Dragons* (copyright 1953) by
Robert Penn Warren are reprinted by permission of
Random House, William Morris Agency, Inc., and A.
D. Peters and Company. Excerpts from *Promises: Poems
1954–1956* (© 1957) by Robert Penn Warren are reprinted by permission of Random House and
Eyre & Spottiswoode (Publishers) Ltd.

Contents

SEVEN AMERICAN STYLISTS

FROM POE TO MAILER

◤ GEORGE T. WRIGHT

Introduction

◤ THE seven writers treated in this volume have been
brought together on a principle somewhat different
from that which governs the other collections in this series. All
seven have published poems, but none of them is thought of
primarily as a writer of verse. All of them happen to have written
long narratives, but we do not think of Poe, Santayana, and
Gertrude Stein as novelists, nor of the latter two as essentially
writers of fiction. Santayana and Warren may be called men of
letters, but even though the others have all produced works of
various kinds — criticism, autobiography, translations, plays,
opera libretti, political commentary, films — the old-fashioned
term sits uneasily on most of them. As American authors go, they
make an unusually cosmopolitan group, but they belong to different eras and no two of them are associated with the same
literary movement. They seem at first about as miscellaneous a
set of distinguished writers as American literature could provide,
but of all seven at least this can be said: that early in any discussion of their work we must talk of style.

If they have this in common, they may have more, and it may

3

tell us something about American literature, or about American stylists, to see what else is shared by authors so diverse as these. They are certainly various enough. Poe, of an earlier period than the others, was dead before the rest were born; Mailer is young enough to be the grandson of Crane or Santayana or Gertrude Stein. The group of seven includes a Spaniard, a Russian, two Jews, and wanderers from Kentucky, New Jersey, Virginia. The father of one was assassinated; one's mother was president of the local WCTU; one has run for mayor of the city of New York. We can find in their number an orphan, an émigré, an Agrarian, a medical student, an aeronautical engineer, a philosopher, and the "husband" of a former brothel-keeper. Three of them (Santayana, Stein, Nabokov) spent most of their lives in Europe; Santayana and Stein died there; so did Stephen Crane. Warren, a southerner, has left the land he writes about; Mailer, a Jew from Brooklyn, keeps voyaging in search of America. By history or intellect, neurosis or circumstance, all have been estranged from at least one country, region, or heritage. Poe alone failed to travel much, not surely by choice, but his tales and poems deny his location, refuse recognizable geographical setting. In one way or another, all these writers have been uprooted; all have lived in a condition of cultural anxiety, have felt the claims of competing cultural or social traditions; all are concerned with questions of personal identity; they interpret the world around them as variously baffling; and they look to style as a resource against what seems to some of them the meaninglessness or the prison of history.

We can hardly read through these seven intelligent and sometimes brilliant essays without noticing that their subjects, for all their diversity, resemble one another in outlook and theme more than we might expect. Searching, all of them, for words with which to say accurately just what happens to anyone in the living of life, these writers, perhaps even more than most American authors, seem very much alone, isolated by their origins or eccentric life-patterns, aloof even from the contemporary literary movements with which some of them have been associated. Poe scorned the transcendentalists, Santayana rebuked the genteel tradition, Crane was not really a naturalist; we cannot sum up Warren in the term Fugitive or New Critic, and Mailer is much more than a "Jewish novelist." Stein and Nabokov, too, are clearly unique and anomalous writers. If we judge from these seven, being an American writer means working things out on one's own, experimenting for years, for decades, at one's desk, and even at one's life, developing the implications of one's own way of seeing the world, of being in the world, of speaking in the world. One's identity has to be forged by continuous exploration of what one is; one's style, one's verbal identity, by continuous attention to what one says.

This persistent absorption in one's own consciousness is likely to result in great egotism or solipsism — not in the modest Santayana, not notably in the courteous Warren, but markedly, sometimes almost monstrously, in the rest. Given the innerness of the modern writer's sources, such a development seems predictable. As the external world grows more uncertain, as experience seems more and more the only guide we have, and our own experience the only reliable guide, writers of talent must watch the flow of life through their own bodies, minds, and speech. All seven of these writers do so vigilantly: they remember and record the turns and tremors of consciousness. The consciousness observed is normally that of a character, who with his situation amplifies and refracts the writer's sense of himself. But several of them have written directly and extensively about themselves — Santayana, Stein, Nabokov, Mailer — and Gertrude Stein has even called one of her books about herself *Everybody's Autobiography*. The writer's consciousness is, in a sense, everyone's; its material may be different, and its habits of imagination and synthesis more spectacularly developed, but "the human mind," which Gertrude Stein discussed at great length, works along the same lines in all of us, so that to examine the process of one consciousness is to see a little how everyone's works.

Except, of course, that everyone's works a bit differently. What happens is different for everyone, and so is everyone's way of taking in what happens. Among the infinite data, however, the writer may show something of the scientist's passion for reporting, like Poe, pathological case histories; for observing, like Crane, the mechanisms of action; or for classifying, like Stein, the types of human consciousness. Every consciousness presented by a novelist like Warren or Mailer is an exhibit, and all the writers under consideration have shown themselves capable of accumulating masses of data to test or corroborate theories of personality, sensibility, or society. As artists they are also capable of making the single detail a telling one, of choosing from among all the data the really significant one, as in Poe's tales of ingenuity and of horror, Crane's striking images, Stein's frequent turns on familiar phrases, or Nabokov's comment on his two meetings with General Kuropatkin (retold by Julian Moynahan): "What pleases me is the evolution of the match theme."

For writers so delicately attuned to the look of reality and the sound of speech, cliché and stereotype are mortal sins. They are sensitive to the slight dislocations of phrase that focus attention; they can use or twist ordinary English syntax to achieve handsome effects. They know how to manage and how to distort a perspective, and all of them — even Santayana in his one novel — have developed distinctive techniques for concentrating meaning in particular symbolic objects, images, or personages. All of them contrive a decor, a surface composed of objects, or of words acting like objects, in combination — one thinks especially perhaps of Poe, Crane, Nabokov, Warren, and Gertrude Stein — each element making its accessory contribution to a whole scenic design. The decor often invests the scene with meaning, if we understand the code, or, as in Crane, empties it of meaning, denies meaning, insists on the disconnection between events and meaning.

And, generally speaking, all these writers stress such disconnections, disjunctions, the absurdity of human life. The world, for all of them, is slippery and deceptive ground. Its oddness and disequilibrium, its patterns that are merely random, mistakes that are merely cryptic, invite our consciousnesses to lose themselves in errors and illusions, in the terror of enclosures and the mockery of mirrors, in the labyrinths of history, art, or dream. Whether we look at language itself (Stein) or the genteel tradition (Santayana), at ordinary or heroic experience (Crane, Mailer), at the psychic life of dreams (Poe) or of guilt (Warren), experience or history tantalizes us with its cunning passages on whose blank walls we try to make out meanings. Our response to this situation may be tragic or comic, or a little of both. We may give up history as bunk or a bad job and reduce experience to a more controllable minimum, abstracting from it the curve of experience itself. In a sense both Stephen Crane and Gertrude Stein do this, and taught Hemingway to do it after them, whittling action down to images, letting narrative and dialogue form themselves around phrases. Another response is to "finger endlessly," as Paul West says of Warren, one's " 'texture of relations,' " to go over the ground again and again as if it were a historic battlefield, which it is. Mailer does this, too. The European-born Santayana and Nabokov, not sharing perhaps the deep-guilt–ridden heritage of the others in this book, accept the absurd situation with greater magnanimity; if humor and humanity cannot make it less absurd, they can at least make us more resilient.

Poe, to be sure, is in a house of his own, a house which, as Richard Wilbur has shown in a classic essay ("The House of Poe," included in Robert Regan's *Poe: A Collection of Critical Essays*), is symbolic of the body and is deteriorating. If all his work, as Wilbur suggests, is an allegory of Poe's continuing desire to escape from life, his prose style is suited to this purpose: remote from everyday use, unnaturally elevated and grandiose, yet superbly paced and linked so as to involve the reader deeply in Poe's dream, in his fiction. Something of the sort is true of all the other writers: all of them, at least, invent their own forms of fiction — autobiographical, critical, and personal as well as novelistic. In trying to steady reality, to keep life from disintegrating entirely (not that Poe would mind) in the abyss between the uncertainties of outer event and the instabilities of inner design, they create styles and structures that are as protean and deceptive as the reality which these reflect: Poe's nightmare images, susceptible of many interpretations; Stein's cheerful enigmatic compositions; Crane's dazzlingly decorative images that warn us not to misread them, or even not to "read" them or reality at all; Santayana's voluminous urbanity, and his ironic *Bildungsroman* about a hero prepared at great length and cost for a life he never gets to lead; Nabokov's halls of mirrors, the images endlessly doubling, the style constantly mocking and undermining its own expansiveness; Warren's elaborate proofs that nothing is provable, his tireless probing of motives to show that ultimately they elude research; Mailer's stylish dance through his changing selves. Ironies and ambiguities evolve, it seems, their own structures and styles, and when the theme is deflation, as it often is with these writers, the styles and structures may at times be hilariously funny, intentionally in Stein, Nabokov, and Mailer, inadvertently in Poe.

The working out of such forms may be seen as a phase in the history of poetry. All these writers have come to literature during that long period, our own, in which poetry is turning into prose. It is not merely that they have all published poems as well as prose, nor that most of them make use, in prose, of techniques traditionally associated with verse — sound effects, sudden intensities, complex metaphors and other figures, and the natural syntax of colloquial speech. But the use of such techniques in prose has come at a time when traditional verse has been going slack. Iambic pentameter, the instrument superbly fitted to express the Renaissance struggle between divine authority and the rebellious human soul, has gradually lost its power to shake us, for the natural universe we have been living in since at least Wordsworth's time has no quarrel with psychological process. Our age may seem violent enough, but the epic struggles between the temporal and the eternal that Shakespeare needed the great measures of iambic pentameter to display have been superseded in modern literature by inconclusive campaigns in behalf of the uncertain aspirations of divided and dubious bumblers. What a difference there is between the Renaissance author's efforts at self-definition ("What is man?") conducted within a framework of more or less known quantities (God, evil, death) and the modern author's search for identity ("Who am I?") conducted within a framework about which nothing at all is known for sure! Meter is expressive of that framework, that known or even unknown quantity which, whatever its exact nature, stands behind the world of experience. But the modern world of experience has no such divine counterpart; it stands on its own, its own guarantor, its own authority, and the language in which a writer can ask serious questions about it must almost certainly be the language of experience itself, the language of speech, words breathed — a loosened or free verse perhaps, or, better still, a casual prose quickened by the figures of poetry.

This seems to me at least a useful way to regard these authors and other writers whose prose fulfills conditions of design and effect that once were fulfilled by verse. Critics nowadays, in order to make observations about style, will frequently arrange in verse form the prose lines of Mark Twain or Hemingway or the Bible. They do this because we are used to thinking of poetry as written in lines of somewhat varying length, and the successive phrases and clauses of some authors seem to correspond to breaths. Richard Bridgman, for example, in his illuminating book *The Colloquial Style in America,* arranges prose from *Huckleberry Finn* like this:

> Then she got to talking about her husband,
> And about her relations up the river,
> And her relations down the river,
> And about how much better off they used to was . . .

and so on. In fact, of course, traditional English verse is almost never written this way. Even Dryden and Pope, for whom the line is a distinct unit, have much more going on within it, and Shakespeare and Milton regularly run phrases over the line endings, make sure there is tension, not congruence, between phrase and line:

> Besides, this Duncan
> Hath borne his faculties so meek, hath been
> So clear in his great office that his virtues
> Will plead like angels trumpet-tongued against
> The deep damnation of his taking-off . . .

We would hardly want to arrange the lines by phrase, thus:

> Besides, this Duncan hath borne his faculties so meek,
> Hath been so clear in his great office
> That his virtues will plead like angels trumpet-tongued
> Against the deep damnation of his taking-off . . .

In such an arrangement all the feeling goes slack. It does not go slack in Twain, or Whitman, because their words are composed according to a different principle.

What is poetic about the fictions of Poe, Crane, Stein, Nabokov, and Mailer in particular will not be made visible if we print their prose as verse. We can feel, nevertheless, in these writers, and perhaps in Warren and Santayana as well, certainly in other Americans such as James and Faulkner, the same urgency we have always sensed in great poets, the compelling need and the energy to measure their experience by their language. The measuring instrument, however, is no longer metrical; the order crucial to poetry arises from the disposition of images, tones, perspectives; and poetry, drifting toward prose since before Poe was born, is written by anyone who masters the new keyboard. Life (English speech) is no longer struggling against a rigid order (meter) but against madness and meaninglessness: a situation in which the most helpful writing will probably be the prose or near-prose work which from a base of relative disorder retrieves an unlikely and miraculous form. Mailer tells us that "Style is character," and by this standard even the most bizarre of the writers before us is a solid citizen. But it is also possible to say that nowadays style is poetry and to claim for these seven stylists the name of poet.

ROGER ASSELINEAU

Edgar Allan Poe

THE most contradictory judgments have been passed on Edgar Allan Poe's character and works. The Reverend Rufus Griswold, whom he had the unfortunate idea of appointing his literary executor, branded him a perverse neurotic, a drunkard and drug addict "who walked the streets, in madness or melancholy, with lips moving in indistinct curses." For Baudelaire, on the contrary, he was a "fallen angel who remembered heaven," a "Byron gone astray in a bad world." Whereas Emerson looked down upon that "jingle man" who shook his bells and called their sound poetry, Tennyson admired him as an equal and Yeats (on an official occasion, it is true) proclaimed that he was "so certainly the greatest of American poets, and always, and for all lands, a great lyric poet." For James Russell Lowell, he was "three-fifths . . . genius and two-fifths fudge," while Mallarmé piously raised the monument of a sonnet over his grave and Paul Valéry acclaimed the author of *Eureka* as one of the greatest thinkers who ever lived. Writers as dissimilar as Mark Twain and Henry James rejected him, the former because he found him "unreadable" and the latter because it

11

seemed to him that "an enthusiasm for Poe [was] the mark of a decidedly primitive stage of reflection." But William Carlos Williams, for his part, praised him for giving "the sense for the first time in America that literature is serious, not a matter of courtesy but of truth." Who was right? Whom are we to believe? T. S. Eliot who denounced his "slipshod writing" or George Bernard Shaw who found him "exquisitely refined"?

These divergences are indeed perfectly justified and stem to a large extent from the constant contrast between the real and the Ideal (the capital was his) in Poe's own life and from the consequent duplicity (in the etymological meaning of the word) of his personality. Thus, though he would have liked to be of aristocratic southern lineage, he was born in Boston, on January 19, 1809, of poor actor parents who happened to be playing there at the time. His father, David Poe, who came from a good Baltimore family, of Irish descent, was a mediocre actor and a heavy drinker who was soon to desert his wife and vanish forever. His mother, Elizabeth Arnold Poe, seems to have been a charming and talented actress, on the contrary, but she died of tuberculosis in Richmond, Virginia, in December 1811 at the age of twenty-four. This sudden death probably warped Poe for the rest of his life. He was not quite three, but he always remembered — more or less unconsciously — his mother vomiting blood and being carried away from him forever by sinister men dressed in black. He was then taken into the home of John and Frances Allan — hence his middle name. John Allan was a successful and ambitious Richmond merchant. The couple were childless, so they reared the boy as if he were their only son, but they never formally adopted him. In 1815 they took him to England and sent him to private schools there, notably to Manor House School at Stoke Newington which Poe later used as a setting for the childhood of his hero in "William Wilson." The boy was athletic and brilliant. His foster parents, especially Mrs. Allan, doted on him, but as he moved through adolescence this apparently fortunate situation quickly deteriorated; he felt more and more insecure and estranged from his schoolmates because of his lowly origin and more and more antagonistic to Mr. Allan out of love for his valetudinarian foster mother — a standard Oedipus relationship. Being a precocious and passionate boy, while still at school he fell in love with the beautiful young mother of one of his friends, Mrs. Jane Stanard, whose memory inspired the first of his poems "To Helen," and with a young neighbor, Sarah Elmira Royster, but her parents disapproved of him since he was penniless and the courtship was soon broken off.

Although his practical-minded foster father wanted him to work as a clerk in his business, Poe managed to be sent to the University of Virginia in 1826. There he studied French, Spanish, Italian, and Latin, read Byron and Campbell, and had an excellent scholastic record. But the University of Virginia in those days was a wild, dissolute place (like Oxford in "William Wilson"). Poe got into difficulties almost at once because Mr. Allan had parsimoniously not provided him with enough money to pay for his fees and other necessities; then he took to drinking and gambling, accumulating debts in excess of $2000. His foster father refused to pay his "debts of honor," so Poe could not remain at Charlottesville. It was the end of his dream of a university education and he decided to break with Mr. Allan. He left Richmond in March 1827 for Boston, his birthplace, and enlisted in the army as a common soldier under the name of Edgar A. Perry. He was stationed for over a year on Sullivan's Island in Charleston Harbor, which he would describe in "The Gold Bug." Surprisingly enough, he adapted very well to military discipline and quickly rose to the rank of regimental sergeant major, the highest noncommissioned grade in the army. Yet he soon became tired of the routine of military life in peacetime and fretted at the thought of serving out his full five-year term of enlistment — or rather he now dreamed of becoming an officer like his colonel whom he admired. He wrote repentingly to Mr. Allan and reconciled with him after the death of Mrs. Allan in February 1829. With Allan's support he got his discharge and an appointment to West Point which he entered on July 1, 1830.

During this period of nearly perfect social adaptation he must have cherished dreams of an entirely different kind, though, for in the summer of 1827, while still at Boston he published at his own expense a thin volume, *Tamerlane and Other Poems*, "by a Bostonian," which passed unnoticed. That he did so at such an early date (he was only eighteen) in spite of his reduced circumstances shows his faith in himself and his belief that he had something original to say. Undiscouraged by the failure of this first volume, he published a second one at Baltimore in December 1829: *Al Aaraaf, Tamerlane, and Minor Poems*. As the title shows, it was a revised and enlarged edition of his first book. It received hardly more critical attention than its predecessor.

At West Point, the same thing happened as at the University of Virginia. Mr. Allan, who had remarried in the meantime, did not provide Poe with adequate funds. In January 1831 Poe wrote to him: "You sent me to W. Point like a beggar. The same difficulties are threatening me as before at Charlottesville — and I must resign." He kept his word. Though he had been a very good student until then, he decided to have himself expelled by deliberately cutting classes and disregarding orders. He was therefore court-martialed for "gross neglect of duties" in January 1831 and left West Point the following month.

Once again, though more destitute than ever, he succeeded in 1831 in publishing a new edition of his poems, simply entitled *Poems*, Second Edition. The appearance of this new book at such a time proves his extraordinary perseverance, but he was again ignored by critics. Yet the book included "To Helen," "Israfel," "The City in the Sea," "The Sleeper," "Lenore," "The Valley of Unrest," and an interesting introductory statement of poetic principle, "Letter to Mr. _____ _____."

By now Poe was in the greatest difficulties. He had settled in New York, but could find no job there. His pathetic calls for help to Mr. Allan remained unanswered. He devised all sorts of wild schemes — he thought for a time of joining the Polish army — which came to nothing. He was eventually obliged to take refuge with his aunt, Mrs. Clemm, in Baltimore. Baltimore was then an active publishing center and it was natural for him to seek employment there now that he had made up his mind to live by his pen.

Having failed to attract attention as a poet, he turned to story writing and worked frantically. In 1831 he competed for the prize offered for the best short story by the Philadelphia *Saturday Courier*. He submitted five: "Metzengerstein," "The Duke de l'Omelette," "A Tale of Jerusalem," "A Decided Loss," and "The Bargain Lost." He did not win the prize, which was given to a mawkish tale, but all five of his stories were later published in the *Courier* (in 1832). It must be admitted that only one of them was first-rate: "Metzengerstein." Poe had by then embarked on an ambitious project: he had planned a series of tales supposedly told by members of a rather farcical literary group, the Folio Club, in imitation of Boccaccio's *Decameron* and Chaucer's *Canterbury Tales,* a prefiguration in a way of Dickens' famous Pickwick Club. But he could find no publisher for his stories, and in at attempt to make a breakthrough he once more entered a contest in June 1833. The competition was organized by the Baltimore *Saturday Visiter* and Poe sent one poem, "The Coliseum," and six stories: "Epimanes," "MS. Found in a Bottle," "Lionizing," "The Visionary," "Siope," and "A Descent into the Maelström." This time he won the short-story award with "MS. Found in a Bottle" and his troubles were temporarily brought to an end, for one of the judges of the contest, a wealthy lawyer and amateur novelist, John P. Kennedy, befriended him. "I found him in Baltimore," Kennedy wrote in his journal in 1849, "in a state of starvation. I gave him clothing, free access to my table and the use of a horse for exercise whenever he chose. In fact, I brought him up from the verge of despair."

On Kennedy's recommendation Poe became assistant editor of the *Southern Literary Messenger* published at Richmond by T. W. White. Poe now went through a period of emotional instability during which he apparently resorted to the bottle to steady his nerves. He was no habitual drunkard and never wrote under the influence of drink, for he was very frugal and of a sober inclination, but he was extremely sensitive and given to excruciating fits of depression so that he could not at times resist the temptation to use alcohol as a sort of moral anesthetic. Unfortunately he was inordinately affected by even one glass and then lost all sense of dignity and decency. As he put it himself: "My sensitive temperament could not stand an excitement which was an every-day matter to my companions." In any event, after a month, White discharged him but relented when Poe pleaded to be reinstated.

Poe brought Mrs. Clemm and her daughter Virginia to live with him in Richmond and in May 1836 he married his young cousin, who was boldly declared to be "of the full age of twenty-one years," while actually she was not quite fourteen and looked very immature. In all likelihood the marriage was never consummated, but Poe felt very happy with his child-wife ("Sis") and with Mrs. Clemm ("dear Muddy") as mother-in-law and devoted housekeeper.

This was a period of intense production for Poe. He wrote stories, many forceful and slashing reviews in the manner of the Edinburgh reviewers, waging war on mediocrity, trying to enforce high literary standards, attacking "the heresy of the didactic," and denouncing plagiarism even where there was none. Unfortunately his efforts were often wasted on rather trivial works. He also composed a drama in verse, *Politian,* set in Renaissance Italy in the manner of Byron and Shelley, and *The Narrative of Arthur Gordon Pym,* two installments of which appeared in the *Messenger* and which was published in book form in 1838. This was his only attempt at a long story, but it is in fact a series of separate short stories strung together. Under his dynamic editorship, the *Southern Literary Messenger* became the leading review of the South and its subscription list rose, in a year's time, from five hundred to nearly thirty-five hundred. But White objected to Poe's continued intemperance and resented his editorial authority and even his success. He dismissed him in January 1837. Poe then went to New York in the hope of finding another editorial position there. He was unsuccessful and in the summer of 1838 moved to Philadelphia where he lived for the next five years and became in July 1839 the editor of *Burton's Gentleman's Magazine.* Under the pressure of financial need he wrote unceasingly — in particular a piece of hack work, *The Conchologist's First Book*, for which he was (justly) accused of plagiarism in his turn, but also "Ligeia" (for the *American Museum*), "The Man That Was Used Up," "The Fall of the House of Usher," "William Wilson," "The Conversation of Eiros and Charmion," and "Morella" (for the *Gentleman's Magazine*). Soon, however, the story of his editorship of the *Southern Literary Messenger* repeated itself. Burton and Poe quarreled over editorial policies and Poe was fired in the summer of 1840.

In that year he at last found a publisher for a collection of his stories, which appeared in two volumes in Philadelphia under the title *Tales of the Grotesque and Arabesque*. They were well received by critics, but sold rather slowly. So Poe's financial problem remained unsolved and, after he had failed to find backers for a literary journal called *The Penn Magazine* of which only the prospectus was ever printed, he joined the staff of *Graham's Magazine* and became its editor in April 1841. This was another very productive period. It was then that he published his reviews of Longfellow's *Ballads* and Hawthorne's *Twice-Told Tales* in which he defined his conception of poetry and fiction, and such stories as "The Man of the Crowd," "The Murders in the Rue Morgue," "The Island of the Fay," "The Colloquy of Monos and Una," "Eleonora," "The Oval Portrait," and "The Masque of the Red Death." Yet for all his success and brilliance he once more lost his job, in May 1842, after only thirteen months, for the same reasons as before.

His dismissal from *Graham's Magazine* did not interrupt his creation of fiction, but he found it very difficult sometimes to place his stories. He sold "The Mystery of Marie Rogêt," "The Pit and the Pendulum," "The Tell-Tale Heart," and "The Black Cat" for paltry sums to second-rate magazines. In April 1844, realizing that he could not make a living in Philadelphia as a free-lance writer, though he had won a $100 prize for "The Gold Bug" in 1843, he moved to New York which was to remain his home until his death five years later. But he encountered the

same difficulties in earning a living as in Philadelphia, though at
first he scored a few resounding successes. Thus he had hardly
settled there when, on April 13, 1844, he published in the *New
York Sun* what is now known as "The Balloon Hoax," a tale in
the form of a news item. It appeared under the caption "Astound-
ing News by Electric Express via Norfolk! The Atlantic Crossed
in Three Days — Signal Triumph of Mr. Monck's Flying-
Machine . . ." The description was so graphic that everyone was
taken in. But Poe was none the richer for it and the only job he
found was that of assistant editor of the *Evening Mirror*. It was
in this periodical that "The Raven" first appeared on January 29,
1845. The poem immediately caught the imagination of the
public and was reprinted all over the country and even abroad
in all kinds of newspapers and magazines, but Poe pocketed only
a few dollars for his pains. However, 1845 was on the whole a
lucky year for him. In July there appeared another collection of
his *Tales* (only twelve of them, though) and in November another
edition of his poems under the title *The Raven and Other Poems*.
Besides, he was offered a better position as assistant editor of the
weekly *Broadway Journal* of which he soon became the editor.
He even obtained control of the paper and thus very nearly
realized his ambition of becoming the sole proprietor of a periodical, but the *Broadway Journal* died on his hands during the
first weeks of 1846. Despite all his feverish exertions — and though
he then wrote such a fine story as "The Cask of Amontillado" and
such a brilliant essay as "The Philosophy of Composition" — he
had been growing poorer and poorer all the time and was in such
distress at the end of 1846 that the *New York Express* and the
Philadelphia *Saturday Evening Post* asked his friends and admirers to come to his aid. He was then living with Virginia and
Mrs. Clemm in a diminutive wooden cottage at Fordham and
Virginia, though dying of consumption, had to sleep in an un-
heated room. After six years of marriage she had become fatally
ill and her slowly progressing illness between 1842 and 1847
had driven Poe to distraction.

Virginia eventually died on January 30, 1847, and Poe broke

down though he felt relieved in a way from "the horrible never-ending oscillation between hope and despair." Thus, like the hero of one of his own tales, he was constantly threatened and tortured by the pendulum of fate swinging between the extremes of the human condition. All his life he craved love and tenderness, but was doomed to lose in turn all the women he loved: his mother, Mrs. Stanard, Mrs. Allan, and Virginia. He longed for wealth and luxury and yet, for all his talent and frenzied efforts, was condemned to destitution. He dreamed of fame and never succeeded in publishing a complete edition of his works or founding a review of his own. When he reached manhood after a sheltered childhood and adolescence he encountered nothing but failures and denials. So, instead of really living, he took refuge from the physical world in the private world of his dreams — in other words, in the world of his tales — and gradually identified himself with those phantoms of himself who haunt his stories. As is frequent with artists, nature in his case imitated art. He became the spiritual brother of his doomed heroes. His life was quite literally "a descent into the Maelström," a slow, inexorable descent into the abyss which attracted him irresistibly and was to claim him at forty years of age. He remained perfectly lucid to the end, but, unlike the hero of "A Descent into the Maelström," he lost the will to extricate himself from the whirlpool which was sucking him down. His art failed to save him. His works reflect this double aspect of his personality: the abandonment of the self-destructive romantic artist and the self-control of the conscious and conscientious craftsman, the passivity of the dreamer indifferent to all that exists outside his dream world and the restless activity of a keen mind always on the alert.

Portraits of Poe always show him fullface, but the only really revelatory portrait of him would be a head with a double profile, like that of the Roman god Janus, one side turned toward reality, the other toward dreams. Poe was himself perfectly aware of this duality. When describing the detective who appears in several of his tales, C. Auguste Dupin, he pointed out: "I often dwelt meditatively upon the old philosophy of the Bi-Part Soul, and amused

myself with the fancy of a double Dupin — the creative and the re-
solvent." He divided his tales into tales of imagination and tales
of ratiocination. The former were written by a Dionysiac and
inspired creator, the latter by a lucid and impassive analyst.

The tales of imagination are the undisputed domain of fear.
Poe again and again tries to make us experience the same feelings
as the narrator of "The Fall of the House of Usher": "a sense of
insufferable gloom pervaded my spirit . . . There was an iciness, a
sinking, a sickening of the heart . . . There can be no doubt that
the consciousness of the rapid increase of my superstition . . .
served mainly to accelerate the increase itself. Such, I have long
known, is the paradoxical law of all sentiments having terror as a
basis. . . . An irrepressible tremor gradually pervaded my frame;
and, at length, there sat upon my very heart an incubus of utterly
causeless alarm." The irrational fear which rises gradually and
eventually invades the whole being soon leads Poe's heroes to
insanity and death.

The world of Poe's tales is a nightmarish universe. You cross
wasted lands, silent, forsaken landscapes where both life and
waters stagnate. Here and there you catch sight of lugubrious
feudal buildings suggestive of horrible and mysterious happenings, like the gloomy abbey in which the hero of "Ligeia" takes
refuge "in one of the wildest and least frequented portions of fair
England." The inside of these sinister buildings is just as disquieting as the outside. Everything is dark there, from the ebony
furniture to the oaken ceiling. The walls are hung with heavy
tapestries to which mysterious drafts constantly give "a hideous
and uneasy animation." Even the windows are "of a leaden hue"
so that the rays of either the sun or moon passing through fall
"with a ghastly lustre on the objects within." To make things
worse, it is usually at night in the ghastly (one of his favorite
adjectives) or red-blood light of the moon that Poe's tales take
place — or in the middle of terrific storms lit up by lurid flashes
of lightning. In this strange world even the baptism of Morella's
daughter takes place at night! His heroes are tortured solitaries,
with a tainted heredity, addicted to drink or drugs. They know

that they are condemned sooner or later to lose their minds or their lives and presently indeed they die or kill before our eyes under horrifying circumstances. Metzengerstein is a victim of "morbid melancholy" and "hereditary ill-health." The nervous illness of Roderick Usher passes from hypochondriacal hyper-esthesia to delirious telepathy. The odious protagonists of "The Tell-Tale Heart," "The Imp of the Perverse," and "The Black Cat" suffer from irresistible homicidal manias and in "Berenice" Egaeus is impelled by a furious "monomania" to finish off the girl he loves in order to possess himself of her teeth. In this ghoulish universe love turns to vampirism and sadistic necrophilia.

Such an accumulation of horrible details inevitably leads the reader to ask himself whether Poe was sincere when he wrote these tales, whether they were the gratuitous play of his imagination or the true expression of a terror which he really felt in his inmost heart. There is room for hesitation, for there was in Poe's time a strong taste for Gothic romances and fantastic tales which he seems to have shared and at any rate deliberately exploited. He mentions Mrs. Radcliffe at the beginning of "The Oval Portrait" and on several occasions praises William Godwin's *Caleb Williams*. Moreover he must have read the works of Charles Brockden Brown and we know that he admired Hawthorne's tales. He must also have been acquainted with E. T. A. Hoffmann's tales — with "Das Majorat" in particular, at least in the summary which Walter Scott gave in his essay on Hoffmann, for there exist some striking similarities between this tale and "The Fall of the House of Usher."

Some critics have therefore claimed that Poe was a mere mysti-fier who wrote his stories only to please the public and follow the current fashion. Indeed more than once he himself pretends to be joking and describes horrible events with apparent unconcern. At the beginning of his career, in 1835, he wrote to White: "The sub-ject [of "Berenice"] is by far too horrible, and I confess that I hesi-tated in sending it to you especially as a specimen of my capabili-ties. The Tale originated in a bet that I could produce nothing ef-fective on a subject so singular, provided I treated it seriously."

The next year, referring to his early tales, he wrote to Kennedy: "Most of them were *intended* for half banter, half satire — although I might not have fully acknowledged this to be their aim even to myself." And finally, eight years later, in "The Premature Burial," he spoke of tales of horror with surprising skepticism. After a misadventure which was in itself a parody of the tale of horror, since he merely dreamed his premature burial, the supposed narrator declares that from then on he completely changed his way of life and got rid of his morbid obsessions by ceasing to read Edward Young's *Night Thoughts*.

Thus Poe's attitude toward his own tales is much more complex than is commonly realized. He is never completely taken in by his own imagination. His apparent frenzy is always accompanied by lucidity. His fear is often tinged with skepticism — but conversely his skepticism with fear as is shown by the concluding lines of "The Premature Burial": "Alas! the grim legion of sepulchral terrors cannot be regarded as altogether fanciful — but, like the Demons in whose company Afrasiab made his voyage down the Oxus, they must sleep, or they will devour us — they must be suffered to slumber, or we perish."

So, for all his gibes and feigned detachment, fear finally prevails and there is no denying that his "tales of imagination" were not mere literary exercises or hoaxes. They wholly committed him. His own tragic life is the best proof of it. He has sometimes been accused of being a histrion, but if it is true that he sometimes behaved like one, he forgot he was playing a part and killed himself in the last act with a real dagger (figuratively speaking). He declared himself in 1840 in the preface to his *Tales of the Grotesque and Arabesque*: "If in many of my productions terror has been the thesis, I maintain that terror is not of Germany but of the soul."

This terror which haunted his soul, like any form of fear, whatever its occasion or immediate cause may be, was in the last analysis a panic fear of death, as appears in particular in the vivid descriptions of the deaths of his characters — of Ligeia especially. Sometimes it takes the form of a fear of the void, an insufferable vertigo and an unspeakable horror which overwhelms the hero's soul just as he is going to be swallowed by a bottomless pit, as in "MS. Found in a Bottle." Arthur Gordon Pym disappears in the same way in an awful white chasm at the end of the narrative which recounts his adventures. Only the hero of "A Descent into the Maelström" escapes a similar fate thanks to his Dupin-like coolness and power of observation. At other times Poe imagines final annihilation in the form of an absolute silence suddenly spreading over the whole world and filling all creatures with terror, as in "Silence — A Fable" and the sonnet also entitled "Silence."

This fear of death and engulfment by nothingness (or God?) which constitutes the very matter of most of Poe's tales is not exceptional per se. All men experience it, but it reaches a rare degree of intensity in his works and often takes the form of phobias and manias of a decidedly abnormal character. He thus describes with a curious complacency, as if they were his own, cases of morbid claustrophobia in "The Premature Burial," at the beginning of "The Pit and the Pendulum," and in the first episode of "The Narrative of Arthur Gordon Pym." On other occasions Poe visibly takes pleasure in accumulating macabre and loathsome details. He seems to have a partiality for corpses in a state of advanced decay and never fails to emphasize the nauseating smell which they exhale — in "The Facts in the Case of M. Valdemar," for instance, when M. Valdemar's body which had been kept for seven months in a cataleptic state suddenly disintegrates. There are even times when this fascination with corpses takes the form of true necrophilia as in "The Oblong Box" and the case of Egaeus in "Berenice" is still clearer since he goes as far as digging up the body of his beloved.

Some of Poe's tales also contain undeniable traces of sadism. His half-mad murderers delight in torturing their victims and eventually kill them with devilish savagery. "The old man's terror *must* have been extreme," jubilantly exclaims the murderer of "The Tell-Tale Heart." We are frequently made to witness the dismemberment of corpses, horrible mutilations or scenes of cannibalism as in "The Narrative of Arthur Gordon Pym." Even in such a sober tale as "The Murders in the Rue Morgue," Poe cannot resist the temptation of giving all kinds of precise details about the horrible condition of the victim's corpses. In "The Pit and the Pendulum," in spite of all the pity that Poe seems to feel for the unfortunate hero, we may wonder if in his inmost heart he does not secretly admire the Inquisitors' demoniac ingenuity.

Side by side with these signs of sadism, there are also unmistakable indications of masochism, which Poe in "The Philosophy of Composition" sympathetically calls "the human thirst for self-torture." Most of his sick heroes are afflicted with it. It is this perverse instinct which impels them to sink deeper into their nightmares and eventually surrender to madness and confess their crimes publicly at the end in order to be punished and thus suffer still more. In its extreme form this neurosis completely neutralizes the instinct of self-preservation and turns into a passionate desire for self-destruction. This is precisely what happens to Metzengerstein, Roderick Usher, and all the murderers who people Poe's tales. They are all irresistibly attracted and fascinated by death.

Thus Poe constantly allows unavowable thoughts and feelings to rise from the inmost recesses of his soul and gives shape in his tales to horrible imaginings. He dreams aloud and we witness the extraordinary adventures which he took pleasure in inventing because he was not allowed to live them. His heroes are projections of his real and secret self which, for fear of being condemned and suppressed, his social self was obliged to keep hidden. At the beginning of "The Man of the Crowd" he declares: "It was well said of a certain German book that 'es lässt sich nicht lesen' — it does not permit itself to be read. There are some secrets which do not permit themselves to be told." He was unable completely to hide his own thoughts, though. Impelled by the same desire to confess as so many of his characters, he gave free play to the obsessions which tortured him and lent them to his heroes in order to revel in them by proxy. His tales — especially those which he called "tales of imagination" — were not the result of a conscious effort, but were to a large extent dictated to him by his subconscious cravings, as Gaston Bachelard has shown in his books on the four elements. They are not gratuitous inventions or intellectual fabrications, but veiled confessions. Besides, the return of the same themes and the permanence of certain phobias or manias show that Poe was a prey to well-defined obsessions and obeyed irresistible motivations.

Hence the special quality of the fantastic element in his tales. For we must here use the word "fantastic" rather than "supernatural." Poe himself used it in "The Island of the Fay": "These fancies, and such as these, have always given to my meditations . . . a tinge of what the every-day world would not fail to term fantastic." By this word he probably meant the intrusion of mysterious elements upon the world of the senses, but this intrusion in his case always took place without the exterior intervention of specters, monsters, devils, or miracles. In his tales terror intrudes into the everyday world in a more subtle way. It is aroused by the visions and hallucinations of his characters. The fantastic element is thus here of a subjective, or more precisely oneiric, origin. No ghosts or supernatural happenings are needed. We deal only with nightmares described as such — though sometimes an objective element is slyly added as in "Metzengerstein" when the portion of the tapestry representing the horse of one of the Berlifitzings suddenly vanishes at the very moment when the selfsame horse appears alive in the yard of the castle. We might think that Metzengerstein is the victim of an illusion if he were the only witness to this disappearance, but since it is also observed by one of his pages, we must admit that it is an objective phenomenon and not a mere hallucination. Exceptionally in this particular example, fantasy yields to the supernatural, but everywhere else it is linked up with morbid states which become the source of frightening and phantasmagoric visions. As Baudelaire noted, the fantastic element in Poe's tales is grounded in *"exceptions* in human life and in nature . . . hallucinations . . . hysteria usurping the place of the will, contradiction set up between the nerves and the mind, and personality so out of joint that it expresses grief with a laugh. He . . . describes . . . all that imaginary world

which floats around a high-strung man and leads him into evil."
"Poe is a writer who is all nerves," he concluded. Indeed, in
"Shadow — A Parable," Poe makes this statement which is tanta-
mount to a confession: "There were things around us and about
of which I can render no distinct account — things material and
spiritual — heaviness in the atmosphere — a sense of suffocation —
anxiety — and, above all, that terrible state of existence which the
nervous experience when the senses are keenly living and awake,
and meanwhile the powers of thought lie dormant."

If Baudelaire had written in our time, he would have spoken of
neuroses rather than nerves. Poe is the writer of neuroses. "The
Premature Burial" shows he was fully aware that the epileptic
and cataleptic states of his heroes were the consequence rather
than the cause of their morbid thoughts; he discovered before
Freud that the health of the body depends on the health of the
mind.

The hidden cause of his own neurotic condition — which he desperately tried to escape by drinking and even perhaps by taking
drugs — has been diagnosed by one of Freud's friends and disciples,
Marie Bonaparte. She has set forth her thesis in a bulky book full
of insight and ingenuity whose general conclusions are irrefutable
even if some of her interpretations seem too systematic. According
to her, all the disorders from which Poe suffered can be explained
by the Oedipus complex and the incurable trauma caused by the
tragic disappearance of his mother when he was only three years
old. The image of his beautiful and frail young mother sapped by
consumption seems indeed to have dominated his whole life and
probably explains why he could marry only a child-wife in the
person of his cousin Virginia. It is obvious too that all his "ethereal" heroines (the adjective is his), Berenice, Morella, Madeline
Usher, Eleonora, Ligeia, are mere reflections of that beloved
mother too soon taken from him. Most of them, besides, are
introduced to us as cousins of the narrator and close kin to his
mother. These lucid and translucid women, lucid like himself and
translucid like his mother, inspire his heroes with intellectual
rather than sensual passions, with passionate friendship rather

than desire. Everything happens as if Poe had forever exhausted all the possibilities of love in his relation with his mother and he or his heroes could only love sick or dying women like his own mother. Love and death are indissolubly merged both in his works and in his life.

Thus Poe's fantastic tales, which on account of their very nature should be quite impersonal, in fact plunge their roots to the inmost recesses of his being. Each of them in a way masks the mouth of a cave in the darkness of which creep monstrous creatures, the author's obsessions and phobias. Or, to use another image, each of his tales is a palimpsest and we must try to read under the legible text the almost completely faded scrawl which it hides and which will clarify everything if we succeed in deciphering it. "The supposition that the book of an author is a thing apart from the author's *Self* is, I think, ill-founded," he once declared.

Like Baudelaire, his French translator and counterpart, Poe could have addressed his reader as "hypocritical reader, my brother!" Whether we like it or not, we feel secret bonds with him and his heroes — who at times look strangely Kafkaesque or Faulknerian. Indeed they are both romantic figures and prefigurations of the twentieth-century existentialist hero. They live in an empty, dehumanized, and dechristianized world, plunged in deep melancholy, trailing clouds of glory (and European romanticism), absolutely pure and sexless, refusing to notice the turbid waters in which their dreams sink their snakelike roots. They are often shut up in a secluded place of no exit. They are dark Narcissuses involved in a desperate search for their identity and haunted by an obscure sense of guilt; they feel alienated from the world that surrounds them. They spend their time talking with their double (the narrator) or trying to guess his thoughts (Dupin whose intellect tries to identify itself with that of his opponent) or they struggle with him and finally kill him like William Wilson and, in a way, Prospero in "The Masque of the Red Death." Whether they kill their double (and consequently themselves) or some apparently alien victim, they do so in order to find and define themselves. "I kill, therefore I am." But self-knowledge thus leads to nothing but self-destruction. The application of Socrates' advice "Know thyself" here only results in the realization that the self is bound to die, will sooner or later be sucked in by nothingness. A rather despairing conclusion.

Though he was always unconsciously guided by the secret obsessions of his imagination, Poe did not follow his inspiration blindly. Another faculty constantly interfered. Even in his fantastic tales he never lets himself go. There is method in his madness. Madness, moreover, is not incompatible with reason, as he himself observed on several occasions, notably in "The System of Doctor Tarr and Professor Fether." It sometimes consists in stubbornly making right deductions from wrong premises. Poe, at any rate, knew how to impose a strict discipline on his nightmares. The data of his morbid and undoubtedly disordered imagination are always controlled by a severe method and presented in the form of a clear and logical train of events bound together by connections between causes and effects. In other words his reason always rules his creative activity. He wanted it so.

According to him, inspiration and reason are compatible; they even harmoniously combine with each other. In his fantastic tales he has succeeded in balancing the two opposite faculties, but so great was the power of reason over him that he composed under its exclusive guidance a series of tales which he rather pedantically called "tales of ratiocination": "The Murders in the Rue Morgue," "The Purloined Letter," "The Gold Bug," "The Mystery of Marie Rogêt," and "Maelzel's Chess-Player." In these tales he behaves as a perfect rationalist and even goes so far as to deny the existence of the supernatural. "In my own heart," he makes the narrator of "The Mystery of Marie Rogêt" declare, "there dwells no faith in praeternature. That Nature and its God are two, no man who thinks will deny. That the latter, creating the former, can, at will, control or modify it, is also unquestionable. I say 'at will'; for the question is of will, and not, as the insanity of logic has assumed, of power. It is not that the Deity *cannot* modify his laws, but that we insult him in imagining a possible necessity for modification." Poe thus fully shares the views of the scientists for whom the only existing phenomena are those of the physical world obeying a set of immutable laws which can be rationally accounted for and expressed in mathematical formulas. We are a long way from the state of mind of the narrator of "The Fall of the House of Usher" whose intelligence on the contrary capitulates before a number of strange happenings which he considers inexplicable: "I was forced to fall back upon the unsatisfactory conclusion, that while, beyond doubt, there *are* combinations of very simple natural objects which have the power of thus affecting us, still the analysis of this power lies among considerations beyond our depth."

Thus reason triumphs in the tales of ratiocination and Poe again and again sings its praises: "As the strong man exults in his physical ability," he exclaims at the beginning of "The Murders in the Rue Morgue," "delighting in such exercises as call his muscles into action, so glories the analyst in that moral activity which *disentangles*. He derives pleasure from even the most trivial occupations bringing his talent into play. He is fond of enigmas, of conundrums, hieroglyphics; exhibiting in his solutions of each a degree of *acumen* which appears to the ordinary apprehension praeternatural."

Poe here describes his own tastes and activities. He was passionately fond of riddles and puzzles. When he was editor of *Graham's Magazine* he wrote a series of articles on cryptography and claimed in one that he had defied the readers of the *Alexander's Weekly Messenger* to send him a cryptogram which he could not decipher. He had received, he said, about one hundred coded messages all of which he had succeeded in decoding, except one which he had proved to be indecipherable. He was very proud of his ability — though professionals nowadays look down upon him as a mere amateur — and he paraded it in particular in "The Gold Bug."

He applied his ingenuity to all kinds of other problems. In "Maelzel's Chess-Player" for instance, he proved that this famous automaton which had just been exhibited in a number of American cities could be nothing but a machine with a man hidden inside. His demonstration in seventeen points is conducted with impeccable logic and his conclusions are incontrovertible. Poe, besides, exhibits a truly scientific spirit by fastening on a seemingly trivial detail — the fact that the automaton always used its left hand — and by basing all his reasoning upon it. For as he points out in "The Murders in the Rue Morgue," "it is by these deviations from the plane of the ordinary, that reason feels its way, if at all, in its search for the true."

In his review of *Barnaby Rudge* in *Graham's Magazine* in February 1842, Poe described how, while this novel was appearing serially, he had succeeded in identifying the murderer by reasoning from the data supplied by Dickens in the first seven pages. True, his predictions, which he published in the Philadelphia *Saturday Evening Post* on May 1, 1841, did not prove correct, but the fault was not his, he asserted, but that of Dickens, who had not been perfectly consistent. His own reasoning had been faultless and therefore his "prophecy should have been true," he claimed.

Poe did not grapple only with imaginary police problems; he also undertook to solve a case which had thwarted all the efforts of the New York police. It was the murder of a girl called Mary Cecilia Rogers whose body had been found in the Hudson River. The press at the time had claimed (without evidence) that she had been killed by a gang of ruffians. In "The Mystery of Marie Rogêt" Poe transferred the murder to Paris in order to put the matter in the hands of Dupin, the imaginary hero of "The Murders in the Rue Morgue." He then succeeded in proving that the murderer was in fact the lover of the girl, a sailor in all likelihood, and he subsequently maintained (in a footnote added to later printings of "The Mystery of Marie Rogêt" and in a letter to a friend) that his deductions had been correct: the culprit, a naval officer, had confessed his crime (or rather his share of responsibility for the death of Mary Rogers, who had succumbed following an attempted abortion) before two witnesses.

Poe could take to pieces with the greatest skill any intellectual mechanism or solve any kind of problem, but he could also do the reverse and build up piece by piece the most plausible and convincing hoax in the world, as he did when he published "The Balloon Hoax" in the *New York Sun* in 1844. "The Murders in the Rue Morgue" is a feat of the same kind since Poe had to organize and combine the details of the murders with the same regard for logic and consistency as if he were reporting them for a newspaper. It only remained for him then to tell the events in the reverse order, beginning with the still warm bodies of the victims and working his way back from there to the murderer. Contrary to what the reader may think, the author's ingenuity here does not consist in unraveling the threads of a complex plot, but in weaving a strong web, as Poe himself pointed out in a letter to the poet and critic Philip Pendleton Cooke: "Where is the ingenuity of unravelling a web which you yourself (the author) have woven for the express purpose of unraveling? The reader is made to confound the ingenuity of the supposititious Dupin with that of the writer of the story." At any rate, whether the creative process works backwards or forwards, the interest of this kind of tale is essentially of an intellectual order. The author poses such a complex problem that the reader is unable to solve it, but the author helps him, proves in turn the absurdity of a number of hypotheses, and eventually reaches the only possible solution. What matters is the discovery of the culprit and not the analysis of his or her motives. The human or psychological interest is therefore completely lacking — especially in "The Murders in the Rue Morgue" in which the murderer is not even a man but an orangutang.

So, by applying the most rigorous logic to the writing of fiction, Poe discovered the detective story. Voltaire, it is true, had already created Zadig, but Dupin and his companion were the immediate predecessors of Sherlock Holmes and Dr. Watson and through these had a numberless posterity. However, Poe only exceptionally gave free play to his faculties of analysis and deduction. Most of the time, he preferred to combine them with his imagination and the dark forces of his subconscious. He succeeded in effecting the difficult synthesis of these antagonistic elements thanks to a deliberate strategy of applying to the data provided by his imagination a number of well-defined aesthetic principles.

It is remarkable that even in his very first tales, though he wrote them when he was hardly over twenty, Poe reached mastery of his art. He owed it not only to his full knowledge of the requirements of this difficult genre which demands both conciseness and concentration, but also to the conscious and deliberate fusion of his visionary faculties and his analytical intelligence. In "Magazine-Writing — Peter Snook," he lays it down as a principle that "There is no greater mistake than the supposition that a true originality is a mere matter of impulse or inspiration. To originate is carefully, patiently, and understandingly to combine."

Thus, for Poe — whether he wrote in prose or verse — inspiration was necessary, but not sufficient. He reached at a very early date a voluntarist conception of literary creation which he set forth in several critical essays, "The Philosophy of Composition," "The Poetic Principle," "Fancy and Imagination," and in reviews of Longfellow's poems, Dickens' *Barnaby Rudge,* and above all Hawthorne's *Twice-Told Tales.* All these essays overlap and repeat each other, which proves Poe's belief in the importance of his thesis. And that he should have felt it necessary to write all this dogmatic criticism shows how deeply convinced he was of the power of reason in this field.

To begin with, Poe asserts that inspiration is a legend and a myth and those who claim to have written under its influence are only imposters. According to him *poeta fit, non nascitur,* you are not born a man of genius, you become one, provided you are sufficiently diligent — and intelligent, for everything depends on the will and a judicious application of the intellect. To prove the truth of this paradox, Poe gives as an example the one of his works which had met with the greatest and most immediate success, "The Raven." He takes it to pieces in "The Philosophy of Composition" in order to show "that no one point in its composition is referable either to accident or intuition — that the work proceeded, step by step, to its completion with the precision and rigid consequence of a mathematical problem."

Yet we cannot take Poe's word for it and blindly accept his thesis that a poet is not an inspired artist but a clever technician knowing how to obtain a deliberately chosen effect by appropriate means. Baudelaire for all his sympathy with such an aesthetics could not help voicing some doubts when he commented on "The Philosophy of Composition": "Did he make himself, by a strange and amusing vanity, much less inspired than he naturally was? . . . I should be rather inclined to think so." Indeed how can we put stock in Poe's so-called confession and believe that "The Raven" was the work of Poe-Dupin alone without the help of the other Poe, the inspired neurotic? It is impossible in particular to believe that his famous refrain was not given to him after long gropings (he had already used "no more" in the "Sonnet — To Zante" and "The Haunted Palace"). Besides, we do know that "The Raven" was not the result of a few hours' lucid work. Its composition was spread over several months. He let it grow organically as it were (conformably with the precepts of romantic aesthetics) and this at a time when Virginia was dying and he was reduced to nearly complete destitution. It is not surprising under such circumstances that "The Raven" should have spontaneously expressed his agony, his haunting fear of the future, his terror at the thought that his beloved wife was soon to disappear forever. It is not a feat of virtuosity, but a cry of pain — even if its form has been cleverly wrought. Poe's account of the genesis of this poem is nothing but an a posteriori analysis. In fact, "The Raven" was to a large extent the result of inspiration, imposed on the poet before being perfected by the craftsman. In a way he confessed this semi-mystification in one of his "Marginalia": "It is the curse of a certain order of mind, that it can never rest satisfied with the consciousness of its ability to do a thing. Not even is it content with doing it. It must both know and show how it is done."

Poe, however, did not underestimate the importance of intuition as this note shows: "That the imagination has not been unjustly ranked as supreme among the mental faculties, appears from the intense consciousness, on the part of the imaginative man, that the faculty in question brings his soul often to a glimpse of things supernal and eternal — to the very verge of the great secrets . . . Some of the most profound knowledge — perhaps all *very* profound knowledge — has originated from a highly stimulated imagination. Great intellects *guess* well." But for all the intense awareness of what he owed to inspiration, Poe nevertheless preferred to lay emphasis on analysis and conscious arrangement, all those aspects of the creative activity which can be clearly defined and, to some extent, codified, with regard to the tale as well as poetry.

Poe considered the tale a superior form of art: It is superior to the novel, according to him, and even, to some extent, to poetry: "the tale has a point of superiority even over the poem. In fact, while the *rhythm* of this latter is an essential aid in the development of the poem's highest idea — the idea of the Beautiful — the artificialities of this rhythm are an inseparable bar to the development of all points of thought or expression which have their basis in *Truth*. But Truth is often, and in very great degree, the aim of the tale."

But in order to deserve this eminent status in literature the tale must meet well-defined requirements. And at this point Poe — like Aristotle in his *Poetics* — formulates a number of rules, the first of which bears the name of "unity or totality of interest." It could more simply be called the rule of "unity of effect or impression" — and it is meant to apply to poems as well as tales. Poe defines it in his review of Longfellow's *Ballads*: "in pieces of less extent, the pleasure is *unique,* in the proper acceptation of this term — the understanding is employed, without difficulty, in the contemplation of the picture *as a whole*; and thus its effect will depend, in great measure, upon the perfection of its finish, upon the nice adaptation of its constituent parts, and, especially, upon what is rightly termed by Schlegel *the unity or totality of interest*." As the quotation shows, Poe had borrowed his theory from August Wilhelm Schlegel whose *Lectures on Dramatic Art and Literature* had been translated into English in 1815. He may have read extracts from them in *Blackwood's Magazine* and elsewhere and he also may have found some of these ideas in the *Biographia Literaria* in which Coleridge uses the phrase "unity of effect." For once Poe frankly acknowledged his debt.

Granting the principle of unity of impression, there remains the problem of determining how it can best be obtained. According to Poe, the first requirement is brevity. One can create an effect of totality or unity only in a sufficiently brief piece. And this is the reason why he thought a poem must not exceed "what can comfortably be read at one sitting, that is to say about a hundred lines, for, if two sittings be required, the affairs of the world interfere, and every thing like totality of effect is at once destroyed." As regards prose, conditions are different. The reader can endure more without having to stretch out his legs. It seemed to him therefore that the ideal length of a short prose narrative was that of a text requiring "from a half-hour to one or two hours in its perusal." In his opinion, such a narrative is superior to a novel which "deprives itself, of course, of the immense force derivable from *totality*" simply because it cannot be read at one sitting.

The second requirement to be met in order to obtain unity of effect is of the same kind as the first one and directly derives from it. A narrative can be brief only if the action which it recounts takes place in a fairly restricted space. Poe gives this rule a rather barbarous name. He calls it "close circumscription of space." It is much the same thing as the rule of unity of place prescribed by Aristotle, but it is less rigid. The author is not required to keep the actors in one room, he is merely advised not to let them stray away too far from a central point.

As to the third requirement, it is reminiscent of Aristotle's rule of unity of action. Poe does not give it any name, but it concerns the plot and consists in asserting that all the details of a narrative must be closely subordinated to the whole. A tale must be self-sufficient and "should contain within itself all that is requisite for its own comprehension" and nothing else, a prescription which is curiously consonant with the principles of New Criticism.

In practice Poe used two main methods to obtain that impression of unity and homogeneity which he valued so much: subjective narratives and what he called "concatenation." Indeed all his tales are told in the first person singular, the narrative being placed either in the mouth of the hero or in that of his confidant. This device enabled Poe to link up the incidents with one another by placing them inside one consciousness, and at the same time to fuse them into one by means of comments whose presence under such circumstances seems quite natural. He was aware of the advantages of this method, for in reviewing one of Captain Marryat's books he wrote: "The *commenting* force can never be safely disregarded. It is far better to have a dearth of incident, with skilful observations upon it, than the utmost variety of event, without." Authorial comment, he affirmed in the review of a novel by William Ainsworth, has "a binding power" which gives unity to the most desultory narratives. On the other hand, he always strove to relate closely to one another the various incidents of a tale by very carefully establishing connections between cause and effect — which made D. H. Lawrence protest that Poe was "rather a scientist than an artist." According to Poe this is, on the contrary, the supreme skill which enables the artist to rival God, as he claimed in *Eureka*: "In the construction of *plot*, for example, in fictitious literature, we should aim at so arranging the incidents that we shall not be able to determine, of any one of them, whether it depends from any one other or upholds it. In this sense, of course, *perfection* of *plot* is really, or practically, unattainable — but only because it is a finite intelligence that constructs. The plots of God are perfect. The Universe is a plot of God."

Another of Poe's preoccupations was the creation of verisimilitude. In his critical essays, however, he hardly touches upon it because, in his opinion, it was the natural result of that concatenation at which he aimed all the time. Yet in one of his reviews he incidentally reveals one of the devices he used to convince the reader of the authenticity of the extraordinary episodes he related, namely the extreme precision of some details. He was not the inventor of this technique; he acknowledged it implicitly when he

praised Defoe. His method, however, was somewhat different from
that of Defoe in *Robinson Crusoe* or *A Journal of the Plague
Year* since he had to adapt it to his own purpose. "It consists
principally," he said, "in avoiding, as may easily be done, that
directness of expression which we have noted in *Sheppard Lee*
[by Robert M. Bird] and thus leaving much to the imagination —
in writing as if the author were firmly impressed with the truth,
yet astonished at the immensity of the wonders he relates, and for
which, professedly, he neither claims nor anticipates credence —
in minuteness of detail, especially upon points which have no
immediate bearing upon the general story [for example the description of the House of Usher and the apparently incidental
mention of the fissure in the façade] — this minuteness not being
at variance with indirectness of expression — in short, by making
use of the infinity of arts which give verisimilitude to a narration."

It is thus clear that Poe deliberately applied to the fantastic tale
some of the devices of the realistic novel. He loved small details
and, like Dupin, had a keen sense of observation. Hence his precise descriptions of the setting in some of his tales: the old abbey
bought in England by Ligeia's husband, the castle where Prospero
and his court take refuge in "The Masque of the Red Death," the
school attended by William Wilson in his childhood — hence also
the pseudo-scientific substructure of "The Unparalleled Adventure of One Hans Pfaall." It was his way of rooting fantasy in
reality, but conversely he also had to avoid precision as soon as he
touched on fantasy; he then had to suggest and use, as he said,
"indirect" means of expression. Passages of realistic description
appear in his tales only as isles of light in a dark landscape. He
recommended against accumulating details: "An outline frequently stirs the spirit more pleasantly than the most elaborate
picture." Generally speaking, he had only contempt for pure
realism: "That the chief merit of a picture is its *truth,* is an
assertion deplorably erroneous. Even in Painting, which is, more
essentially than Poesy, a mimetic art, the proposition cannot be
sustained."

Poe's aim was not exclusively truth, but also what he called "passion, or the excitement of the heart," which "although attainable, to a certain extent, in poetry [is] far more readily attainable in prose." Hence his emphasis on the "tone" of the tale aside from the contents, on the impression to be produced rather than on the purely narrative element. Besides, he thought that a tale must not be a mere narrative, for then its "hardness" and "nakedness" would "repel the artistical eye." "Two things are invariably required," he claimed: "first some amount of complexity, or more properly adaptation; and secondly, some amount of suggestiveness — some undercurrent, however indefinite, of meaning ... It is this latter, in especial, which imparts to a work of art so much of that *richness* (to borrow from colloquy a forcible term) . . ."

In other words, the reader must feel beyond the letter of the narrative the presence of a spirit which confers on all the details and incidents a precious but inexpressible meaning. Here Poe joins hands with Coleridge and the German romantics. He wants his tales to bring the reader into contact with what he called "the Ideal" or, as he also said, borrowing the word from August Wilhelm Schlegel, he wants them to be "mystic."

Such was his ultimate aim. His tales were not ends in themselves, but a means to make us feel the mystery and horror of our condition. We must go beyond the surface of his narratives. Most of his texts are only pretexts which he uses to take us beyond appearances. His purpose was not simply to build perfect plots, but to make us share his dreams and through the rational reveal the irrational to us. In this respect, his use of coincidences is characteristic. They are not just tricks. He sometimes multiplies them deliberately to the detriment of verisimilitude, in "William Wilson" for instance, in order to suggest the fatality which crushes man.

All these aesthetic principles often seem to verge on transcendentalism. But Poe, who felt only contempt for Emerson and his disciples, would have indignantly rejected such an insinuation. He equated transcendentalism with the surrender of intelligence and the failure of reason. For his part he was ready to accept the existence of a mystery at the center of the universe, but his intelligence, as *Eureka* shows, strove to pierce it and eventually reached, instead of Emerson's vague pantheism, what Allen Tate has called a form of panlogism. Poe's rationalism, like the hero of "A Descent into the Maelström," resisted the fascination of the abyss and refused to be engulfed by a hazy spiritualism.

However, though Poe tried hard to maintain equipoise on all levels between his reason and his imagination, it is obvious that Roderick Usher repeatedly got the better of Dupin within him. He was closer at heart to his haunted criminals than to his impassive detective. In the last analysis, therefore, for all their rational construction and well-concatenated narrative contents, his tales are lyric outbursts in disguise, in which the "I" of the speaker corresponds less to fictitious characters than to Poe himself if he had let himself go. And this is one of the reasons why he never succeeded in creating any lifelike characters in his tales (his personal experience of life was much too limited). He gave as an excuse that the extreme brevity of the tale does not lend itself to the study in depth of characters, but the true reason was that he was himself the hero of all his tales. If Roderick Usher, Egaeus, Metzengerstein, and even Dupin are all alike, if Ligeia, Morella, and Eleonora look like sisters, it is because, whether he consciously wanted to or not, he always takes the story of his own life as a starting point, a rather empty story on the whole since he had mostly lived in his dreams, imprisoned by his neuroses and obsessed by the image of his dead mother. What he makes the narrator of "Berenice" confess is probably partly true of himself: "The realities of the world affected me as visions, and as visions only, while the wild ideas of the land of dreams became, in turn, — not the material of my every-day existence — but in very deed that existence utterly and solely in itself."

This further explains why he rebelled against the moralizing literature of the America of his time, why he protested against what he called "didacticism." His only care and preoccupation was to take himself, that is to say his dreams, as the subject of his tales under the pretext of entertaining the reader.

What Joseph Wood Krutch has said of his detective stories, that he invented the genre in order not to go mad, applies to all his tales. Describing the arabesques of his reveries in fictional narratives helped him to exorcise his inner demons. But he had still another derivative: humor. Besides his tales of imagination and ratiocination, he also wrote what he called grotesque tales: "The Devil in the Belfrey," "Lionizing," "Four Beasts in One; the Homo-Cameleopard," "Some Words with a Mummy," "The Angel of the Odd," "The System of Doctor Tarr and Professor Fether," "The Duke de l'Omelette," "Loss of Breath," "Bon-Bon," "How to Write a Blackwood Article," "Peter Pendulum," "The Spectacles," "Mystification," "Why the Little Frenchman Wears His Hand in a Sling," "Never Bet the Devil Your Head," "The Man That Was Used Up" (which was taken up by Nathanael West in *A Cool Million*), etc. All these tales, which have often been neglected by critics, are above all parodies now of himself, now of others, or rather of himself as well as others, since he had such deep affinities with the fantastic tales which were then so popular. The lucid reasoner in him could not but make fun of the ghosts conjured up by his neurotic self. Torn by his neuroses, tormented in all likelihood by his sexual impotence, baffled by life, Poe nevertheless refused to acknowledge his defeat and preferred to laugh at his misfortune rather than lament over it. The black humor of his tales expresses this courageously concealed despair; it is a desperate challenge to the blind forces which overcome the defenseless individual. As André Breton put it, it is "a higher revolt of the mind."

"Loss of Breath" is quite characteristic in this respect. Its subtitle, "A Tale neither in nor out of 'Blackwood,' " immediately stamps it as a parody. It is a warning that we must not take it seriously. There is little danger that we should, for the very first lines are made comic by the incongruous contrast between the epic bombast of the tone and the triviality of the subject. Poe's humor here as elsewhere is based on exaggeration and overstatement — as in Dickens. The reader suddenly finds himself in a world of hyperboles in which there is no happy mean between obesity and extreme leanness, between a vociferating voice and a whisper. These absurd contrasts are irresistibly ludicrous and one cannot help laughing, either, at the cascade of misfortunes which happen to the hero with quasi-mechanical regularity. "Mechanics stuck on life is always laughable," as Bergson noted. The reader indulges in all this merriment without any qualms, for though his tormentors break Mr. Lacko'breath's head and arms, cut his ears, disembowel him, and finally hang him, he remains as insensitive to pain as Donald Duck in a Walt Disney cartoon. He is — and so are we — anesthetized by humor. We live with him in a nonsensical world in which man is nothing but a wooden puppet and life and death have no meaning. Everything becomes relative and extremes meet and merge. It is the realm of paradox. The most commonly accepted notions are denied or reversed in the most unexpected manner and with a great show of seriousness. The logic of the tale is impeccable, but all the incidents derive from a deliberately absurd premise, namely that you can lose and find your breath, just as you can lose and find your purse — or a character in a tale of imagination can lose and find his shadow. The starting point is the literal interpretation of a common phrase, "to lose one's breath" — humorists often use this trick — and this provides the first link in a chain of irresistibly comic episodes. The underlying subject, however, is tragic despite the apparently happy ending. It is the story of a newly married man suddenly stricken with sexual impotence and excluded from life. It reveals under the disguise of a farce the secret wound from which Poe suffered all his life, the source of all his torments and terrors. He must have felt that he was making here an involuntary confession, for he originally published this tale under a pseudonym, an Irish one, however ("Lyttleton Barry"), as if he were reluctant to deny his authorship altogether.

Except for a half-dozen very popular poems, Poe is chiefly known nowadays as a teller of tales. The corpus of his poems, besides, is extremely small. Yet his supreme ambition was to be a poet: "Events not to be controlled have prevented me from making, at any time, any serious effort in what, under happier cir-

cumstances, would have been the field of my choice." He ranked
poetry higher than prose (when he was not pleading the cause of
the tale), because it is "the desire of the moth for the star," "the
rhythmical creation of Beauty," and "Beauty is the sole legitimate
province of the poem" — whereas the domain of prose is merely
Truth. In other words, the writing of prose is a human occupa-
tion — whereas, when a poet writes verse, he creates something in
the full sense of the word; he rivals God. Before Whitman, Poe
stripped poetry of all the adventitious elements which tended to
hide it, whether epic, descriptive, or didactic. His aim was pure
poetry, his ideal a sheer lyric outburst. Consequently, he denounced prolixity and, as we have already seen, insisted that a
poem must be short: "a long poem does not exist . . . the phrase,
'a long poem,' is simply a flat contradiction in terms."

Such were the principles he laid down in "The Poetic Principle" (1850). In practice he succeeded only gradually in purging
his own poems of heterogeneous elements. "Tamerlane" (1827)
and "Al Aaraaf" (1829) are long poems somewhat in Shelley's
manner and to some extent tell a story. Even "The Raven" (1845)
is in a way a tale in verse rather than a pure poem. But his ultimate object was a self-sufficient and self-contained poem similar
to the long, smooth, white vault painted by Usher, completely cut
off from the everyday world of common sense and hard material
objects, containing nothing but evanescent and ethereal dream-
ing visions. "Oh! nothing earthly save the ray/(Thrown back
from flowers) of Beauty's eye . . ." he exclaimed at the very beginning of "Al Aaraaf." He aspired after what he called "supernal
Beauty" rather than plastic Beauty, "the Beauty above" rather
than "the Beauty before us." The poet according to him must be
"inspired by an ecstatic prescience of the glories beyond the
grave." It seemed to him that such a form of poetry produced "an
elevating excitement of the Soul" independent of both the
"Heart" (matter, the body) and the "Intellect" (reason). He
wanted the poet's imagination to reach beyond itself, so to speak,
and his ideal was Israfel, the angel "whose heart-strings are a
lute," singing "an unimpassioned song" to spiritual love ("the

true, the divine Eros — the Uranian, as distinguished from the Dionaean Venus").

It is out of this rarefied matter that Poe wrote most of his shorter poems on the twin themes of Eros and Thanatos, love and death — "To Helen" (1831) for instance, which is addressed to an ideal rather than to any real woman, to a goddess from another world whom the poet worships for her holiness rather than her beauty. The last stanza is an apotheosis: Helen is suddenly metamorphosed into Psyche (the soul). The communion of souls replaces the union of bodies. Indefiniteness displaces sensuousness ("The naked senses sometimes see too little — but then *always* they see too much") and the poem becomes something out of space and out of time, a rare aerial orchid without any roots. "For Annie" (1849) in the same way sings the Lethean peace of death:

> Thank Heaven! the crisis —
> The danger is past . . .
> And the fever called "Living"
> Is conquered at last.

"Ulalume" (1847) in the form of strange and infinitely sad images expresses indirectly all the mystery and terror of death — in application of the principle that "the death of a beautiful woman is, unquestionably, the most poetical topic in the world — and equally is it beyond doubt that the lips best suited for such a topic are those of a bereaved lover."

So, in his poetry as in his tales, Poe turns his back on the world of the senses and a poem in his hands becomes an end in itself. He believed in what he called the "poem *per se* — this poem which is a poem and nothing more — this poem written solely for the poem's sake." He would undoubtedly have subscribed to Archibald MacLeish's prescription that "A poem should not mean/ But be." He was already preparing the way for some of the most extreme experiments of the French Symbolists.

He believed in the power of images (or more specifically of sad and dreamy evocations), but also, like the French Symbolists, in music. He wanted the reader "to see with his ear." He was an extraordinarily skillful metrist, passionately interested in prosody

as his essay on "The Rationale of Verse" (1848) testifies. He was
not satisfied with mere harmony, which, according to him, consists of "the regular alternation of syllables differing in quantity"
and is a matter of rhythm. He insisted that over and above harmony there must be "melody," which is a matter of sounds.
Hence his emphasis on rhymes and refrains and his frequent use
of alliterations. "The perception of pleasure in the equality of
sounds is the principle of music," he maintained. In the name of
this principle he multiplied rich and even opulent rhymes and
combined them in ingenious stanzaic patterns in order to obtain,
as he said, both "equality and unexpectedness," both anticipation
and surprise. His supreme aim was incantation, what he called
"the magic power of verse." All the clever prosodical devices he
used and sometimes invented were intended to hypnotize the
reader by appealing almost exclusively to his ear (which is the
most passive of senses) and thus stir emotions and passions at a
deep and almost elemental level.

Unfortunately, however, he had a tendency to overdo it. He too
often and too deliberately strained after effect. At such times his
poems develop mechanically instead of organically. They are the
fruit of artifice rather than art. The excessive accumulation of alliterations and rich rhymes again and again betrays his desire to
show off his technical virtuosity. Though he praises "the concord
of sound and sense principle," he then completely sacrifices sense
to sound and truly deserves the epithet of "jingle-man" which
Emerson applied to him. Aldous Huxley has devastatingly criticized his over-sonorous rhymes: "Poe's rich rhymes . . . are seldom
above suspicion. That dank tarn of Auber is only very dubiously
a fit poetical companion for the tenth month . . . On other occasions Poe's proper names rhyme not only well enough, but
actually, in the particular context, much too well. Dead D'Elormie [in "The Bridal Ballad"] is first cousin to Edward Lear's
aged Uncle Arly sitting on a heap of barley — ludicrous; but also
(unlike dear Uncle Arly) horribly vulgar, because of the too musi-
cal lusciousness of his invented name and his display . . . of an
obviously faked Norman pedigree. Dead D'Elormie is a poetical

disaster." Allen Tate, for his part, objects to the insistence and monotony of Poe's rhythms which, he says, are for the metronome, not the human ear. T. S. Eliot summed up the case by concluding that "his versification is not, like that of the greatest masters of prosody, of the kind which yields a richer melody, through study and long habituation, to the maturing sensibility of the reader returning to it at times throughout his life. Its effect is immediate and undeveloping; it is probably much the same for the sensitive schoolboy and for the ripe mind and cultivated ear."

There is thus a general agreement among writers of the English-speaking world that Poe as a poet has a very limited range and suffers from exasperating defects. Yet he has been praised to the skies by such French poets as Baudelaire, Mallarmé, and Paul Valéry. The reason for this discrepancy is that these poets because of linguistic differences have not felt the vulgarities of Poe's manner. They have been sensitive only to the high seriousness of his poetic quest and been filled with admiration for the boldness of his attempt to express the inexpressible by means of words. Poe himself had declared this to be his purpose: "There is a class of fancies . . . of exquisite delicacy, which are *not* thoughts, and to which, *as yet*, I have found it absolutely impossible to adapt language. . . . Now so entire is my faith in the *power of words,* that, at times, I have believed it possible to embody even the evanescence of fancies such as I have attempted to describe."

Such was his ambition — or, according to some, his megalomania — that he considered no undertaking too difficult for his genius and he even attempted to solve the riddle of the universe in the middle of his distress after the death of Virginia. The result was a supreme "prose-poem," *Eureka.* The title itself is a shout of triumph: "I have found! I have found the answer!" Poe-Dupin had decoded the secret message of God thanks to his usual combination of intuition and deduction. In this brilliant essay written in lucid, unpretentious prose, Poe expounds a cosmogony, "a survey of the universe" contemplated in its oneness and diversity. It is a

grandiose vision based on the findings of Newton, Laplace, Leib-
nitz, Alexander von Humboldt, and other cosmologists and Poe's
conclusions are quite consonant with the conclusions of contemporary physicists. He makes a distinction between the universe
of stars studied by astronomers, which is limited, and the universe of space, which contains it and is infinite, its center, in
Pascal's phrase, being everywhere and its circumference nowhere.
An irresistible intuition, which is the sum of shadowy and elusive
inductions and deductions in his inmost mind, makes him posit a
God in the middle of this infinite void space, a God that is "not-
Matter," therefore Spirit, who originally created matter by dint of
volition out of his Spirit or from Nihility — pure matter in a state
of absolute "simplicity," i.e. of oneness, which then exploded into
apparently infinite multiplicity and diversity. Thus the physical
world in Poe's hands becomes essentially energy, perpetual motion, permanent tension between centrifugal and centripetal
forces, between attraction which is of the body and repulsion
which is of the soul, or between gravity and electricity. Because
"the atoms were, at some remote epoch of time, even *more than
together* . . . because originally and therefore normally they
were *One* . . . now, in all circumstances, they struggle *back* to
this absolutely, this irrelatively, this unconditionally *one*," as the
law of gravity shows. This "awful Present" leads to a "still more
awful Future," for all will eventually coalesce and return to Unity
and therefore to that Nothingness which both fascinates and
frightens so many of Poe's heroes: "The final globe of globes will
instantaneously disappear, and . . . God will remain all in all."
A tragic denouement to a perfect plot. *Eureka* in a way enlarges
the dimensions of the cosmos of Poe's fantastic tales. It celebrates
in metaphysical terms both the irresistible dynamism of life and
the terror of death. It posits the essential unity of the cosmos
toward which all his characters irresistibly gravitate.

   The story of the cosmos does not stop there, however; there is a
postscript to it, for Poe imagines the processes of diffusion and
concentration may be reversed forever and forever, "a novel universe swelling into existence, and then subsiding into nothingness,

at every throb of the Heart Divine," that is to say of his own heart, since we are part and parcel of the spiritual ether which pervades all matter, of "this Divine Being, who thus passes his Eternity in perpetual variation of Concentrated Self and almost Infinite Self-Diffusion." At the end of *Eureka*, the poet becomes God or God becomes the supreme poet.

Actually this apotheosis never took place — in this world at least. After he had written *Eureka*, Poe was torn by the two opposite forces of attraction and repulsion which he had described. He craved for death and wrote to his aunt and mother-in-law, Mrs. Clemm: "I must die. I have no desire to live since I have done 'Eureka.' " And at the same time he was frantically looking for a substitute for Virginia (and his mother) among a group of widows whom he courted all at once, rushing from one to the other, trying to make them promise to marry him. He thus went to Richmond in July 1849 to call on his childhood sweetheart, Mrs. Sarah Elmira Royster Shelton. On the way back he stopped at Baltimore and no one knows what happened to him there. A few days later he was found unconscious in a gutter and taken to a hospital. He died there without regaining consciousness on October 7, 1849, at the age of forty.

Two days later, the Reverend Rufus Griswold, his treacherous literary executor, launched him on his checkered posthumous career by declaring that in Poe "literary art had lost one of its most brilliant but erratic stars." From then on Poe was to be reviled by some and extravagantly lauded by others. His main weakness, besides the ethereality of his matter, is indisputably his style. Although Walter de la Mare thought that his "heightened language" captures the fancy, most readers find it on the contrary irritating, pretentious, verbose, needlessly mannered and stilted. D. H. Lawrence in particular writes: "Poe has been so praised for his style. But it seems to me a meretricious affair. 'Her marble hand' [Ligeia's] and 'the elasticity of her footfall' seem more like chairsprings and mantel-pieces than a human creature." But the most savage criticism came from Aldous Huxley in "Vulgarity in Literature." According to him Poe "is, as it were, one of Nature's

Gentlemen, unhappily cursed with incorrigible bad taste." He cannot resist the lure of paste jewels. He loves superlatives and, contrary to what Pudd'nhead Wilson and Ezra Pound were later to recommend, he never uses a noun without coupling it with an adjective preferably vague and suggestive of gloom, horror, vastness, strangeness, or indefiniteness.

Despite this proliferation of adjectives, Poe's language gives an impression of poverty and monotony, at least as far as the vocabulary of sensations is concerned. His is an intellectual style. He is not really interested in the physical world. The only precise sensuous details that he mentions are visual (sight being the most intellectual of our senses) and refer to colors — especially black, gray, and white (a sinister color with him), followed far behind by red and brown, the colors of blood, but even then he is more interested in displaying his verbal virtuosity by playing with such words as "ebony," "sable," "swarthy," "dusky," and "inky" for "black" than in defining a sensuous quality.

This lack of sensuousness was, however, to some extent deliberate and consistent with that "ideality," as he called it, with which he wanted his tales to be permeated. "The indefinite," he claimed, "is an element in the true ποίησις (poiesis)." He had therefore to wrench the reader from his usual surroundings by using "rare and radiant" words and that is why he systematically preferred Latin terms to common words of Anglo-Saxon origin. In the fantastic world of his tales, grass is never green but "verdant," an illness becomes "a malady," an outline "a contour." His characters do not see the sky but "heaven" or "the firmament," and they speak an outlandish language: "The days have never been when thou couldst love me — but her whom in life thou didst abhor, in death thou shalt adore."

The reason for Poe's relative failure is the discrepancy between the irrational nature of what he wanted to convey and the imperturbably intellectual character of his means of expression. In his writings, as in life, even when raving mad, he always behaved and expressed himself like an eighteenth-century gentleman. He felt like a romantic and even like a twentieth-century neurotic, but described his disintegrating personality in the prim and elegant language of an English essayist of the age of Steele and Addison, or of a romancer of the Gothic school. Whitman realized this and appraised him with his usual uncanny insight: "I was not an admirer [of Poe's poems], tho' I always saw that beyond their limited range of melody (like perpetual chimes of music bells, ringing from lower b flat up to g) they were melodious expressions, and perhaps never excell'd ones, of certain pronounc'd phases of human morbidity."

And yet it works. The charm operates. We cannot read or reread his best tales and poems without a thrill. Though his heroes behave in a Grand Guignol manner in rather inauthentic settings and speak an unreal language, we feel a secret kinship with them. The same nightmarish monsters which haunt them roam the deeper layers of our minds. Their fears and obsessions are ours too — at least potentially. They echo in our souls and make us aware of unplumbed depths in our inmost hearts.

■ NEWTON P. STALLKNECHT

George Santayana

DESPITE his firm and well-deserved reputation as a man of letters, George Santayana will be remembered, as he himself would have wished, primarily as a philosopher. This is not because his more strictly theoretical studies overshadow his other writings. It is rather that his memorable achievements as a poet and as a novelist, as a literary critic and as an observer of modern life, are throughout philosophical in spirit. Santayana's concept of philosophy reflects this attitude. "I should not give the title of philosopher to every logician or psychologist who, in his official and studious moments, may weigh argument against argument or may devise expedients for solving theoretical puzzles. I see no reason why a philosopher should be puzzled. What he sees he sees; of the rest he is ignorant; and his sense of this vast ignorance (which is his natural and inevitable condition) is a chief part of his knowledge and of his emotion. Philosophy is not an optional theme that may occupy him on occasion. It is his only possible life, his daily response to everything." Indeed everything that Santayana touched seemed to turn to philosophy. It is for his broad comprehension, his patient and persistent thoughtfulness, usually unmoved by the pressure of contemporary opinion, that we most admire his work.

To be sure, such thoughtfulness can constitute a limitation as well as a virtue. Ideas may solidify into preconceptions and impose a burden on the imagination. Thus Santayana's poetry and his fiction, however charming or enlightening, sometimes lack that adventurous immediacy of encounter that distinguishes the cry of a living occasion from a more deliberate meditation. His poems and the incidents and characters of his novel may at times appear as aptly chosen and elegantly executed supplements to philosophical reflection, in which understanding takes dominion over imagination. On the other hand, in his theoretical works, imagination, serving as a handmaiden to understanding, often clarifies and enlivens the progress of Santayana's argument. His choice of words is happy and invigorating even when his style is most literal. His more figurative language is often brilliant. Lucid metaphor lends his utterance a power of communication that the clichés of professional philosophy often lack, while marginal example and analogy indicate the direction of this thought and give it a concrete reference so that, as the argument unfolds, the reader feels its continued pertinence to the world of his experience.

One must admit that Santayana's work as a philosopher is not distinguished by any radical originality of doctrine. In the academic histories of American philosophy he will receive briefer notice and occupy a more modest position than his contemporaries William James, C. S. Peirce, and John Dewey. But Santayana's work taken as a whole, if we consider the scope of his thought and the variety of literary form in which it is expressed, seems as rich an offering as that made by any thinker of our century. In his work, religion, arts and letters, science, and social policy receive generous consideration and the common sense of the layman is treated with respect. All these are seen as contributing to the conscious self-interpretation of the individual in whose life civilization is realized. Although he hesitated to use the word — since its use might seem to ignore, at once, the values of religion and our sense of dependence upon nature — we may do well to think of him as a humanist, perhaps the greatest humanist of his period. Santayana's work as a whole may be characterized as a voluminous essay on man and on man's interpretation of his own situation. This essay, a long-sustained meditation, offers us, on the one hand, a perspective of human nature and, on the other, a striking portrait of Santayana himself. In more ways than one, Santayana reminds us of Montaigne. The circumstances of his life bred an independence of thought even surpassing that of the French philosopher. Indeed, Santayana may be said to have had freedom — at least an intellectual freedom — thrust upon him.

Jorge Agustín Nicolás Ruiz de Santayana y Borrás was born in 1863 in Madrid of Spanish parents. He remained a Spanish citizen throughout his life. But after his early childhood he saw little of Spain. He was brought to America at the age of nine, to be educated in Boston with the children of his mother's first marriage. Señora Santayana had been married to George Sturgis, a member of a prominent Boston family of international merchants. Before his death, she had promised Sturgis to educate their children in Boston, and she kept her word, although in the end it involved a separation from Colonel Santayana, who found New England and its climate less than congenial. Thus George Santayana's boyhood was spent as a poor relation in the heart of the well-to-do Boston that he was to describe with brilliant irony in the most telling passages of *The Last Puritan*. He studied at the Boston Latin School, acquiring English as a second language which came to replace his mother tongue. Despite the anticlericalism of his parents, Santayana was as a boy attracted by Roman Catholicism. In this he was influenced by his half sister Susana. But almost from the first he maintained an independence of judgment that led him at an early age to the study of philosophy; and his early reading included Lucretius and Spinoza.

At the age of nineteen, Santayana entered Harvard College where he took advantage of the elective system then coming into force to devote himself primarily to philosophy. He wrote poetry from time to time and contributed a number of humorous draw-ings to the *Lampoon*. Both as an undergraduate and as a grad-uate, he studied philosophy and psychology under William James and, like T. S. Eliot after him, he completed his studies by writing a doctoral dissertation under Josiah Royce. Royce persuaded him to write on the philosophy of Hermann Lotze, a German profes-sor who enjoyed a considerable reputation at the time. Santayana would have preferred to work on Schopenhauer as a more con-genial and interesting subject.

After completing his graduate studies, which included a period in Berlin, where he heard Friedrich Paulsen's lectures, Santayana taught at Harvard. He became a very successful teacher, especially of undergraduates, an ornament even to the Harvard department of philosophy, then at the height of its reputation. Among his students may be counted Gertrude Stein, T. S. Eliot, Walter Lippmann, and Bronson Cutting, while Wallace Stevens, as a spe-cial student at Harvard, submitted poetry to him. Santayana lec-tured with an apparently extemporaneous lucidity — which, how-ever, Eliot occasionally found soporific — on Plato and other fig-ures in the history of philosophy and on the philosophy of art, which led to the publication in 1896 of *The Sense of Beauty*, the first important systematic treatment of the subject in America and one that remains a classic in its field. During these years he visited Oxford, where he continued his study of Greek thought, and lectured for a brief period in Paris. From his school days on, Santayana was a prolific and persistent writer and by the early years of this century he had won recognition as a poet, a critic, a philosopher, and a consummate master of English prose.

Never entirely content as a college teacher, required as he said to lecture "under forced draught," and often ill at ease in the cultural climate of New England, Santayana resigned from the Harvard faculty as soon as his circumstances permitted, and from 1912 until his death in 1952, he lived quietly in Europe, at first briefly in Spain, during World War I in England, later in France, and finally in Rome, for some years at a hotel on the Piazza Bar-berini. Santayana's later life was one of "studious ease," devoted to philosophical and literary pursuits. He lived simply in retirement but not in isolation, a bachelor who "like the Pope" did not return visits. During World War II and thereafter until his death, Santayana was cared for — with affectionate concern as his health failed — at the nursing home of the "Blue Sisters" in Rome.

For Santayana philosophy, disciplined by a wholesome respect for the work of the natural scientist, participates with religion and the arts in what he described as the "life of reason." Reason, on this interpretation, is not limited to discursive argument but pursues by any means available an envisagement or adumbration of the values open to human realization. These values are conceived as satisfying the instinctive motivations of human nature, and reason is interpreted as "instinct enlightened by reflection." Thus, throughout his work, Santayana thought of himself as a student of morals concerned with the attitudes and ideals that contribute to the quality of our life.

As a sympathetic critic of religion, Santayana insisted that the vitality of the religious life may spring from the recognition and enjoyment of ideals to which we find ourselves committed quite aside from any belief in their supernatural origin or miraculous revelation. These ideals are entertained in imaginative and symbolic form before they appear as discursive concepts. They may seem to be products of human imagination and Santayana sometimes, especially in his earlier writings, calls them fictions. Yet they are not arbitrary imperatives. Their importance, one might say their authority, springs from their relevance to our experience as they take their place in the life of reason. Thus religion requires no assertion of historical fact and no appeal to the supernatural. For Santayana, reason may clarify but cannot overreach experience. Thus the idea of the supernatural is dismissed along with the central doctrines of traditional religion, the immortality of the soul and the existence of God. Through all his work, Santayana offers a recurrent reminder that our life cannot be divorced from its natural environment within which it must seek its fulfillment. The ways of nature, as open to our observation, remind us to expect no miracles in our favor and to recognize the extent of our ignorance. The very sight of the sea, the mountains, and the stars should teach us humility and warn us, as it did the first philosophers of Greece, not to consider human life or any idealism, however humane, as the "center and pivot of the universe." The heavens themselves declare the "indifferent, non-censorious infinity of nature." There follows a firm refusal to think of our world as motivated by supernatural forces or called into being as the realization of a divine purpose. We have no evidence to support the belief that mind can exist apart from a material milieu from which it draws its vitality; and the unspeakable variety of possible life, whose emerging species are often in conflict, suggests no providential responsibility. Nature, it is true, makes possible our human existence and the occasional emergence of human idealism, but it is not itself subject to the power or the authority of these ideals. As Santayana saw it, the refusal to accept the self-sufficiency of nature impeded modern thought, often making human self-knowledge impossible and clouding the vision even of the great philosophers.

Some students of the history of ideas may choose to classify Santayana's philosophy as post-Nietzschean in character. Like Zarathustra, Santayana faced his world well aware that "God is dead" and that man must take responsibility for the ideals to which he finds himself committed unsupported by a belief in divine revelation. Yet Santayana did not find freedom from supernatural authority an oppressive burden. The resultant responsibility did not breed a malignant anxiety or a sense of bewilderment. The practical wisdom of the Greeks and the insight into human nature offered by Christian thinkers remained sources of enlightment, if considered critically. One may profit by the great traditions without attaching an arbitrary authority to them. It is true that in his earlier years Santayana sometimes felt a sense of loss and thought of himself as an exile from a traditional faith. This attitude is often reflected in his poetry. As he grew older, however, he took increasing satisfaction in his ability to see things clearly and to speak his mind with a quiet assurance. He did not, however, relish controversy, religious or philosophical. His intent lay

in freeing religion from the embarrassment of untenable doctrine
and including it as an effective element within the life of reason.
He was not eager to break with religion, but drastically to purify
it. In the America of the early twentieth century, such an attitude
aroused far greater resistance than it would have a generation
later and called for a greater firmness of character. Thus Santayana mentions the relief that he felt while lecturing at the
Sorbonne, where he no longer had to remind himself that his
ideas might be considered unwholesome.

As he surveyed the American scene, Santayana found the polite
culture of the educated classes less than congenial. He noted, now
with ironic detachment, now with something like compassion, the
agonized conscience or sense of sinfulness that still lingered in
Calvinist New England and elsewhere. This he contrasted with
the self-confident and superficial mysticism of the transcendentalists who had reacted against their Puritan background; also
with the romantic doctrine that the highest achievement of the
artist stands above moral considerations. He found all these attitudes sadly wanting, while at the same time he viewed with equal
suspicion the secular faith in the importance of material progress
that sometimes took the place of these more genteel ways of
thought.

Nor was Santayana ready to accept democratic ideas of government as standing beyond any serious criticism, successful democracy being possible, on his view, only under unusual conditions.
Nonetheless, as a student of social relations and social values, he
recognized clearly that the whole exists for the parts. It is only in
the lives of individuals, in their health and happiness, that social
well-being can be achieved. Such an achievement is by no means
assured. Santayana never argued that history is moving automati-
cally toward a social or political millennium. Thus he held aloof
from the several forms of dogmatic optimism that had tempted
nineteenth-century philosophers. The historical extrapolations of
both liberals and Marxians seemed to him naive, if not dishonest.

Committed, as he was, to the "life of reason," Santayana found
himself, in the first decades of the century, ill at ease as he consid-

ered the intellectual temper of the age both in Europe and in America. In the early years, there were moments when he spoke out in a harsh spirit of denunciation which in later life he would have considered a rather futile gesture. But he was never reconciled to what seemed to him the shallowness, the confused and aggressive sentimentality, and the self-deceit of the time. Competitive nationalism and the dream of unlimited material progress, even if dignified by the myths of creative evolution and human perfectibility, offered no vision of enduring value. The only institutions, religious or academic, capable of resisting the attraction of these brash ideals or idols of the tribe were themselves often too demoralized and disoriented to be effective. As a result the life of reason was impoverished and civilization seemed to be stumbling in a state of aggressive confusion toward a new barbarism or cultural bankruptcy.

To be sure, this attitude of Santayana's was by no means unique. It reminds us, for instance, of the more scornful moments of E. A. Robinson as expressed in his poem "Cassandra":

> Your Dollar is your only Word,
> The wrath of it your only fear.
> . . . .
> You have the ages for your guide,
> But not the wisdom to be led.
> . . . .
> Are you to pay for what you have
> With all you are?

In these famous lines, Robinson spoke with greater power but with no greater bitterness than the young Santayana. Neither writer had to wait for the catastrophe of World War I to free him from the presiding illusions of his generation. In later life, Santayana was able to survey the current scene more patiently, accepting human blindness and perversity without indignation. In his early writing he met with scorn the hypocrisy "That talks of freedom and is slave to riches," a hypocrisy that breeds only conflict and confusion.

> What would you gain, ye seekers, with your striving,
> Or what vast Babel raise you on your shoulders?
> You multiply distresses, and your children
> Surely will curse you.

These forebodings may have been premature but, a full lifetime after their expression, they carry a warning not to be lightly brushed aside.

Santayana's naturalism and his repudiation of the moral outlook of his contemporaries constitute the more negative aspect of his philosophy. This stands as a background for his more positive intention as a moralist to put first things first in the consideration of human affairs. This enterprise was essentially a critique of Western cvilization and was directed toward a reconciliation of Greek and Christian ethics. He willingly endorsed the ideal of self-realization and the harmonious development of the capacities and talents of the individual, although he saw clearly that its pursuit should not tolerate a ruthless self-assertion but should rather be guided by disciplined self-knowledge and tempered by human sympathies and a sense of social responsibility.

On the other hand, he spoke with persuasive eloquence of moments when the sense of selfhood is overcome as the life of the spirit culminates in disinterested intelligence and disinterested admiration, virtues which, he believed, carry with them their own rewards. Santayana describes this maturity or freedom of the spirit as an activity of contemplation. Yet it may achieve not only an intellectual satisfaction but also the enjoyment of things beautiful and the admiration of the many forms of human excellence. The spirit is set free by the happy recognition of things worthwhile in themselves. Such freedom may culminate in a religious affirmation of a way of life. Yet the spirit cannot dominate its world, and its vision is often distracted by hardships and temptations, while its cherished ideals are thwarted by circumstance. The spirit cannot escape disappointment, even disillusion. Still the recognition and enjoyment of ideal possibilities, even though but partially realized, can transform our existence and, as Santayana once put it, help to make a long life worth more than a short one. The spirit need not in the freedom of its transcendence ignore or repudiate its world. Thus Santayana recognized the virtue of Christian charity as a practical expression of spiritual maturity. "Charity will always judge a soul not by what it has succeeded in fashioning externally, not by the body or the words, or the works that are the wreckage of its voyage, but by the elements of light and love that the soul infused into that inevitable tragedy." It is only after we have come fully to recognize the insecurity of our existence and to admit that the human enterprise can achieve no more than a passing shadow, even a caricature, of perfection that we are ready to share fully in such insight.

Here Santayana's philosophy appears as profoundly Christian in moral orientation. Nonetheless there are many readers inclined to interpret the final achievement of the spirit as a subordination of human attitudes and evaluations to the supremacy of aesthetic enjoyment. According to such a reading, imagination may be said to offer us a purely aesthetic perfection that lures our attention away from the shabby incompleteness of our world and reconciles us, at least momentarily, to existence. Such a philosophy, recalling passages from Schopenhauer and Pater, may have briefly appealed to Santayana in his younger days, as some of the sonnets suggest. But in his mature thought Santayana is more inclined to subordinate the aesthetic to the moral. He dismisses the notion of art for art's sake: "beauty, being a good, is a moral good; and the practice and enjoyment of art, like all practice and enjoyment, fall within the sphere of morals." After all, the arts contribute to the life of reason, in Santayana's sense; and this life must make room for many values besides the aesthetic.

This philosophy not only appears in Santayana's more systematic and theoretical writings but is reflected in his poems, his occasional essays, and his novel, *The Last Puritan*. Santayana's attitude reflects the influence of Platonism, of Christian ethics, and of ancient and modern naturalism; and yet, perhaps because of his profound sincerity, it does not seem to be an eclectic compromise but a reconciliation of ideas that we cannot honestly overlook once they are freed from their supernatural entanglements. Santayana was well aware that these ideas belong to our civilization, and he never insisted upon the novelty of his thought. He took pleasure in declaring his debt to his great predecessors and he looked back upon the European tradition in a spirit of gratitude, almost of piety.

His relation to his contemporaries and immediate predecessors, however, was another matter. He was little inclined to commit himself to the narrowing influence of a school or a program, and he preferred to stand alone. It is not, to be sure, difficult to recognize certain affinities: with Matthew Arnold, for example, and with Ritschlian theology. But despite these echoes, Santayana first appeared upon the American scene as an independent, even an isolated, thinker. As a result he has been sometimes misunderstood and the reception of his work has been varied. Its tone has vacillated from an almost reverent admiration to an unqualified hostility. He has been warmly accepted as a champion of sanity, an archenemy of intellectual dishonesty; and he has been condemned now as an aesthete, now as a sentimentalist. To many he has appeared as the prototype of the philosopher for whom contemplation, humane and yet personally disinterested, is a natural and spontaneous attitude, and whose quiet voice clarifies, even epitomizes, our civilization. This estimate has found its most memorable expression in Wallace Stevens' beautiful poem, "To an Old Philosopher in Rome," written at the time of Santayana's death in that city. Stevens, who had since his student days at Harvard followed Santayana's work, saluted him as "The one invulnerable man among / Crude captains," yet added the moving lines "each of us / Beholds himself in you, and hears his voice / In yours, master and commiserable man." Stevens saw clearly that for Santayana the life of the spirit springs from an awareness of things human and mortal: "The life of the city never lets go, nor do you / Ever want it to." Stevens found in Santayana's philosophy a few congenial ideas that are reflected in his own concept of poetry as the matrix and vehicle of a "supreme fiction" that gives meaning to our lives. He praised Santayana as an intellectual and spiritual leader and spoke warmly of the charm of his poetry. This Stevens admired despite the great difference between his own restless and independent style and the more traditional tone of Santayana's verse.

This tribute, although the most eloquent and perhaps the most sympathetic, does not stand alone. Santayana's work has appealed to many people whose background widely differs from that of Wallace Stevens. Justice Oliver Wendell Holmes read his essays with lively interest and he received cordial recognition from such writers as Middleton Murry, Ludwig Lewisohn, Ellen Glasgow, R. P. Blackmur, and Owen Barfield. Professional philosophers including John Dewey, Bertrand Russell, Alfred North Whitehead, and Morris Cohen found much to commend in his more theoretical studies. Russell admitted that Santayana had made clear to him the narrowness of his earlier writings on ethics; and Whitehead was happy to claim Santayana's notion of "animal faith" in support of his own theory of perception. At almost the same time, Walter Lippmann, in his widely read *Preface to Morals*, drew from Santayana the background of a philosophy of disinterested evaluation and commitment.

As a philosopher, Santayana has enjoyed a wider influence among laymen than in strictly professional and academic circles. Unlike the work of James, Dewey, or Whitehead his writings have not encouraged the formation of a school of professional thought, although a few distinguished followers have interpreted and developed his argument with sympathy. Of these Irwin Edman is perhaps the best known, but one should add the names of B. A. G. Fuller, the brilliant historian of philosophy, and John Herman Randall whose widely read *Making of the Modern Mind* contains numerous references to Santayana as a mature representative of modern thought. Many laymen have shared this view; and outside the academic world Santayana's obvious sincerity and his modesty have won the hearts of many. His witty refusal to pose as a polymath, a temptation all too common among professional writers on philosophy, has at once amused and impressed readers. His remark, "I am an ignorant man, almost a poet," has disarmed many critics both literary and philosophical — as also his admission that his own arguments might well have been more cogently stated had he mastered the techniques of mathematical logic. Here Santayana accepted a criticism of his work offered by Bertrand Russell. Russell, however, was generous enough to point out that Santayana's contribution contains more than a little truth despite its literary and therefore, for Russell, primitive style of presentation. Santayana took this criticism in good part. After all, he was addressing a public of thoughtful laymen, not a profession of technically trained specialists; and he preferred to do so.

In America, Santayana's reputation as a critic has in part centered upon the fact that in 1911 he coined a phrase that has been used again and again by other writers. He spoke of the "genteel tradition" in American philosophy and letters, suggesting that polite literature had remained too long under the influence of a Puritan heritage, only to some extent softened by the influence of the transcendentalists. American, or at least New England, culture can hardly be said to have had a genuine youth or spring-time of its own. It acquired at birth the mature, even sophisticated, attitudes of an older tradition. This conservatism, at once timid and haughty, was symbolized by the colonial mansion and its suburban facsimile. It tended to ignore the issues emerging from the new regime of factory and skyscraper and thus to divorce "culture" from "life" to the detriment of both. Santayana's phrase, "the genteel tradition," became a cliché repeated with slight changes of meaning in many noteworthy contexts, among them Sinclair Lewis' speech in acceptance of the Nobel Prize. Such writers as Vernon Parrington and Malcolm Cowley found the phrase a useful one, and for some years it was a commonplace of literary conversation.

Despite widespread recognition, Santayana did not always win the sympathy of his readers. Some who admired his prose found his attitude one of condescending disapproval and, despite his censure of the genteel tradition, of withdrawal from the modern scene. This impression is largely the outcome of Santayana's more than academic readiness to interpret and evaluate the present in terms of the past and his cautious reserve before new ideas and modes of expression. Santayana was, to be sure, no mere antiquarian; and yet after turning the pages of his witty *Dialogues in Limbo,* where he converses with Democritus and Socrates, one might picture him as hesitating upon the threshold of our century and accepting its invitation with courteous, if slightly ironical, reservations, insisting upon bringing with him his own philosophy and his own sense of value.

Even Santayana's kindly teacher William James, who recognized his great talents, praised his work with reservations. Displeased by his rather callow distaste for Browning and Whitman, James spoke of the "moribund latinity" of Santayana's criticism and the fastidious detachment of his "white marble mind." For James, these remarks were little more than friendly banter but they are nevertheless characteristic of a considerable body of adverse opinion. Somewhat sharper is the acid reference by Paul Shorey, the Plato scholar, to Santayana as "that dainty unassimilated man." But perhaps the most trenchant repudiation of Santayana's criticism came from Van Wyck Brooks who found his attitude toward his American predecessors narrowly prejudiced. Brooks's judgment is not without foundation. Santayana's treatment of the transcendentalists was often high-handed. Certainly Emerson had no intention of fostering a genteel tradition and was more hospitable toward new movements than the young Santayana, especially in the case of Whitman.

Some critics have condemned Santayana as a sentimental champion of the attitudes of Roman Catholicism, accepted without its underlying theology. Such comment is less perverse than that interpreting Santayana as an aesthete committed to the dogma of art for art's sake, but it is still wide of the mark. This misconception has been perpetuated by the witticism that for Santayana "there is no God and Mary is his mother." This remark, perhaps initiated in a playful moment by Bertrand Russell, has been repeated so often that it has acquired a spurious authority. Its last

prominent appearance is in a poem by Robert Lowell. Yet it remains a travesty. There were moments, some of them recorded
in his poetry, when Santayana admired the charm of the naive
faith that he had intellectually outgrown; but the respect for the
Christian tradition that characterizes his mature thought was by
no means a sentimental gesture. It sprang from the fact that he
shared with another atheist, the poet A. E. Housman, the firm
conviction that Luke 17:33 expresses the most important truth
that ever was uttered. "Whosoever shall seek to save his life shall
lose it, and whosoever shall lose his life shall preserve it."

Santayana was Catholic in his sympathies only in the sense
that he found Catholicism more congenial than its Protestant opponent. But he belonged to neither group intellectually or emotionally. He did find in Roman worship a greater warmth of
feeling than was apparent in Boston Unitarianism, and certainly
he was dismayed by the aggressive aspects of a Protestantism
that thinks "optimism akin to piety" and "poverty a sort of dis-
honorable punishment." But the Roman attitude toward religion,
centering upon the unqualified acceptance of an institutional
authority, was not acceptable to him. His was not the contrite
or guilty consciousness that Hegel attributed to the Middle Ages.
Surely no one can follow Santayana's reflections on Dante, whose
poetry he recognized as the magnificent culmination of medieval
Christianity, without noticing important reservations. He could
not, for instance, sympathize with Dante's moments of uneasy
fearfulness that seem at times to mar, if not to distort, the virtue
of humility; and he did not hesitate to contrast the courage of
Goethe's Faust with what he took to be Dante's timidity.

It is true that Santayana's air of detachment and cosmopolitan
independence has alienated some readers; and one can understand that the famous words in which he made a virtue of this detachment may seem to many little more than an eloquent exaggeration that, strangely enough, echoes Martin Luther. "In the
past or in the future, my language and my borrowed knowledge
would have been different, but under whatever sky I had been
born, since it is the same sky, I should have had the same philoso-

phy." So sweeping an assumption should hardly be expressed with such an air of confidence. Nor is this self-interpretation quite consistent with Santayana's profound respect for the moral values inherited from the Greek and Christian traditions, under whose influence he lived and thought. However this may be, one might fairly call him a man without a country. After his childhood he was never at home in his native land to which he paid only occasional visits and whose language he found, as a man of letters, not fully at his command; and both in England and in America his attitude was that of a visitor well acquainted with the life and language of the country but still essentially that of a spectator. His habitual attitude was, as he would say, "under whatever sky" — that of the wandering scholar. This suited him well and was profoundly characteristic of his philosophy.

Yet Santayana's contribution as a philosopher and a man of letters has a proper place in the history of American culture. After all, although during the last forty years of his life he lived solely in Europe, he was throughout his career influential on the American scene rather more than elsewhere; and his thinking, despite its independence, may, as he himself admitted, often be interpreted as a response to his encounter with American life and thought, certainly more so than to that of any other country. *The Last Puritan* is as much a comment upon American life, viewed from within, as any work of Henry James or William Dean Howells. Again, some of Santayana's most cogent writing occurs in essays in which he deliberately undertook to influence American opinion. Nonetheless, despite his genuine interest in things American, Santayana felt little attachment and no deep loyalty to the United States. This is clearly apparent to the reader. If we are to profit fully from his criticism of American life, we must accept his occasional outbursts of irritation. In the long run, his prejudices were superficial and his more deliberate judgments intended to be fair. In this connection, one should not overlook that exuberant piece of satirical doggerel entitled "Young Sammy's First Wild Oats," a sprightly comment upon the American imperialism of the Spanish war. One could wish that all criticism of

American policy were as generous, as thoughtful, and as witty. There remains an important ground of difference between Santayana's philosophy of life and American thought whether popular or academic. Santayana did not find in democracy any obvious superiority over other modes of government. He considered Thomas Jefferson a fanatic and he viewed the ideal of popular sovereignty with frank suspicion. Certainly it was not to be saluted as time's noblest offspring whose vices are to be discounted as superficial blemishes. Nor are we to suppose that a universal franchise and a bill of rights can guarantee a sense of fellowship and community or a concern for one's neighbor's happiness. They may, indeed, awaken in some a ruthless competitiveness and in others an aggressive conformity. Santayana's political theory is essentially Platonic. Authority should reside in the decisions of carefully trained and personally disinterested administrators who are dedicated to their vocation. To be sure, Santayana admired some features of the fascist corporate state, but he considered Mussolini an unscrupulous, even a wicked, man. He had no more sympathy for the charismatic adventurer or self-appointed dictator than had Plato.

Santayana's political theory is, philosophically speaking, a restatement of an ancient tradition. If anywhere, it is in his philosophy of art that his thinking approaches genuine originality. Even here his ideas are not revolutionary but his argument frees itself from standardized interpretations and displays a freshness of its own. For Santayana value enters the universe with the emergence of conscious awareness. "The good when actually realized is a joy taken in the immediate." There is no such thing as a value that cannot be enjoyed. This seems most obviously true when we consider the status of the beautiful. Beauty must be defined in terms of pleasure or satisfied taste. It is, indeed, nothing more than pleasure taken directly in the contemplation of an object. "The test is always the same. Does the thing actually please?" To delight in jewels because they are expensive is a vulgar "self-excommunication" from intrinsic enjoyment. To love glass beads for their own sake may be barbarous but, for all that, a genuine appreciation. We do not enjoy the beauty of an object because it reminds us of something else or because it serves as a means to an end. In our enjoyment of the beautiful, our pleasure is inseparable from the presence of an object before our perception. Yet we do not feel that the beautiful object produces our pleasure or comfort as, let us say, a blanket or a bed warmer might do. On the contrary, we take a direct pleasure in the thing itself. This statement might seem a commonplace in the philosophy of art. But Santayana goes further and offers a challenging observation. We are, he insists, moved to recognize our delight as an actual quality of the object, a quality as proper to its existence as its shape or color. The sense of beauty objectifies our pleasure. Our delight is transmuted in a moment of self-forgetfulness into a sense of the object's value. In reality, this value lies in the object's fitness or adaptation to our powers of perception and enjoyment. The sense of beauty carries with it a fleeting intimation that we need not always be at odds with our world. It offers a fulfillment that at times recompenses us for the anxieties and frustrations of our existence.

There are many kinds of beauty since there are many kinds of objects that offer us such direct enjoyment. Thus we can find beauty in the charm of a flower, the harmony of line and color in a landscape or a picture, the "glorious monotony of the stars," the expressive power of a poem or a painting. If we define the sense of beauty as a feeling of objectified pleasure, we must admit that beauty does not arise in isolation from other values, since the enjoyment that we take in a beautiful object always has a character of its own distinct from its purely aesthetic aspect as an objectification of pleasure. There are many kinds of pleasure that can be objectified. Indeed such enjoyment may be directed toward objects of moral significance. Poetry can pass into religion as it celebrates attitudes and ideals whose presence in symbolic form claims our full attention and our spontaneous admiration.

Santayana's best criticism is philosophical in spirit; and his critical essays offer an attractive and informal introduction to his thought as a whole. His studies of individual authors include patient attempts to perceive their characteristic attitudes and to understand the view of things that each has come to accept. His evaluations are presented in terms of his own philosophy. He may, to be sure, speak occasionally of more strictly literary matters. He praises both Shakespeare's exuberance of language, which grants the verbal medium a spectacular prominence of its own and the apparently effortless transparency of Dante's verse. But he does not analyze such features at length, and he does not offer close readings of chosen passages. In his thinking the literary critic is never isolated from the moralist. Thus Santayana's first adventures in criticism contributed as much to a philosophy of civilization as to an appreciation of literature. In his earlier essays, he recognized the cultural importance of imagination, especially the imagination of the poet, as it furthers the life of reason. Poetry may be described as "rational," not because it follows a pattern of discursive argument but because, as in a Sophoclean chorus, it brings a presiding order into our life of thought and feeling, helping us, in the words of Plato's *Timaeus,* "to cope with what is unmeasured and chaotic in our minds." Devotion to this ideal of rational poetry led Santayana at one time to view with condescension the work of those authors who seek something less comprehensive. "To dwell, as irrational poets do, on some private experience, on some emotion without representative or ulterior value, then, seems a waste of time. Fiction becomes less interesting than affairs, and poetry turns into a sort of incompetent whimper, a childish foreshortening of the outspread world."

When such "short-winded" poetry becomes self-confident and assertive, valuing intensity of experience for its own sake, it may be described as barbarous. Poetry of this sort, headstrong and irrational, is to be contrasted with the "victorious" imagination that, overcoming the confusion and vacillations of our daily lives, places us within a "cosmos" or scheme of ideal order and value. Here we may be reminded of Paul Valéry's "hero" who in "Ode Secrète" singles out the constellations and identifies each in an act of pictorial imagination, thus translating mere experience into orientation and taking possession of his world. A victorous imagination takes dominion over our consciousness, synthesizing rather than interrupting experience. As the centuries pass, such dominion may take many forms. Each one of these deserves sympathetic participation, but it was in the poetry of the Greeks that Santayana first discovered the moral power of the imagination. In 1900, he praised ancient literature as happily embodying the life of reason: "The ancients found poetry not so much in sensible accidents as in essential forms and noble associations; and this fact marks very clearly their superior education. They dominated the world as we no longer dominate it, and lived, as we are too distracted to live in the presence of the rational and the important."

Santayana's uncompromising devotion to the ideal of rational poetry led him to condemn Browning and Whitman as gifted barbarians and to regret the absence of a presiding religious or moral commitment in Shakespeare. Santayana sharply rebuked Browning for his failure to grasp the religious spirit that had inspired the Italy to which he seemed so devoted. Browning "saw, he studied, and he painted a decapitated Italy. His vision could not mount so high as her head." It was clear to Santayana that widespread sympathies and alert sensibility even when combined with rare powers of description and expression cannot bring literature to its highest stage of development, since they cannot by themselves or in union bring order and direction into our lives. Thus, in Santayana's early thinking Shakespeare stands below Dante and Lucretius. Furthermore, all theory that supports the maxim "art for art's sake" is grossly inadequate since it praises a moment of aesthetic enjoyment isolated from a more comprehensive sense of value. This conviction led Santayana to write two adversely critical reviews of Croce's *Aesthetic*. In these essays, Santayana is virtually defining his own position by repudiating the thought of the Italian philosopher. Santayana could not tolerate Croce's doctrine that intuitive expression, the act of imaginative synthesis whereby feeling (i.e., any feeling) is embodied in imagery, constitutes in itself the intrinsic value of the arts. For

Santayana, at this period, aesthetic experience enjoys no isolated autonomy. It cannot retain its value if separated from the complex of interests and ideals over which the rational imagination seeks to preside. This attitude was cogently expressed in 1910 in the opening lines of *Three Philosophical Poets.* "The sole advantage in possessing great works of literature lies in what they can help us to become." The function of the critic is that of a cicerone whose interpretation opens the masterpieces of the past to a reading public, keeping "their perennial humanity living and capable of assimilation."

For the poetry of classical polytheism Santayana felt a lively sympathy which he shared with many of the romantic poets, but for reasons of his own. In a few notable passages, he presents us with a charming, if somewhat idealized, picture of ancient poetry. "All that we may fairly imagine to have been in the mind of the pious singer is the sense that something divine comes down among us in the crises of our existence . . . The gods sometimes appear, and when they do they bring us a foretaste of that sublime victory of mind over matter which we may never gain in experience but which may constantly be gained in thought . . . A god is a conceived victory of mind over Nature. A visible god is the consciousness of such a victory momentarily attained. The vision soon vanishes, the sense of omnipotence is soon dispelled by recurring conflicts with hostile forces; but the momentary illusion of that realized good has left us with the perennial knowledge of good as an ideal. Therein lies the essence and the function of religion."

Great poetry need not, however, confine itself to the celebration of human life in mythic fashion. It may concern itself more directly with our place in nature and remind us that we cannot in all honesty hope to escape from our world. This sense of reality is an indispensable element of the life of reason, which owes as much to Lucretius as to Pindar. The materialism as well as the mythology of the ancients deserves respect, not that it presents an accurate account of the origin of things but rather that it is a reminder of our dependence upon them.

The philosophy of Lucretius is one of thoughtful resignation, springing from a wholesome sense of human limitations, human life being but a part of nature. "All things are dust, and to dust they return; a dust, however, eternally fertile, and destined to fall perpetually into new, and doubtless beautiful, forms. . . . To perceive universal mutation, to feel the vanity of life, has always been the beginning of seriousness. It is the condition for any beautiful, measured, or tender philosophy. Prior to that, everything is barbarous, both in morals and in poetry; for until then mankind has not learned to renounce anything, has not outgrown the instinctive egotism and optimism of the young animal, and has not removed the centre of its being, or of its faith, from the will to the imagination."

Santayana interprets the wisdom of Lucretius as centering upon a recognition that "nothing arises save by the death of something else." This fact must be recognized not only by the materialist but by any poet or philosopher who squarely faces the human situation. Death, including the death of each of us, is a moment of nature, in a sense a part of life. We must accept it, as we accept our presence in the world, in a spirit of natural piety. Santayana reminds us, however, that Lucretius' practical psychology is at times faulty. Thus his advocacy of the Epicurean doctrine, that there is nothing to feel in death so that "where we are, death is not; where death is we are not," is hardly a firm bulwark against the dread of mortality. We can take shelter behind it only by ignoring or trying to ignore the fact that the fear of death is often for many of us a love of life. But this love may be more than a mere clinging to existence. It may carry us beyond ourselves in a flood of self-forgetfulness as we discover the ideal perfections that our own existence all too meagerly reflects. The Platonist and the Christian praise this attitude of love and admiration as in itself an approach to an ideal. Such thought reaches its poetic culmination in the myths of Plato and in Dante's great poem on heaven and hell. Dante's vision includes a brilliant hierarchy of possible achievements open to those in whose lives love has healed the moral and spiritual blindness by which human nature is constantly threatened. This is a blindness capable of terminating the growth of the spirit and reducing it to a state of permanent and hopeless frustration, where the love of life has yielded to despair.

But Santayana remains a naturalist. For him, love, humility, self-forgetfulness, and self-transcendence may free the human spirit without the benefit of supernatural interference; nor need we think of salvation as a metaphysical escape from our world. Yet we may willingly forgive Dante his supernaturalism and cherish his ideal of salvation which may help us to accept our destiny in peace of mind, a peace not purchased, as that of the Stoics and Epicureans so often has been, at the expense of human sympathies. For all his supernatural trappings, Dante may help us to recognize that love may be its own reward. We may even profit by the celestial cadre of Dante's poetry. It offers more than fanciful embellishment or marginal illumination. It contains a symbolic language which, when properly read, clarifies our sense of value. All told, Dante stands as the type of a consummate poet. Despite his medieval contrition and his exaggerated fearfulness, his moral vision is clear and confident and his sense of value deeply significant even for those who cannot accept the literal truth of his world drama. When discussing Dante, Santayana brought to full and detailed exemplification the ideal of poetry that was first sketched in 1900 in the opening pages of *Interpretations of Poetry and Religion,* where he had written: "Poetry is called religion when it intervenes in life; and religion, when it merely supervenes upon life, is seen to be nothing but poetry . . . For the dignity of religion, like that of poetry and of every moral ideal, lies precisely in its ideal adequacy, in its fit rendering of the meanings and values of life, in its anticipation of perfection."

These words apply happily to Dante's achievement as Santayana conceives of it. But this attitude is a transitional one, and the argument of *Three Philosophical Poets* carries us beyond any unqualified approbation of Dante. Dante, although a consummate poet and unrivaled as a master of supernatural symbolism, lacks Lucretius' concern for the goings-on of nature considered without reference to any possible anthropocentric interpretation. What is more, Dante lacks Goethe's Faust-like eagerness, characteristic of many romantic artists, to participate imaginatively in the manifold possibilities of human experience, each to be enjoyed for its own sake, without references to the values established by a comprehensive philosophy of life. Thus Santayana's treatment of Dante in *Three Philosophical Poets* marks a significant departure from his earlier position.

Santayana had learned from William James rather more than the latter recognized when he censured his pupil's "moribund latinity." Under James's tutelage, Santayana came to give full attention to the rich detail of immediate awareness taken *in concreto,* the "unadulterated, unexplained, instant fact of experience," accepted with a minimum of intellectual assumptions. The character of such experience may be slurred over by a mind unable or unwilling to free itself from the pressures of tradition or prejudice. Such an attitude can undermine the life of reason, and isolate from reality the cultural life of a whole nation. On the other hand, sheer sensation is just as barren as any dogma arbitrarily taken to be self-evident. The poet who merely swims "out into the sea of sensibility . . . to picture all possible things, real or unreal, human or inhuman, would bring materials only to the workshop of art; he would not be an artist." For Santayana a mind may be free, sincere, and articulate, and yet remain bewildered. Experience accepted as an end and a justification of life is a self-defeating ideal that can result in the restlessness and recurring ennui, the sense of frustration, with which the enthusiasm of the romantic so often ends. It can also invite a self-centered irresponsibility, which Santayana found in Goethe and so sharply condemned, perhaps caricatured, in the witty dialogue of *The Last Puritan.* At no time could Santayana abide the romantic theology that justifies Faust's ultimate salvation.

The Santayana of *Three Philosophical Poets* tries deliberately to avoid extremes. Although himself no Kantian, his literary theory echoes the seminal insight of Immanuel Kant upon which so much of modern philosophy is founded. "Concepts without perceptions are empty, perceptions without concepts are blind," or, as Santayana would prefer to say, bewildered. Experience must seek understanding or wander in confusion; yet understanding must be continually refreshed by experience or it will wither into a narrow and brittle ideology, a genteel tradition, remote from life and increasingly irrelevant to our experience. Thus the supreme poet will not be one to confine himself to the imaginative envisagement of a comprehensive ideal. Whatever his sense of value, he will recognize our place in the world, accepting our physical predicament and repudiating too eager an anthropomorphic interpretation or evaluation of nature. At least, he will always recognize that our ideals do not shape or control our world. Nor will his idealism constitute a barrier between his thinking and that of other men. He will be able to comprehend with sympathy the experience of life open to those who do not share his vision. He will be at home, like Shakespeare, in the pluriverse of human affairs, ambitions, and ideals as they appear among men of varied and contrasting temperament and background. Yet he will hold firmly to the idealism that has taken shape within his own experience.

Santayana hastens to remind us that this "supreme poet is in limbo still." For all his virtues he does not exist. The supreme poet is himself an ideal. Once we are willing to admit that, although reflecting a genuine possibility, the supreme poet has not existed and may never exist, we find ourselves inclined toward a far more tolerant consideration and grateful acceptance of those poets who do. Santayana was no longer eager to condemn irrational poetry, and he ceased to use such terms as "barbarous" or "childish" when writing of famous men. In fact, his thinking seemed in later years to be moved by his growing disapproval of a certain narrowness which he felt to be present in the criticism of the neo-humanists, like Irving Babbitt, and more especially in that of T. S. Eliot. As the years pass, we find Santayana defending Shakespeare against Dante in reply to Eliot. The fact that Shakespeare, unlike Sophocles or Dante, does not offer us a vision of the best to be enjoyed, so to speak, in its own right need not keep us from recognizing the moral significance of many passages and incidents in his plays. The nihilism of Macbeth's "Tomorrow and tomorrow and tomorrow" is not to be condemned, as T. S. Eliot once supposed, as a statement of an inferior or truncated philosophy. Taken in context, this passage may be seen magnificently to epitomize the state of mind and the view of life that Macbeth at the end of his career cannot escape, a fact which he, being still something of a hero and thus unable wholly to deceive himself, remains capable of grasping. Read in this way, the speech is a noble one and its connotations within the structure of the play are by no means nihilistic. Macbeth's cry of despair tells us more of "moral evil and of good" than most poets — and most philosophers — ever succeed in doing. As a moralist, Santayana cannot help but admire, and even participate in, the many human perspectives that Shakespeare sets before us. To be sure, his many insights are not subordinated to any central or overarching ideal, expressed either as concept or symbol. Nor is any supernatural support recognized or invoked. Again and again, Shakespeare penetrates and evaluates the manifold complexities of human motivation, of human actions, their character and consequences, without trying to reduce his concrete pluriverse to an ordered cosmos. Tragedy and comedy may be found on every hand but there is no inclusive world drama or divine comedy. Santayana was well aware that our modern world is not a cosmos and that the poet must be, in Stevens' phrase, a "connoisseur of chaos." Although he is privileged in his own life and work to resist the pressure of what he may call "absolute" fact, he must not overlook its presence or seek wholly to triumph over it.

Perhaps this later attitude of Santayana's is expressed most happily in his warm appreciation of Charles Dickens, whose novels he praises in the same spirit that led him to revise his opinion of Shakespeare. Dickens, far more than Shakespeare, is "disinherited" in that his thinking is not organized about ideas. He derives, in fact, little or nothing from the great traditions of thought. Yet Dickens' sympathetic participation in life is complete and genuine, for he feels the presence of good and evil intensely and finds people more important than institutions. But, despite his humanity, Dickens is a master of "pure" or "merciless" comedy. In a few exuberant sentences, perhaps the finest that he ever wrote although he once called them sophomoric, Santayana paid his respects to comedy of this sort and to the naive but uncompromising wisdom that lies behind it.

The most grotesque creatures of Dickens are not exaggerations or mockeries of something other than themselves; they arise because nature generates them, like toadstools; they exist because they can't help it, as we all do. The fact that these perfectly self-justified beings are absurd appears only by comparison, and from outside; circumstances, or the expectations of other people, make them ridiculous and force them to contradict themselves; but in nature it is no crime to be exceptional. . . . If Oedipus and Lear and Cleopatra do not seem ridiculous, it is only because tragic reflection has taken them out of the context in which, in real life, they would have figured. If we saw them as facts, and not as emanations of a poet's dream, we should laugh at them till doomsday; what grotesque presumption, what silly whims, what mad contradiction of the simplest realities! Yet we should not laugh at them without feeling how real their griefs were; as real and terrible as the griefs of children and of dreams. But facts, however serious inwardly, are always absurd outwardly; and the just critic of life sees both truths at once, as Cervantes did in *Don Quixote*. A pompous idealist who does not see the ridiculous in *all* things is the dupe of his sympathy and abstraction; and a clown, who does not see that these ridiculous creatures are living quite in earnest, is the dupe of his egotism. Dickens saw the absurdity, and understood the life; I think he was a good philosopher.

As we have seen, Santayana's criticism grew more generous and more tolerant with the years, and he came gradually to recognize many achievements that he had once been inclined to overlook. He admitted that successful poetry need not be rich in wisdom or perceive the moral burden of life. It may, in a spirit of sheer lyricism, confine itself to a moment of awareness if only "it utters the vital impulses of that moment with enough completeness." By 1922 he had outgrown his outright condemnation of "short-winded" verse and anticipated Wallace Stevens' belief that the poem may be the cry of an occasion. This late attitude remained, however, one of toleration. Santayana never retreated from the position that great literature must clarify our sense of ultimate values.

Santayana has spoken of Emerson as one "whose religion was all poetry, a poet whose only pleasure was thought." These words we might well apply to their author, at least while we consider his achievement as a poet. In a remarkably honest and astute passage of self-criticism, Santayana has characterized his own verse in almost similar terms. Santayana's poetry reflects for the most part his earlier conception of literary value, and of this he was clearly aware. His poems do not, as a rule, spring from the "chance experience of a stray individual." They contain, on the contrary, passages of sustained meditation, in fact, his philosophy in the making. His poetry lacks, as he himself readily admitted, that "magic and pregnancy of phrase" that constitutes the "creation of a fresh idiom" and marks the highest achievement of the poet. But readers generally respect the thoughtfulness of his verse and enjoy the "aura of literary and religious associations" that surrounds it. In his poetry, Santayana's acceptance of tradition both of theme and of style may amount to submissiveness that welcomes and celebrates a rich heritage of idea and feeling. His poems transpose ideas into a pictorial imagery traditionally appropriate and realized in an elegant, although rarely a very powerful, diction.

Much of Santayana's poetry seems today flaccid and without energy. In his prose, he aimed at clarity of thought and invited the sympathy of the reader, subordinating all matters of style to these intentions. In his verse, form and manner often seem to have been ends in themselves and thus to resist the full realization of meaning. And yet at least once or twice Santayana completely escaped these limitations. The lines on Cape Cod are translucent and flawless and quite without any distracting artificiality. In this poem, language, rhythm, and imagery yield fully to the sense of forlorn exile that is sustained throughout. The scene becomes a haunting symbol of loneliness, an end of the world, whose beauty lives in its very desolation. In his early life, Santayana sometimes thought of himself as an exile, and these lines spring from an experience as deeply felt as that in any of the sonnets, less doctrinaire in concept, and more spontaneous in expression.

> The low sandy beach and the thin scrub pine,
> The wide reach of bay and the long sky line,—
> O, I am far from home!
> . . . .
> The wretched stumps all charred and burned,
> And the deep soft rut where the cartwheel turned,—
> Why is the world so old?

We may compare the sad monotone of the Cape Cod shoreline with the rich and sensuous charm of the Mediterranean, celebrated in the sapphic stanzas of Santayana's fifth ode. This poem is less haunting and more contrived than the lines on Cape Cod and not as obviously a personal confession. Yet the Northman's longing for the southern sea and the sense of fulfillment with which he returns to it reveal the nostalgia of the author. This nostalgia, or sense of alienation, inspired much of Santayana's poetry. As he outgrew it, his need to express himself in verse seems almost to have evaporated.

One should not overlook Santayana's occasional success as an author of light verse. His parody, or rather his translation into modern dress, of Shakespeare's "When in disgrace with fortune and men's eyes" is brilliant, a very acceptable poem in its own right, free of the archaic artificiality of his own earlier sonnets. I have already mentioned "Young Sammy's First Wild Oats" which may today remind us of some of Auden's more whimsical work. It is a masterpiece of its kind. Its wit is penetrating and the apparently careless verse suits the convivial occasion on which the poem was read. The author of such spirited yet good-natured polemic could have made of himself, had he wished to do so, a very formidable pamphleteer. One might add that the poetic dialogue in Santayana's closet drama, when satirical in spirit, comes at times

suddenly to life and deserves consideration apart from its otherwise rather undistinguished context.

In his novel, *The Last Puritan,* Santayana presented a brilliant
picture, now ironical, now sympathetic, of the America that he
had known and known well before he retired to Europe. His attention is turned for the most part to the manners, attitudes, and
beliefs of well-to-do and cultivated people in New England and
New York. There are memorable glimpses of life at Harvard as
well as pictures of Eton and scenes from British clerical and scholastic life, some sympathetic and some downright hilarious in
their irony. These, along with many scenes from his memoirs,
Persons and Places, establish their author's reputation as an acute
and witty observer of life and manners. Beneath these superficial adornments, *The Last Puritan* develops a somber theme
that is central to Santayana's philosophy. Santayana describes in
the person of Oliver Alden a human life distorted and frustrated
by an unrelenting obsession, an "absolutist conscience," perhaps
more Stoic than Puritan, that suspects all motives not presented
as obligations. A sense of duty, often a rationalized acceptance of
convention, overwhelms all other springs of action, darkens the
vision, and thwarts the achievement of a generous and gifted
youth, who is alienated from his world and deprived of the ability
to enjoy things freely and for their own sake. As Santayana points
out in the Prologue, Oliver felt it necessary always to be master
of himself. For Santayana this insistence indicates a spiritual immaturity, although it may well appear as an infirmity of noble
minds; and in Oliver's case it was indeed just this. In his life, the
spirit wished always to govern and was never content merely to
understand or to enjoy. A strict moral judgment too often took
the place of spontaneous admiration and a watchful self-scrutiny
made self-forgetfulness and self-surrender almost impossible. Thus
the spirit deprived itself of its richest fulfillment.

It is owing to Santayana's skill as a literary portraitist that
young Alden appears throughout as a sympathetic figure. He
might so easily have seemed a stuffy and conceited prig. But, as
Santayana makes clear, his instinctive kindliness, his modesty, his

sincerity, and perhaps a certain naiveté protect him from a self-righteous respectability. After all, his conscience is not aggressive. He tolerates other attitudes with patient generosity as he considers his family and his friends, treating even his tyrannical mother, a truly decadent Puritan, with courtesy while learning to ignore her inept sarcasm. He is kindly and tolerant and profoundly honest, but, as he grows to maturity, less and less capable of carefree enjoyment.

Even as a schoolboy, Oliver came to interpret all his relationships as obligations and to see his life as a network of minor commitments extending from athletic competition, which came to bore him, to all sorts of family duties including eventual matrimony. He is at last freed from this self-imprisonment by the frankness of the young lady whom for some years he had intended to marry and whom he had treated with an exemplary chivalry. Love, she tells him, must be happy, natural, and unreasoning and she makes it clear that she would have preferred the attentions of his debonair cousin. Oliver accepts this rebuff with outward calm, but he is profoundly shaken by the picture of himself that has been set before him. He feels that he has in a sense lived the life of a conscript and in profound relief, almost enthusiasm, he promises himself a new freedom. Yet only in the vaguest terms can he tell himself what this freedom will be like — a freedom that he is never to experience since a few months after his change of heart he is killed in a motor accident.

Santayana surrounds Oliver Alden with a number of fascinating characters. His cousin Mario Van de Weyer, kindhearted and often irresponsible, with a bubbling sense of humor, finds something enjoyable in almost any situation, if only its incongruity; and he seems disposed by nature to a happy acceptance of his lot. He is sometimes baffled, but not repelled by Oliver's unrelenting self-criticism; while the wealthy Oliver often feels himself responsible for his cousin's well-being. Neither character is morally complete. Mario makes himself too easily at home in his world, while Oliver is never sure of himself and there is always something clumsy about his earnestness. Oliver's uncle Nathaniel, whose conscience stands beyond self-criticism, presents in his humorless self-assurance and intolerance an inversion of Puritan integrity. The fact that we find Nathaniel credible and enjoy his outrageous, even heartless, eccentricities reminds us of Santayana's debt to Dickens. There are also Oliver's father, Peter Alden, the restless dilettante whose life is one long fruitless escape from Nathaniel and from Oliver's mother; the saintly and poverty-stricken Vicar who understands Oliver without being able to help him; the Vicar's son, captain of Peter Alden's magnificent yacht, a cheerful and plausible rascal whom the young Oliver at first mistakes for a hero; Oliver's young German governess in whose kindly soul the wisdom of Goethe and the philosophy of the romantics have inspired a muddled sentimentalism; and Oliver's cousin, the sharp-tongued cripple Caleb Wetherbee, a Catholic convert who spends his wealth trying to introduce into New England a truly medieval monasticism. Each of these finds a place in Santayana's philosophy and there are times when this is perhaps a shade too obvious especially in the case of cousin Caleb. Still, it is quite possible to enjoy Santayana's book for just what he tells us it pretends to be — a memoir written by a retired professor of philosophy concerning one of his favorite students whose short life has reflected the virtues and the grave limitations of a dying tradition. The reader makes the acquaintance not only of the student and his friends and relatives, but also briefly of the professor himself; and they are all very interesting people. They are perhaps rather larger than life in that they are remarkably articulate and their attitudes very well defined. But in most cases we may welcome them for that very reason. Even so, our enjoyment of *The Last Puritan* is not purely intellectual. To the humane reader, Oliver is more than an example or a period piece. He appears as a very decent and gifted young man who deserves a happier life than he has been able to find for himself. After all, there are still many people who can draw from their own experience a ready sympathy for his predicament.

The Last Puritan was not published until 1936, although Santayana had returned to the manuscript off and on over many years. The story, however, is brought to a close with Oliver's sudden death shortly after the Armistice of 1918. The American reader of the mid-thirties might perhaps have wondered — as might the reader of today — what sort of a person Oliver would have become had he lived through the moral confusion of the twenties and faced the social challenge of the great depression. Santayana seems also to have asked himself this question. There is a brief suggestion in the Prologue that we might have found Oliver active in left-wing, perhaps revolutionary, circles, accepting the need of radical reform as a compelling source of obligation. He might even have been capable of "imposing no matter what regimen on us by force." This dismal picture seems hardly consistent with Oliver's state of mind before his death. At that time, he was more ready than ever before to accept the "miscellaneous madness" of the world, to "practise charity," and to keep himself "as much as possible from complicity in wrong." One would hardly expect a new authoritarianism to follow upon so sober a moment of open-mindedness. Strangely enough, it may well be that the reader's — the American reader's — confidence in Oliver Alden surpasses Santayana's. The air of futility that surrounds the last events of the story may not seem inevitable to everyone. Then for the first time Oliver was ready to face his world, free of the narrow preconceptions of his upbringing, ready to understand attitudes that had been beyond his scope — perhaps even to understand, or to begin to understand, the wisdom of his friend and teacher, the retired professor of philosophy.

Over the years, Santayana's orientation as a philosopher changed but little. In his later writings, however, the skeptical caution, always latent in his thought, received a greater emphasis. As always, he accepted the results of scientific inquiry as constituting our most trustworthy knowledge of the world. Yet, he insisted, we must recognize that our knowledge, however well founded in observation and however consistently formulated, remains the product of human thinking subject to the limitations of our situation and to assumptions that this situation forces upon us. Knowledge is interpreted as springing from belief and belief from something very like instinct. In the 1920's, Santayana argued that in a viable philosophy of life insistence upon intellectual certainty surpassing that of practical belief is out of place. He undertook to support this observation by considering, or reconsidering in the spirit of the early modern philosophers, just how far we may go toward claiming certain or irrefutable knowledge of any kind. This led him to an exercise, somewhat in the manner of Descartes' *Meditations,* concerning "those things of which we may doubt." He carried these skeptical reflections well beyond the limits reached by Descartes and came to rest in a position remarkably similar to that from which David Hume had challenged the philosophers of the eighteenth century. Like Hume, he turned away from the pursuit of certainty toward an examination of the effective beliefs that are taken for granted in our overt behavior.

No statements concerning the existence of things in a world around us or concerning our own existence as thinking beings can escape all possibility of doubt, that is, if we think of doubt as a purely intellectual exercise. Descartes cannot help us here. The famous *cogito ergo sum* — "I think, therefore I am" — does not carry the mathematical certainty that Descartes attributed to it. The skeptical exercises by which he challenged our commonplace perceptions and the familiar propositions of our common sense cannot be brought to a halt so easily. If we follow in Descartes' footsteps, rigorously demanding an absolute certainty, we will end with accepting the reality, not of an enduring thinking subject, but of something far "thinner" and much less satisfying — a moment of isolated sentience, of truncated consciousness. Such a position may be described as a "solipsism of the present moment." This radical skepticism, although, as Santayana believed, internally consistent, springs from a narrow and academic interpretation of the life of reason. The reasoning by which we live is not to be divorced from the common sense that presides over our daily behavior. As Santayana had insisted in his earlier writings, reason is to be defined as "instinct enlightened by reflection," and the primitive beliefs that guide our conduct are instinctive in nature. These beliefs are as indispensable to our conscious life as breathing is to our bodily existence. Without them, we would be overwhelmed by the restless multiplicity of sensation and feeling that constitutes the raw material of our stream of consciousness. This flux of sheer sensibility does not yield us a picture of things and events until we subject many of its fleeting elements to a scheme of interpretation, until we recognize them as symbols indicating the presence of enduring objects in a world of objects spatially related to our own bodies. We do not derive this interpretation from experience, since without such interpretation we have no experience worth the name, only a whirl of sensation and feeling. Without the initial aid of instinctive interpretation our awareness would lack the continuity even of a dream and conscious selfhood, as we come to know it, would be impossible.

These primordial beliefs are practical in function rather than strictly representative. Their value lies in their contributing toward our survival, not in their grasping the nature or penetrating the structure of things. They support certain attitudes of alertness that further our safety and well-being, and in doing so they give us our first dim sense of ourselves and of our world, comprising what Santayana has called the "original articles of the animal creed." Here we find such effective, although inarticulate, beliefs as that things seen may be edible — or dangerous; things lost or sought may be found. These beliefs or attitudes involve others more fundamental: that there is a world or arena of possible action spread out in space wherein we as moving organisms may operate, that there is a future relevant to these operations that may offer us threats or attractive incentives, and that seeming accidents may have concealed causes. Such assumptions, made without deliberation, constitute what Santayana calls "animal faith," about which our perception of things and our knowledge of the world has gradually taken shape. These assumptions are supported, even encouraged and reinforced, by experience, but they are by no means self-evident propositions in their own right or what Descartes would call "clear and distinct ideas." They are

taken for granted in action rather than established by argument
or intuitive insight. Nature, or the "realm of matter," in which
as living organisms we find a place, enters our thinking as the
realm of possible action. The patterns of time and space, enduring
substance and casual efficacy, about which our idea of nature is
built may well be no more than useful rules of thumb, in themselves gross oversimplifications of reality. Yet these schemes of
interpretation, however imperfect, bring our thinking into a
rough and ready contact with the world around us, and they
contribute to our sense of our own existence. We think of ourselves as caught up in the goings-on of nature to which we must
adapt our behavior if we are to survive. Animal faith carries with
it an anxious sense of our dependence upon things that we can
only partially control, that at once support and threaten our
existence.

Such being its origin, our knowledge, even when refined by
the mathematics of science, must remain tentative. One of the
chief functions of philosophy is to remind us of the shallowness
of our understanding of things and the massive background of
our ignorance. We can readily tease ourselves out of thought by
asking ourselves, for instance, whether our physical world has
had a beginning in time, whether it is infinite or finite in extent,
whether time is unreturning or circular, discrete or continuous.
Absolute truth lies quite beyond our reach and the very idea of
truth brings upon us a sense of humility.

There is a difference, however, between humility and frustration. The natural sciences are self-correcting modes of inquiry
and we may hope to render the view of things that animal faith
has opened to us more extensive and more consistent even if it
can never approach completeness. And, after all, human well-
being does not require omniscience. It is far more important that
we know what we want than what we are made of. A sense of
direction is more satisfying than a knowledge of our origins. To
achieve it, we must ask ourselves what possibilities of life we find
most worth pursuing. In answering this question in patience and
honesty we complete the living pattern that nature has, so to

speak, offered us. In doing so, we are not, as Bergson, Sartre, or Whitehead would insist, fashioning our lives or creating ourselves. We are discovering a path upon which we have already unknowingly set foot, or, to put it in another way, in our discovery, one of nature's uncertain and vacillating variations shapes into something approaching completion. In these moments, we do not seek to initiate, to control, or to create. Our attitude is one of grateful acceptance, a serendipity, even though the ideal that we contemplate has come to our attention in the restless activity of our own imagination. For us, the worth of the ideal lies in its drawing us out of our self-centered anxieties into a moment of disinterested admiration. Such admiration, if it resists inevitable distractions and disappointment, adds a new quality to our existence.

These ideals, whose presence before our imagination can transfigure our lives, receive a new interpretation in Santayana's later philosophy. Ideals are not facts of nature or of history since neither nature nor human nature attains perfection. Nature and history afford only the occasions upon which our imagination grasps the ideal, be it of animal adaptation to circumstance, of social justice, or of individual integrity. Here we may follow Plato. Strictly speaking, ideals do not exist. They are not features of the concrete world. In Santayana's later vocabulary, they are called "essences" rather than existing things. They belong, not to the "realm of matter," the world of interacting concretions that come to be and pass away, each in its time, but to an order or realm of timeless, or unchanging, entities. This approaches orthodox Platonism, but Santayana finds it necessary to add a reservation. Ideals as timeless entities do not exercise an influence upon the goings-on of nature. Here, despite the skeptical caution of his later thinking, Santayana remains fully convinced that the origin and development of life are subject to a contingent interplay of forces and conditions in no way directed toward or controlled by an ideal perfection. Ideals do not exist in nature nor are they supernatural powers influencing the course of nature or of history. They need not, however, be described as fictitious products of hypocrisy or of wishful sentimentality. In the life of the individual they may play a very different role. Here they may stand as genuine objects of prolonged and discriminating reflection.

The universe of discourse to which ideals belong is part of a wider "realm of essence." For Santayana, as for Whitehead, this realm or order includes many items besides the ideals of human life. It includes all objects directly open to our attention rather than those merely postulated as objects of belief, actually enduring for a time as features of the concrete world. Thus I believe in the enduring existence of my watch while at a given moment I may glimpse patches of color that support this belief. A shade of color is an essence as is also a spatial pattern like that of the circle. But my watch, unlike an essence, is a concrete existent and as such, unlike an essence, has a history of its own. It was manufactured at a certain time and place under certain specific, even unique, conditions. It has been subject to many influences of wear and tear and of climate. It has been repaired just so often and in just so many ways. No such history belongs to or characterizes an essence. The color yellow and the pattern circle are exempt from such conditioning, although they may serve as indications of the watch's presence and may be mentioned in our description of the watch. We may, on the other hand, contemplate essences that do not indicate existent things as well as those that qualify our belief in them. Consider the structures of certain non-Euclidean geometries.

Ideals occupy a position of their own within the realm of essence. They are not like colors or familiar shapes. They do not indicate actual conditions in the concrete world, past, present, or future. Yet their presence before our attention may manifest a sense of direction on our part, even though they are, so to speak, beyond our reach and will never be completely realized. In this respect, ideals are like targets on which we cannot hope to hit the center, but whose presence brings order out of random play and makes evaluation possible. Perhaps they should be compared to targets seen through shifting mists so that their very discernment calls for concerted effort. Here our analogy breaks down, since the ideal, unlike the marksman's paper target, may appear as an object beautiful in itself. Any essence that as an ideal offers a disinterested self-transcendence to human beings, if only perhaps to a few, belongs to the "realm of the spirit" and commands the respect of any student of human nature. The essences that constitute the realm of the spirit may appear as surpassingly beautiful as we center upon them — or objectify in them — our most sincere and enduring admiration.

The ultimate justification of philosophy and the arts lies in the fact that they may help the individual toward a spiritual affirmation according to his own vocation. Their function is to enlighten, not to command. Such enlightenment dawns upon us gradually as the enjoyment of essence becomes richer and more deeply influences our lives. In Santayana's later philosophy the enjoyment of beauty of any kind and the intellectual discovery of form, pattern, or structure may involve the apprehension of essences usually unnoticed or beyond our ken. Like physical health, the delight that we take in such discovery of essence has a worth of its own while making possible the realization of greater values. Philosophy and the arts, indeed all intellectual and aesthetic activity, encourage the practice of detachment from the unstable confusion and insecurities of our daily experience. In this detachment, when our attention is happily concentrated upon welcome essences, we have a foretaste of the freedom that may accompany an enduring self-transcendence.

The process of enlightenment may take many forms as the spirit emerges from its lowly origins. Santayana considered with sympathy the paths toward self-transcendence apparent in the great traditions, Indian, Greek, and Christian. As he considered the contemporary scene, he noted with lively interest that his account of the enjoyment of essence bears a close resemblance to that so brilliantly recorded by Marcel Proust, although for Proust it is recognition of an essence long forgotten and suddenly recalled that brings us the deepest satisfaction. Santayana made clear that the recovery of the past meant far less to him than to Proust. The discovery and isolation of an essence do not of themselves lure us into the past. On the contrary, they make time irrelevant as we rest momentarily content in our vision, free from any regret or anxiety, free, indeed, from that instinctive uneasiness that has inspired our animal faith. This sense of freedom awakens the spirit and encourages its search for ideals worthy of an enduring commitment.

The contrast between animal faith and spiritual contemplation constitutes the central theme of Santayana's later philosophy. Without the first man cannot live; without the second he cannot hope to live well. Thus the life of reason must include a defense of the life of the spirit. From its first awakening the spirit may be distracted by practical anxieties, and its contribution may be undermined by intellectual dishonesty or distorted, even annulled, by an insistence upon the exclusive authority of a single insight. Santayana's career as a philosopher and a man of letters was devoted to protecting the life of the spirit from these indignities.

▼ JEAN CAZEMAJOU

Stephen Crane

▼ S OME writers work their way up to popularity in a long
     and difficult climb; others hit upon success almost over-
night. Stephen Crane's second novel, *The Red Badge of Courage,*
met with triumphal acclaim early in 1896, but he lived long
enough to enjoy only a few years of controversial fame.

Experimenting in various media — journalism, fiction, poetry,
playwriting — Crane was for his contemporaries above all a pic-
turesque figure of the world of the press. His professional commitments kept him in close touch with the life of his country, and
he explored slums and battlefields with unabating eagerness, seeing war in two brief conflicts in 1897 and 1898. The conjunction
of highstrung temperament and obstinate neglect of his health
brought Crane's life to an early close when he was not yet
twenty-nine.

During the two decades following his death, in 1900, he was to
be almost forgotten. Then in 1923 Thomas Beer published an
impressionistic biography which served to focus attention on
Crane once more, and *The Work of Stephen Crane* (1925–27),
edited by Wilson Follett, made most of his writings available to

90

a scholarly audience. This limited edition contained laudatory prefaces by creative writers such as Amy Lowell, Sherwood Anderson, H. L. Mencken, and Willa Cather, a few assessments by professional critics, and reminiscences by fellow journalists. Crane's reputation was also enhanced by the faithful support of some of his friends, especially Edward Garnett, Joseph Conrad, H. G. Wells, and Ford Madox Hueffer, later known as Ford Madox Ford. The thirties saw in him a champion of the cause of the comman man, and the forties continued to fit him into a realistic tradition; in the next two decades he appeared to critics primarily as a symbolist, but a wide range of interpretations confronted the student with a mass of conflicting scholarship. In 1950 John Berryman's *Stephen Crane* established him as an American classic. The Modern Library edition of *The Red Badge of Courage* came out the following year with a preface written by R. W. Stallman, whose extensive work on Crane, climaxed by his monumental biography in 1968, has aroused much enthusiasm and controversy. D. G. Hoffman's *The Poetry of Stephen Crane,* a very lively and perceptive study, appeared in 1957. Since 1951 there has also been a steady outpouring of articles, dissertations, monographs, and reprints. When, in the summer of 1966, a *Stephen Crane Newsletter* was founded and began to be issued regularly by Ohio State University, Stephen Crane had come into his own.

With deep roots in the soil of New Jersey he appeared extremely proud of his American heritage. One of his ancestors bearing the same name had, according to Crane, "arrived in Massachusetts from England in 1635." The man who wrote *The Red Badge of Courage* was, on his father's side, descended from a long line of sheriffs, judges, and farmers, and another Stephen Crane had been one of the leading patriots of New Jersey during the Revolution; in his mother's family, as he humorously put it, "everybody, as soon as he could walk, became a Methodist clergyman — of the old, ambling-nag, saddle-bag, exhorting kind."

Born in a Methodist parsonage in Newark, New Jersey, on November 1, 1871, Stephen was the fourteenth child of Jonathan Townley Crane, D.D. He grew up in various parsonages in New Jersey and New York State, his father being, according to the custom of his church, shifted from one charge to another every two or three years. The death of Dr. Crane in Port Jervis, New York, in 1880 brought this itinerancy to a close. Still a child when his father died, Stephen always cherished his memory.

After the death of her husband Mrs. Crane returned to Newark for a while, but soon made a permanent home in Asbury Park, New Jersey, which was a new stronghold of American Methodism. There she settled in 1883 and, that same year, was elected president of the Woman's Christian Temperance Union of Asbury Park and Ocean Grove. Frequently lecturing in neighboring towns, she occasionally traveled to distant cities as a delegate of that organization. A well-educated woman, she also dabbled in journalism to eke out her meager resources and reported on the summer religious meetings on the New Jersey shore, contributing mostly to the *New York Tribune* and the *Philadelphia Press*. She suffered from mental illness for some months in 1886 and was to die in 1891. Her religious zeal did not inspire a similar response in Stephen and he left the fold of the church; but he remained dominated by fundamental religious precepts and patterns — charity, fraternity, redemption, and rescue — which he usually kept at an earthly level.

At the age of fourteen he left Asbury Park to go to the Pennington Seminary, a Methodist academy in New Jersey, and thus attended a school over which his father had ruled for ten years (1849–58). He did not complete the four-year course there but transferred in the middle of the third year to Claverack College and Hudson River Institute, a semi-military Methodist school near Hudson, New York. He stayed there from January 1888 to June 1890. His university education lasted only one year: it began at Lafayette College, a Presbyterian institution at Easton, Pennsylvania, where he spent the autumn term of 1890, and ended at Syracuse University the following June. All these schools stressed religious and classical studies and at no time did the young man feel any sympathy for these two branches of knowledge. He was already a rebel resolutely hostile to formal education and preferred to study "humanity."

Crane suffered both from his mother's moral severity and from her physical neglect of him, but in Asbury Park he enjoyed a happy freedom near the "soft booming sound of surf." The deaths of his father, his sister Agnes, his brother Luther, and finally his mother must have made his childhood and adolescence a period of many severe trials. Three of his older brothers played the part of father-substitutes, offering either material assistance or a questionable but attractive model. William, who became a lawyer in Port Jervis in 1881, and Edmund, a man of limited education but of generous heart who, in 1894, settled at Hartwood, near Port Jervis, often helped the young man in his financial difficulties at the beginning of his literary career. Jonathan Townley Jr.'s bohemian tastes exerted a powerful influence on his younger brother; almost twenty years older than Stephen, he was in the late 1880's the coast correspondent of the *New York Sun,* the *New York Tribune,* and the Associated Press in Asbury Park and so a well-known regional journalist. Stephen, as early as 1888, began helping him in his reportorial work on the New Jersey shore. His oldest sister, Nellie, who then kept an art school in Asbury Park, may have introduced Stephen to the world of color and prepared him for an aesthetic exploration of his environment.

Stephen Crane's sensitivity was thus early aroused and developed through a gradual training of his faculty of observation: Methodism forced him to probe his own soul, journalism taught him how to note facts with accuracy, and art provided his craving for reality with chromatic patterns.

After publishing a few pieces in *Cosmopolitan* and the *New York Tribune,* a paper for which he wrote his "Sullivan County Sketches," boyish tales of the woods, in the early part of 1892, he was fired by the *Tribune* for an ironic article about a parade of workers in Asbury Park, and became a free-lance journalist in New York. (This brief report had expressed, in the tone of a sententious aesthete, his mild amusement at the sight of "an uncut and uncarved procession" of men with "principles" marching past a "decorous" throng of "summer gowns" and predatory Asbury Parkers.) Then began his apprenticeship in bohemianism in the metropolis, where he lived with struggling young artists. Occasional visits to his brothers Edmund and William helped him keep from starving; they provided him with handy refuges where he could escape from the hardships and turmoil of New York. His pride, however, prevented him from making frequent use of them. In 1893 he published his first book, *Maggie: A Girl of the Streets,* under a pseudonym and at his own expense. The audacity of the subject did not deter Hamlin Garland and W. D. Howells from praising that novel, but they were almost the only critics to notice it. They both encouraged him to write proletarian sketches, some of which appeared in the Boston *Arena* and others in the *New York Press,* enabling him to attain some financial security. His picture of the big city was centered around the life of the underprivileged in their ordinary setting, the southern tip of Manhattan.

Gradually acquiring self-reliance, experience, and ambition, he immersed himself in the most significant venture of his literary life, the writing of *The Red Badge of Courage,* an imaginative reconstruction of a Civil War battle; it was first printed in an abbreviated form as a newspaper serial distributed by the Bacheller Syndicate in December 1894. The success of the story led to an assignment as roving reporter in the West and Mexico at the beginning of 1895. When he came back in May, his first volume of verse, *The Black Riders,* had just appeared in print and proved that the young man was impelled by the spirit of religious and social rebellion. Appleton published *The Red Badge* as a book in New York in October 1895, and the London firm of Heinemann included it in its Pioneer Series at the end of November. Warmly received by English reviewers, it soon became a popular novel in the United States as well and its tenth American edition was issued in June 1896.

In that year Crane's celebrity reached a peak. All at once

praised, parodied, and harshly criticized, he found it difficult to cope with success. Going from one apartment to another in New York and probably from one girl to another, he ended up challenging the impregnable metropolitan police force on behalf of a prostitute who claimed she was being unjustly harassed. Then, rushing into escape, he accepted a commission to report the insurrection in Cuba against Spanish rule, but his ship sank off the coast of Florida on January 2, 1897, and he returned to Jacksonville, where before sailing he had met Cora Howorth (known there as Cora Taylor), the proprietress of the Hotel de Dream, a somewhat refined house of ill-fame. She had already been married twice and, at the time of her first meeting with Crane, was thirty-one years old. They were to live together for the rest of his life. His previous adventures with women had been inconclusive episodes. At the age of twenty he had fallen in love, at Avon-by-the-Sea, a resort near Asbury Park, with a certain Helen Trent, who was already engaged. In 1892 a love affair with a young married woman, Lily Brandon Munroe, enlivened his summer in Asbury Park and inspired some of his more moving love letters. Nellie Crouse, a provincial maiden whom he met at a social tea in New York, flirted with him by mail but finally rejected him. In 1896 he started sending money to Amy Leslie, a former actress now past her prime who had become a drama critic for the *Chicago Daily News.* He kept doing so until January 1898, when she succeeded in having a warrant of attachment issued against him to recover $550 of the $800 she had allegedly given him in 1896 to deposit for her. The details of their relationship remain somewhat obscure but, in November 1896, when he set out for Florida, he was probably fleeing from her as well as the New York police.

The year 1896 was not marked by any really new work from his pen, except his "Tenderloin" sketches for the *New York Journal*: Crane was too busy with his public and private life. *Maggie,* made respectable by the success of *The Red Badge* and slightly revised, came out under his real name, accompanied by another tale of the slums, *George's Mother,* which had been completed in November 1894. A volume of war stories, *The Little Regiment,* appeared in New York late in 1896 and in London in February 1897.

Crane's longing for adventure had apparently been only whetted by the shipwreck off Florida, in which he nearly lost his life; periodically the urge to see violent action was aroused in him. The Greco-Turkish war, which he covered in a disappointing manner for the *New York Journal* and the *Westminster Gazette,* took him to Europe in the summer of 1897; his bad health interfered with his reportorial duties in Greece, but he saw enough fighting to conclude on his return to London that *"The Red Badge* [was] all right."

Obviously conscious of the impossibility of introducing his "wife" — there is no record of a marriage ceremony — to his family, and still afraid of retaliatory action by the New York police, he decided to stay on in England after the Greek war was over. His shipwreck had inspired him to write a brilliant short story, "The Open Boat," which *Scribner's* printed in June 1897. About the same time he published *The Third Violet,* a novel based on his experiences in the highly contrasted worlds of Hartwood, New York, and New York City. Crane's stay in England did not provide the writer with a fresh batch of literary topics but it did enable him to see his own life in a new perspective. Many of his western adventures and several accounts of urban poverty went into a volume published in 1898 under the title *The Open Boat and Other Stories.* This volume, which contains seventeen tales, gives a sample of Crane's best talent. His meeting with Joseph Conrad brought him into contact with a writer whose aesthetics was very close to his own. In his "villa," situated on the borderline between Oxted and Limpsfield, Surrey, where he settled in the fall of 1897, Crane was not far from Ford Madox Hueffer and Harold Frederic. A few English Fabians, the Sydney Oliviers and the Edward Garnetts notably, lived in the vicinity.

In 1898 he was hired by Pulitzer to write for the *New York World* and, seeing war for the second time, reported the Spanish-American conflict, which left deep scars on his body and mind; the symptoms of the tuberculosis that was to prove fatal had already set in. In the fall he lingered in Havana where he served as special correspondent for the *New York Journal* and wrote the first draft of a novel, *Active Service,* based on his Greek assignment.

Early in 1899 he was back in England and, because of harassing creditors in Oxted, decided to move from Surrey to Sussex, his new English residence being the medieval manor of Brede Place situated near Rye on the charming Sussex coast. There his literary production reached a peak, but his efforts to avoid bankruptcy proved vain in the face of a rising tide of debts and recurring signs of failing health. He kept writing doggedly, now coaxing, now threatening his literary agent, James B. Pinker, from whom he tried to obtain more and more advances, and even the best work of this period shows the effects of haste and worry. Drawing upon his recent experiences, he completed a series of eleven fictional and autobiographical accounts of the Cuban war, which were posthumously collected in *Wounds in the Rain* (1900). He also wrote thirteen children's stories which first appeared in *Harper's Magazine* and were assembled in book form after his death under the title *Whilomville Stories* (1900). In the course of 1899 three other books saw print: a volume of verse, *War Is Kind,* containing a variety of poems whose composition embraced a period of seven years; *Active Service,* a novel which he himself regarded as second-rate; and the American edition of *The Monster and Other Stories.* Reminiscing about his family's role during the Revolutionary War, he composed three "Wyoming Valley Tales" and, creating an imaginary country, chose it as the setting for a series of archetypal battles, the "Spitzbergen Tales," which began to appear in English and American magazines in 1900.

Taking a mild interest in Cora's passion for entertaining, he watched streams of guests come to visit him in his dilapidated mansion, among whom were some distinguished writers (Conrad, Wells, Henry James) and many parasites. He decided or was persuaded by Cora to arrange a Christmas party for his literary friends, producing an original play for the occasion. The play

was very aptly called *The Ghost* and, in spite of a widely adver-
tised collaboration with famous English and American authors,
most of it was written by Crane himself. During the festivities
he almost died of a lung hemorrhage. He was to drag on for a
few more months, his body and his brain gradually weakening,
but he went on writing to his deathbed. With the help of Kate
Lyon, Harold Frederic's mistress, he turned out a series of articles
on nine great battles of the world for *Lippincott's Magazine,* out-
lined the plot and wrote the first twenty-five chapters of *The
O'Ruddy,* a picaresque novel of the eighteenth century with an
Irish hero and an English setting. But it was left uncompleted
when Crane died on June 5, 1900, in Badenweiler, Germany,
where Cora had seen fit to take him in the idle hope of a miraculous recovery from tuberculosis. Crane's friend Robert Barr
agreed to write the final chapters of the novel which, after picaresque ups and downs, was eventually published in New York
in October 1903.

The inescapable trait of Crane as a writer is his desire to express his own mind candidly, regardless of accepted opinion, conventions, and satirical attacks. The world first appeared to him
with the colors, shapes, and sounds of the Psalms and of Wesleyan
hymns, and he unconsciously made frequent use of the rhythms
and imagery of Biblical stories. His parents' participation in charitable work encouraged his interest in slum life, and he soon discovered, through his own deep concern with the mainsprings of
fear, a strange curiosity about war.

In Crane's generation "low life" was a subject of reportage,
fiction, and melodrama. When he moved into this area of literature he did so with the seriousness, the intentness, and the acute-
ness of a minister's son who had received his training as a journalist. Even if he did not know New York well at the time he wrote
Maggie, he must have caught by then a few glimpses of the
poorer districts of the American metropolis, which was so close to
Asbury Park where he lived between his stays at boarding school
or college.

The approach to slum life of Crane's first novel was new in
that it did not preach and did not encourage "slumming"; it
simply aimed, he said, to "show people to people as they seem[ed]
to [him]." Maggie is the daughter of the Johnsons, a family of
poor tenement dwellers living on the lower East Side of Manhattan. A large part of the story is devoted to drinking bouts, and
Maggie's home is the scene of a daily fight for survival. We thus
attend the growth and brutal extinction of the heroine who has
"blossomed in a mud-puddle" to become a "pretty girl" strangely
undefiled by her surroundings. She tries to escape the degrading
atmosphere of her home by working in a collar-and-cuff factory,
but soon discovers the dull routine and corruption of the sweat-
shop. Then Pete, a commonplace bartender, comes into her life,
and to Maggie he seems to be "a supreme warrior," "a knight."
He takes her to dime museums, beer gardens, and theaters, and
thus satisfies her vague and romantic longings for culture and
refinement. Seduced and abandoned by her lover, rejected by her
drinking mother and callous brother on "moralistic" grounds,
Maggie finally turns to prostitution. Shortly afterwards, "upon a
wet evening," she abruptly ends her life in the East River while
in the distance "street-car bells [jingle] with a sound of merriment."

The problem this story hinges on is not primarily a social one,
and Crane is not merely content with studying the causes and
consequences of prostitution. Mainly concerned with the "soul"
of the young prostitute, he tries to challenge the beliefs of Sunday
school religion. Can an "occasional street girl" be expected to end
up in Heaven, irrespective of the indignant frowns of "many
excellent people"? The answer is never made explicit in a narrative brimming over with irony, but it could not be other than
positive. Maggie falls because "environment is a tremendous
thing in the world," because she herself is romantic and weak, and
also because nobody is interested in her fate. She, however,
redeems herself by committing suicide, her only possible escape
from a life of moral degradation. By so doing she undergoes an
ironic purification in the foul waters of the East River while her

brother Jimmie, who had "clad his soul in armour," and her mother, who belatedly "ferg[ave]" her, are allowed to continue their degenerate lives of vice and hypocrisy in the human jungle to which they are perfectly adapted.

As a first novel *Maggie* revealed on the part of the author a deep seriousness and the powerful urge to gain an audience. It posited the imperative need for a new ethical code and, through a consistent use of irony, debunked the false values worshiped by society and exposed the part played by collective passivity in the destruction of innocence. "Indifference is a militant thing," Crane commented in a story of 1897; this idea is implied throughout *Maggie*. Much of this early Crane is reminiscent of the young Zola's passion for social rescue which found its most moving expression in *La Confession de Claude* (1865). The critics who wonder whether *Maggie* should be called a tragedy or a melodrama raise a fruitless issue, because the book is undeniably filled with pity and fear, and Howells was right when he discovered in it "that quality of fatal necessity which dominates Greek tragedy."

George's Mother is a companion piece to the drama of the New York prostitute, and it takes up again the problem of the corruption of innocence, this time in the person of a young workingman, George, who has recently settled in New York and lives in a tenement with his widowed mother, a very religious woman. The path leading to George's physical and moral destruction opens early in the story when he meets a former acquaintance, a certain Jones who introduces him into a circle of alcoholics. He thus misses work one day and invents a lie as an excuse for his absence. His mother, who tries to keep him from drifting, induces him to go with her to a prayer meeting which only "prov[es]" to him again that he [is] damned." Plunging more resolutely into drink and dissipation, the young man inflicts great moral torture upon his mother who finally dies, worn down by disappointed expectations. The last scene shows her in the grips of her death agony, while her son, hastily called to her bedside, suddenly feels "hideous crabs crawling upon his brain." This book shows more interest in abstract ideas than in real people; it demonstrates the baneful effects of Sunday school religion upon George, who seeks refuge from it in drink, and the failure of this primitive faith to succor the mother in her sorest need. It also points to the impossibility of communication between human beings. The power corruptive influences and environment exert on immature minds is here again illustrated. This rather flimsy novel raises a number of issues but solves none and throughout are heard distinct echoes of Crane's conflict with his own mother.

The confined world of *George's Mother* could easily be contrasted with the maelstrom of life in Crane's New York City sketches, which he ranked among his "best work." He started his field study in the poorer districts of southern Manhattan, observing the motley streams of passers-by on Broadway, breadlines, crowds gathering outside cheap lodging houses, jingling streetcars, fires, Italian fruit-vendors, tramps, policemen, and here and there his camera eye stopped on a detail, a "tiny old lady" lost in "the tempest of Sixth Avenue," or two children fighting for a toy. His sympathy drew him instinctively to the cause of the common man, but he was more inclined to study the actual working of minds than the possible consequences of economic systems. In his study of the "Tenderloin," undertaken for the *New York Journal* in 1896, he calls up a picture of restaurants, dance halls, and opium dens where, beneath the superficial gaiety, slumbers the fire of an ever-present violence.

His technique in these city sketches follows three main patterns: that of the journey of initiation, exemplified by "An Experiment in Misery" and "An Ominous Baby"; that of canvas painting, in "The Men in the Storm," "An Eloquence of Grief," and "The Auction"; and that of the parody, in some of his "Tenderloin" stories. The reporter-errant selects a certain situation which becomes a pretext for a psychological study of urban conflicts. To him "the sense of city [was] battle."

How did Crane's war novel, *The Red Badge of Courage*, come into being against this background of urban literature? The book is not an ordinary Civil War novel. Although the theme is

the baptism of fire of a Union private, Henry Fleming, during
the battle of Chancellorsville, the tone is psychological rather
than military. Its main characters are most of the time designated
as figures in an allegory, "the tall soldier," "the loud soldier,"
"the tattered man," "the man of the cheery voice"; and the protagonist, usually referred to as "the youth" in the early chapters,
only acquires his full identity in Chapter XI.

The author's observation of "the nervous system under fire" is
conducted on the level of Henry's restless mind; before the battle
we witness the premonitory misgivings of this farm boy in uni-
form; then comes his moment of reassurance after a first on-
slaught of the enemy has been repulsed. A second attack launched
against his side causes his sudden panic and flight. Driven by
shame to wander on the fringe of the battlefield, he seems to be
helplessly floating in a nightmarish atmosphere; this, for our
cowardly private, is the beginning of a journey of expiation. He
meets a "tattered soldier" whose wounds and embarrassing questions increase his sense of guilt. The two men are caught up in
the procession of wounded soldiers who make their way to the
rear. Among them they see Henry's friend, Jim Conklin, the
mortally wounded "tall soldier" who, after horrible sufferings
climaxed by a gruesome "danse macabre," dies under their petri-
fied gaze. After this shattering experience Henry abandons the
"tattered man" whose very presence seems to him an accusation.
Retreating Union soldiers fly past him and one of them, whom
the youth tries to question, knocks him down with the butt of his
rifle, ironically giving him the "red badge of courage" he had
been longing for. After regaining consciousness Henry meets a
man with "a cheery voice" who takes him back to his regiment
and, from then on, the protagonist's attitude is altogether
changed. He feels full of aggressive but specious self-confidence
and, because he does not reveal the real cause of his wound, derives much unmerited respect from his fellow soldiers for his
ostensibly courageous conduct. The last chapters show him
turning into a daredevil, fighting at the head of his unit during a
victorious charge, but at the end of the story — which is no

pamphlet for recruiting officers — Henry's regiment finds itself recrossing the river it had crossed a few days before and thus going back to its previous position on the other bank of the Rappahannock as if nothing had happened. Henry's first impression had been right after all: "It was all a trap."

A constant ironic counterpoint aims to debunk the traditional concept of glorious war. The whole thing seems absurd: generals shout, stammer, and behave childishly on the battlefield; Henry's wound confers upon him a spurious glory; Wilson, the "loud soldier," has become as meek as a lamb in the last chapters, and the whole tumult has resulted in no gain of ground for the Union forces and no loss for the Confederates. What remains in the mind of the reader is a series of confused movements with, from time to time, "men drop[ping] here and there like bundles" and, in the protagonist's "procession of memory," sad nerve-racking images suddenly blurred with a sense of relief when the "sultry nightmare [is] in the past."

Like all the great classics of literature *The Red Badge of Courage* speaks of different things to different minds. However, only an oversimplified interpretation could see in Henry's final charge the proof that he has become, as he himself thinks, "a man." The pattern of this book is that of a spiritual journey, but the final goal remains in doubt when we reach the conclusion: "Over the river a golden ray of sun came through the hosts of leaden rain clouds." The youth, in his baptism of fire, has acquired self-knowledge and experience, but a radical change has not taken place within him: he remains, in his heroic pose at the end, just as grotesque as the fearful "little man" he was at the beginning. The dialogue he has been carrying on with his own conscience often contains overtones of legalistic chicanery: it is a constant search for excuses to justify his cowardly conduct. Occasional flashes of inner sincerity are defeated by his attempts to demonstrate that what he did was logically and morally valid, but his arguments would fail to convince anyone and only add to his torment. Through a series of excruciating experiences which follow his shameful act he manages to keep his secret and even to rise in stature in the eyes of his regiment. But, instead of closing the book with a reassuring epiphany, the author preserves the ironic structure throughout. Henry's conscience is still disturbed when the book ends, and his concealed guilt spoils "the gilded images of memory."

The Red Badge of Courage contains the account of a half-completed conversion. It is only in a satellite story entitled "The Veteran" that Henry pays the full price for his "sin" and goes through the final stage of his itinerary of redemption. Then, by belatedly but unequivocally confessing his lack of courage on the battlefield, he purges himself of his former lie. In the last scene of "The Veteran," determined to save two colts trapped in his burning barn, he plunges into the flames never to come out, thus making a gesture of genuine and unconventional bravery. Rejecting his previous irony, Crane presents here a real conversion, grounded on cool, selfless determination and not on spurious enthusiasm as was Henry's sudden reversal of mood on the battlefield.

In Crane's war novel religious imagery prevails, centered on an itinerary of spiritual redemption which leads not to eternal salvation but to a blissful impasse. Alone in the middle of the forest the hero discovers the imaginary "chapel" with its "columnlike" trees where a "hymn of twilight" is heard. When the "tall soldier" dies, wildly gesturing in his final agony, he seems to resemble "a devotee of a mad religion"; most significant in the same creative process is Henry's illusion after his cowardly flight: he looks for "a means of escape from the consequences of his fall" and, unable to reach redemption through mere introspection, returns to "the creed of soldiers." But his final charge does not purge him of his guilt in spite of a temporary exultation due to the repression of his fear; "the ghost of his flight" and "a specter of reproach" born of the desertion of "the tattered man" in his sorest need keep haunting the youth at the close of the book. Some obvious similarities with the theme of concealment in Hawthorne's fiction can also be noted: "veil" metaphors and similes clustered around the character of Henry Fleming keep recurring in the narrative. In

Chapter I the hero "wish[es] to be alone with some new thoughts that [have] lately come to him"; in Chapter VII he "cring[es] as if discovered in a crime" and, under the burden of his hidden guilt, soon feels that "his shame [can] be viewed." But an ironic glimmer of hope reappears in his consciousness when he imagines that "in the battle blur" his face will be hidden "like the face of a cowled man."

Beside this procession of religious images there appears here and there a scattering of scenes with animal characters which seem to be fables in miniature. The style abounds in symbolic rabbits, squirrels, horses, cows, and snakes which form a conventional bestiary by the side of a Christian demonology swarming with monsters directly borrowed from Biblical literature.

Another facet of this book is its consistent use of legalistic terminology. A dossier is being minutely, if inconclusively, revealed to us: the youth of this story approaches his problem of fear in a logical manner and determines to "accumulate information of himself"; at first he tries to "mathematically prove to himself that he [will] not run from a battle." Then, after experiencing his shameful flight, he acts as his own lawyer and attempts to present a convincing defense of his case: "He had done a good part in saving himself, who was a little part of the army. . . . His actions had been sagacious things. They had been full of strategy. They were the work of a master's legs." A strong ironic coloring, one of the main characteristics of Crane's style in the whole book, can easily be detected here. Henry is constantly trying to show his actions to advantage; when he returns to his regiment after his cowardly escape, he even considers using the "small weapon" — a packet of letters — which Wilson in a panic had left in his hands before the battle. This "exhibit" would, Henry thinks, "prostrate his comrade at the first signs of a cross-examination."

The mechanistic imagery of *The Red Badge of Courage* already adumbrates the development of Crane's war motif in his writings after the Cuban conflict of 1898, and serves to highlight the complexity and destructiveness of modern war: "The battle was like the grinding of an immense and terrible machine to him. Its complexities and powers, its grim processes, fascinated him. He must go close and see it produce corpses."

If military courage had been one of the values pitilessly probed in *The Red Badge of Courage,* it also furnished the central topic for a satellite story entitled "A Mystery of Heroism." Private Fred Collins ventures into no man's land under the pretext of procuring some water for his company; but in fact his action has been prompted by the desire to prove to himself that he is not "afraid t' go." After being "blindly . . . led by quaint emotions" he returns unscathed to his lines, but the author wastes no sympathy on his "heroic" deed. "Death and the Child" deals with the same theme, the scene being now the Greco-Turkish war of 1897; the central character, a war correspondent, soon sees his battle fury die out and, instead of fighting by the side of the soldiers of his mother country, flees and encounters a child who asks him this embarrassing question: "Are you a man?"

In his reporting of the same war and of the Cuban conflict Crane fell in with the conventions of his time and did not aim at more than ordinary journalistic style. But when reworking his factual accounts of battles and recollecting his war experiences in tranquillity he achieved the spare and severe economy of *Wounds in the Rain,* a moving and realistic adaptation in fiction of his own adventures with the American forces sent to Cuba in 1898. His protagonist then ceased to be a dreamy amateur like Henry Fleming in *The Red Badge* or Peza in "Death and the Child," and the figure of Private Nolan, the regular, as anonymous and unromantic as any true regular, stood out in the foreground. Crane was now dealing with war as a special trade, and his soldiers at work were shown to be "as deliberate and exact as so many watchmakers." In "The Price of the Harness" he went beyond the phantasmagoria of his early definition of war and made of "a great, grand steel loom . . . to weave a woof of thin red threads, the cloth of death," the essential metaphor of his battle symbolics. Henceforth, in the logbook of the war correspondent, what had been in *The Red Badge* a "monster," a "dragon," or a "blood-swollen god," gradually came down to the lowly estate of "death, and a plague of the lack of small things and toil." Crane could not have gone any further in deglamorizing that image of "vague and bloody conflicts" which had once "thrilled [Henry Fleming] with their sweep and fire."

A gradual reduction of the concept of war to the archetype can be found in Crane's later stories, if we leave aside as mere potboiling and unoriginal work his *Great Battles of the World*. It is in the "Spitzbergen Tales" that the war metaphor is suddenly brought down to its essentials, the taking of a coveted hill, the storming of a redoubt, or a burial scene on the front line. The typical hero of most of these stories is no longer a private but a noncommissioned or low-ranking officer, the problem of conduct being then studied in an almost abstract context and the main issue being the duty of the responsible professional toward his command. Primarily concerned with war as a personal test, Crane avoided the approach of the historian, that of the strategist, and deliberately worked out that of the moralist.

To him war, in its various manifestations, was the alpha and omega of human life, essentially a testing ground, but adventure could be a fair substitute. Sent to the West and Mexico by the Bacheller Syndicate as a roving reporter early in 1895, he drew upon his tour for a few outstanding stories. His shipwreck off the coast of Florida in January 1897 furnished material for "The Open Boat," a tale which won immediate recognition and found in Conrad and H. G. Wells two faithful admirers. The latter even went so far as to say about it: "[It is], to my mind, beyond all question, the crown of all his work."

Stephen Crane depended on adventure, vicarious or real, as fodder for his imagination. He had to *feel* intensely to *write* intensely. As soon as the pace of his life became relaxed because of illness and a general weakening of his spiritual energy, he was compelled to turn to his childhood reminiscences, also fraught with intense emotions, or to an archetypal war metaphor in order to write successfully.

The short stories "The Blue Hotel," "The Bride Comes to

Yellow Sky," and "The Open Boat" outline his personal attitude toward the literary utilization of experience. Although fond of exotic settings and people Crane is not a local colorist. The colors of his adventures are the colors of his soul. For example the real fight that he saw in a saloon in Lincoln, Nebraska, which is supposed to have been the germ of "The Blue Hotel," was transmuted by him into a moral study on the theme of collective and individual responsibility. The narrative in this tale is conducted on two levels, straight storytelling and ironic counterpoint. A Swede who has lived for ten years in New York and is now traveling in the West experiences forebodings of violent death and is eventually justified in his fear, since he meets his doom at the hands of a professional gambler. Crane, however, succeeds in keeping up the suspense by leading his main character into ominous situations at the Palace Hotel which are ironically deflated and prove harmless to the frightened hero. Once the latter feels that all danger is over and is about to celebrate his escape from the hotel in a neighboring saloon, he is stabbed to death by a gambler whom he wanted too insistently to befriend. Crane here comes back once again to an analysis of fear. In the Swede's mind this feeling follows a pattern similar to that of Henry's itinerary in *The Red Badge*: from timidity to unrestrained arrogance. Both Henry and the Swede are intoxicated, the former with a belatedly discovered battle fury, the latter with repeated drinking. Crane also explores the comic overtones of violence, and notes the grotesque fall of the Swede's body, "pierced as easily as if it had been a melon." The protagonist obviously brought about his own destruction, but the writer is not just censuring one man's attitude, and the easterner, Mr. Blanc, who acts as point-of-view character, declares: " 'We are all in it! . . . Every sin is the result of a collaboration.' " Once again the creator of *Maggie* stigmatized the unpardonable sin, indifference: no one had done anything to prevent the final denouement from taking place. The hotelkeeper and the bartender had provided drink; the other "collaborators," Johnnie excepted, since he had been most active in arousing the Swede's anger, had each exhibited a different form of passivity.

"One Dash — Horses" is another study of fear, this time in a Mexican setting. In its gaudy and alluring garb this tale reads like a direct transcript of experience, but the narrative is not limited to the account of a thrilling manhunt; Crane is more interested in exploring the psychological springs of fear and the power of illusion. The young American and his guide are afraid of the Mexican bandits, and the latter are terrorized by the thought of the mounted police — the "rurales" — but it is an abstract stereotype of the traditional enemy which causes this feeling in both cases. The Mexican bandits prove to be playthings in the hands of the gods, and the arrival of a group of prostitutes scatters to the winds their plans of murder and plunder; later on, when their lust has been appeased and they have resumed the chase, a detachment of rurales frightens them away without firing a single shot. The real power of the story lies in its subtle use of irony and in its cascading evocations of fear in a Western-style pursuit.

In "The Bride Comes to Yellow Sky" Crane reached a peak in his exploration of the humorous overtones of fear. A favorite of the author himself and of many of his admirers, "The Bride" raises the western story to the level of the classic by consistently applying to a trite but dramatic situation the powerful lever of irony. It deals with a very unromantic event, the homecoming of a town marshal after his wedding with a plain-looking and timid bride. This town marshal is afraid of nothing except public opinion and, since his marriage was secretly arranged, he fears the hostile reaction of the inhabitants of Yellow Sky, an obvious projection of Crane's own predicament in his life with Cora. When, after walking through the deserted town, the couple reach the door of their home, they meet Scratchy Wilson, the local outlaw. A bloody encounter to come, we might think, but in fact nothing happens: the outlaw is defeated by the mere sight of the town marshal seen for the first time as a married man and walking home unarmed. "Defeated by a woman's mute presence"

might have been the headline for such a story if it had been printed in a "yellow" newspaper. Crane thought that "The Bride" was
"a daisy," and he was right. From beginning to end this charming tale proves that the whole mystique of the wild West was for
him nothing but a game, and he enjoyed watching this game in
its closing stages.

But no judgment of Crane's ability as a storyteller can be
reached without a proper assessment of "a tale intended to be
after the fact" entitled "The Open Boat," which relates the concluding phase of an almost fatal adventure. The newspaper report
he sent to the *New York Press* in January 1897, immediately
after his shipwreck, gave a detailed account of every episode
excluding the "thirty hours" spent in an open boat. It took a few
weeks for the definitive story to crystallize in his mind as a parable of human existence. We follow the ordeal of four survivors
during their long wait in a lifeboat, their desperate attempts to
reach the shore after their ship has sunk. Finally the captain decides to risk steering the frail dinghy through the breakers: the
four men — the captain, the cook, the oiler, and the correspondent — have, each of them, felt the "subtle brotherhood" born of
their shared distress and struggle. Once in the breakers the boat
is overturned and the oiler is killed. The other three set foot
safely ashore. Crane never wrote a more orderly tale: the correspondent, acting as point-of-view character — although he is also
a participant — helps to bring the main facets of the story into
focus. We learn much about the transformation of his mind in
the crucible of experience. This shipwreck is for him a journey
leading from cynicism to humility. But here again Crane retains
the ironic approach, especially when he shows the correspondent's
indignation leveled at the serene indifference of God. "Ship-
wrecks are *apropos* of nothing" puts into a nutshell the meaning
of the whole story. There is the world of facts on one side and
the world of ideas and literature on the other, but facts as such
do not exist to *prove* anything. However, some lessons can be
drawn from the chaos of experience if men manage to be "inter-
preters." Crane's message here is one of endurance, brotherhood,

and stoic acceptance of man's fate; his vision of the universe is one in which man appears frail and insignificant when isolated but surprisingly strong in a united effort. Ruthlessly debunking all the conventional views about heroism, he seems to imply that the only courage worthy of esteem is unobtrusive, silent, and more self-denying than self-assertive.

The true power of this story comes from a style which, in descriptive passages, is almost that of a prose poem. The dialogue, spare and accurate, gives balance to the general tone. According to Edward Garnett, Crane's art at its best was "self-poising as is the art of the perfect dancer." Joined to the grace of the dancer we find in this tale of human frailty a superb control of emotion which makes it a masterpiece of classical art, the epic flow of the narrative being constantly tempered and toned down by gentle touches of irony.

There always remained in Crane, as Alfred Kazin has pointed out, "a local village boy." Essentially American in his stance, although a rebel against many things American, he willingly spoke about his experience of the small town. Far from idealizing his vision, he set it against the background of his urban and cosmopolitan environment and judged it unemotionally.

The Crane brothers loved the countryside of Sullivan County, New York, where they fished, hunted, rode horses, and camped during the summer months. The hills, mountains, and valleys of this still rather wild area form a recurrent image in many of Stephen Crane's stories, poems, and prose poems. Although he used this background indirectly in his fiction, he made of it the infrastructure of his vision of the world.

The Third Violet reflects a deep attachment to the colors and shapes of Sullivan County. It exploits both the popular theme of the "summer hotel" and Crane's own experience at the Art Students' League in New York. In this novel the author has captured some of the flavor of bohemianism, but his treatment of this subject lacks originality. *The Third Violet,* which won very little applause from critics except for Ford Madox Hueffer, is saved from mediocrity by contrasting vignettes of rural and urban

life. This book hints at the difficult struggle of young artists with
the commercial values of their age: Hawker, a young painter,
goes to Sullivan County where his farmer parents live; he is
merely in search of peace and inspiration but, in a neighboring
hotel, the summer has brought adventure in the shape of a rich
New York heiress, Miss Fanhall. It is love at first sight and the
novel abounds in meetings and vapid conversations between the
two lovers and a few other characters, a "writing friend" of
Hawker's called Hollanden, a rival in love, named Oglethorpe,
who is the irresistible rich suitor, and a group of irresponsible
young artists belonging to Hawker's circle in New York. Among
the latter stands out a rather colorful young model in love with
Hawker, Florinda. We close the book unconvinced by the plot
which, with the gift of a final violet symbolizing the reconciliation of the two lovers, seems to be heading for a conventional
epilogue. Crane did not want his novel to end tragically as his
real-life romance with Nellie Crouse had done.

"The Monster," a story set in a rural background, can be regarded as one of the most important of his short works. It is
centered on the disastrous consequences of a generous action:
a doctor's son has been rescued from his burning house by a
Negro servant, Henry Johnson, whose face is "burned away." Out
of gratitude the doctor decides to nurse his heroic servant and
insists on keeping him in his reconstructed house, but the sight
of the "monster" frightens everyone in the neighborhood; the
doctor soon becomes an object of opprobrium and loses much of
his practice. A deputation of influential citizens tries to persuade him to compromise with public opinion and asks him to
turn Henry over to an institution, but the doctor remains ada-
mant. The last scene shows him returning from his rounds and
finding his wife crying over the teacups of guests who have not
come. This brilliant exposition of village mores is enhanced by
symbolic touches which, in the laboratory scene during the fire,
reach a climax with the lurid vision of threatening and fantasti-
cally colored shapes. Besides the fear born of physical danger,

the author probes the blind unreasoning panic generated by the sight of the harmless and horribly maimed Negro, and the many anxieties caused by public opinion. He has also, by the very choice of his protagonist, indicated that true heroism is not the privilege of the whites alone.

Crane began reminiscing about his early youth when he had used up the store of material born of his adult experience. Port Jervis, New York, was the nucleus around which *The Whilomville Stories* took shape. It is "any boy's town" but also a very specific one within easy reach of New York City, yet quite provincial and sleepy with its backdrop of fields, rivers, hills, and forests, a place where boys and girls can roam at peace except when under the ferule of their school or Sunday school teachers. The fields are close by and the farmers' slow and benevolent manner offers a sharp contrast to the "barbarous" habits of the villagers who give tea parties, launch into charitable campaigns, and, in the summertime, entertain relatives from the city.

The rural life depicted by Crane is more civilized than that Mark Twain had evoked before him; it is less sentimentally reconstructed than the *Boy's Town* of W. D. Howells. Abhorring as he did the "Little Lord Fauntleroy" craze which had swept his country in the 1880's, Crane did not hesitate to show us real children. He is aware of their tastes and distastes and conscious of their cruelty — at times they appear to him as "little blood-fanged wolves." In fact, more than a picture of childhood, he gives a picture of town life, since the children project an image of their parents' world stripped to its essentials. Although fond of the company of youngsters and a great favorite with his nieces, Crane was not holding a brief in favor of youth. To quote Robert Frost out of context he "lov[ed] the things he love[d] for what they [were]"; his children were, like their adult counterparts, charmingly deluded in their vision of the world, and we can safely smile at their innocent pranks, for Crane did not allow them to give free rein to their worst instincts. At the critical moment something happened: a bully relented or an adult came into

view, and none of these little dramas of the backyard turned into
a real tragedy.

By profession a journalist and a writer of fiction, Crane had a
higher regard for his poetic endeavors than for the rest of his
literary work. He preferred his first volume of verse, *The Black
Riders,* to his *Red Badge of Courage* because "it was a more
ambitious effort. My aim was to comprehend in it the thoughts
I have had about life in general while 'The Red Badge' is a mere
episode in life, an amplification."

But he did not observe the traditions and conventions of poetic
expression respected by most of his contemporaries, except isolated rebels like Walt Whitman and Emily Dickinson. Alfred
Kazin has called Crane "our first *poète maudit*" and such a label
fits him to perfection, for he regarded poetry, more than prose, as
a vehicle for ideas generally unconventional or iconoclastic.

It is easy to find models for the patterns if not for the tone of
Crane's early verse. He had obviously read Biblical parables, and
some of the work of Emily Dickinson, Whitman, Ambrose Bierce,
and Olive Schreiner, but his poetry remained essentially the expression of his own vision.

The sharpness and brevity of the sixty-eight pieces forming
his *Black Riders* remind many readers of Emily Dickinson's great
verbal economy. Like that of the poetess of Amherst his voice
was one of protest. His own rebellion went against the God of the
Old Testament, and he strove to debunk a cluster of false values,
especially ambition, conformity, worldly wisdom, military glory,
and traditional religion. The universe pictured by Crane in his
poetry has elements of pessimism which have caused some critics
to regard it as naturalistic, but the poet also exalts the positive
virtues of love, endurance, and self-reliance. Crane feels a great
admiration for the "little man" who keeps facing the mountains
fearlessly, for the lonely individualist who "sought a new road"
and "died thus alone," for "they said he had courage." The first
themes of his poetic vision radiate from a central concern, the
problem of man's relation with God. Even earthly love can be

poisoned by the idea of sin and man must free himself from his
obsessive fear of God and from the network of illusions woven by
his imagination. Crane's rebellion was sound but the occasionally
crude phrasing of his protest and the printing of the volume in
small capitals made it fair game for the parodists.

His second book of poetry, *War Is Kind,* contained thirty-seven
poems: fourteen of these had already been printed between 1895
and 1898; a group of ten love poems called "Intrigue" and some
of the remaining pieces belonged to a second poetic output. The
iconoclastic note had not died out and the author went on debunking the outward forms of religious ritual:

> You tell me this is God?
> I tell you this is a printed list,
> A burning candle and an ass.

But his poetry gradually became more concrete and more socially
oriented. Instead of dealing with abstract imaginings, vague and
remote parables, it drank deep from the fountain of experience.
His bitter satire on the popular glorification of military courage
in such a poem as "War Is Kind" (which, although the initial
piece in the second volume, belongs to the first period) had been
expressed along general lines. With "The Blue Battalions" and
the poems inspired by the Spanish-American war, Crane did not
hesitate to present war as the utmost form of God's playful
fancy and violently denounced the exploitation of "patriots" by
"practical men" as well as the imperialistic overtones of America's
help to the Cuban rebels.

Several poems stigmatized other forms of exploitation of man
by man. The gaudy and showy splendor of the mansions of the
new rich aroused his metaphoric ire with a vision of

> . . . a crash of flunkeys
> And yawning emblems of Persia
> Cheeked against oak, France and a sabre,
> The outcry of old beauty
> Whored by pimping merchants
> To submission before wine and chatter.

And he ironically rejected the basic injustice of laissez-faire economics:

> Why should the strong —
> — The beautiful strong —
> Why should they not have the flowers?

If the theme of love had, in the poems of the first poetic manner, taken on few romantic dimensions except in the sheltering gesture of a woman's "white arms," the second volume of verse and some posthumous poems enable us to probe deeper into Crane's house of love. "On the desert" and "A naked woman and a dead dwarf" fly the banner of Baudelairean decadence most clearly and remind us of "La femme et le serpent" and, as has been recently pointed out, of a prose poem by the French Symbolist entitled "Le fou et la Vénus." "Intrigue," the last section of *War Is Kind,* represents Crane's attempt to bring into focus the many components of his love poetry: sensuality, sin-consciousness, and jealousy form the dark side of man's central passion, but Crane's bitter lyricism is spoiled by hackneyed romantic imagery, skulls "with ruby eyes," cracked bowls, castles, temples, daggers, and specters.

He discovered a better instrument for his highly sensitive nature in the prose poem. "The Judgment of the Sage" and "The Snake" are true fables and the same ingredients are found in them as in his verse; but, whereas the verse rejects all traditional rules (rhyme, regular meter, and very often stanzaic form), the prose poems retail a classical mode of expression. They remind us of Baudelaire's utilization of the same medium, but here again Crane's manner remains distinctly his own. He thus studied some archetypes, those of charity, material success, earthly conflict or cosmic battle. "The Judgment of the Sage," which raises the ghost of a Kantian dilemma, briefly tells us the story of a vain quest, that of worldly wisdom. Should we practice charity "because of God's word" or because the beggar is hungry? Crane does not solve this riddle; God seems to play with man his eternal game of hide-and-seek and keeps him on the run. "A Self-Made Man" parodies the Horatio Alger type of success story. " 'To succeed in life . . . the youth of America have only to see an old man seated upon a railing and smoking a clay pipe. Then go up and ask him for a match.' " "The Voice of the Mountain" and "The Victory of the Moon" are focused on the conflict between man and a mysterious cosmic power which can occasionally be defeated by "the little creature of the earth." With "The Snake" the inevitable fight for survival is brought to its emotional climax: the two most antagonistic creatures in the world, man and the snake, confront each other in a ruthless duel in which the principals fight with equal arms, the snake with its venom and man with his stick. If the snake is defeated it is not for lack of courage. Thanks to a clever manipulation of language Crane combines in a unified whole the simplicity of the fable, the logical structure of the sermon, and the raciness of the tall tale.

His poetry at times foreshadows imagism, as Carl Sandburg pointed out in his "Letters to Dead Imagists," but some pieces of the second volume of verse show a tendency to explode the small abstract capsule of the early poems. It is difficult to say where Crane's real poetic genius lies, whether in his spare, concise parables, in his longer symbolistic compositions, or in his prose poems. He worshiped brevity as the first tenet of his literary creed, but he was also touched by the wave of decadent aesthetics that Copeland and Day, his publishers, who were also the American publishers of the *Yellow Book,* had helped to introduce into the United States. There was, however, too much love of moral integrity in Crane for him to become a true decadent. In his verse he often displayed the pathetic agony of a fallen albatross, but the prose poem was perhaps the literary instrument whose scope and subtle rhythm best suited his genius.

Crane's style has a certain number of idiosyncrasies: it is primarily the language of a writer in transition betraying an inner conflict between a romantic tradition and realistic impulses. He began with what he called his "Rudyard-Kipling style" and the "Sullivan County Sketches" contain the germs of most of his future work, displaying as they do a love of abstraction and a systematic use of color, patterning the narrative with structural irony, and building up an oneiric atmosphere laden with threat. It is a gradual mastery of form that we witness in the passage from the style of the early years to that emerging between 1894 and 1898.

Impelled by a desire to control the deep stirrings of his soul, he soon declared that he wished "to write plainly and unmistakably, so that all men (and some women) might read and understand." Crane's literary aesthetics was close to that of the French master of the short story, Guy de Maupassant. According to the author of *Pierre et Jean*, "Les grands artistes sont ceux qui imposent à l'humanité leur illusion particulière." Such a position might very well have been defined by Stephen Crane who wanted the writer to tell the world what "his own pair of eyes" enabled him to see and nothing else. Maupassant's universe, however, differed significantly from Crane's: whereas the French writer often indulged in an excess of sensual evocations, Crane preserved throughout his writing career the viewpoint of the moralist and usually conveyed his ethical comments by means of ironic counterpoint.

He was deeply conscious of man's littleness and of God's overbearing power. Man's wanderings on the earth were pictured by him as those of a lonely pilgrim in a pathless universe. Crane's phraseology comes directly from the Bible, the sermons, and the hymns which had shaped his language during his youth. The topography of his stories, where hills, mountains, rivers, and meadows appear under symbolic suns or moons is, to a large extent, an abstraction fraught with religious or moral significance. With its "monsters" of various kinds and its "dragons," the demonology of *The Red Badge of Courage* evinces a truly apocalyptic quality. In Crane's best work the imagery of the journey of initiation occupies a central position and reaches a climactic stage with some experience of conversion. He did not accept, it is true, the traditional interpretation of the riddle of the universe offered by the Methodist church. Nevertheless he constantly used a Christian terminology, and the thought of "sin" inspired his characters with guilty fears and stirred up within them such frequent debates with a troubled conscience that it is impossible to study his achievement outside a religious tradition.

But he did not remain a prisoner of the stylistic patterns which he derived from his revivalist heritage. New York street life very early made an impact on his language, which thus acquired its liveliness and its ability to picture violence in colorful terms. Crane's dialogues abound in expletives, in stereotyped phrases, in phonetic transcriptions of common verbal corruptions and dialectal idiosyncrasies. Yet they never fall into the trap of over-specialization. His ear was good, whether he listened to Irish, German, Italian, or Cuban immigrants in New York, to farmers in Sullivan County, or to Negroes in Port Jervis, but he never tried to achieve a perfect rendering of local dialect. In *The Red Badge of Courage* he used dialogue to introduce some degree of differentiation between Henry Fleming and his comrades but, on the whole, Crane's characters all speak one language which is Crane's own, a youthful and casual version of the American vernacular of the 1890's often heard in artists' studios and among students.

Language is in the mouths of his central characters a stylized medium carrying universal overtones, and this trait reveals an essential aspect of his fictional techniques, namely the dramatic approach. He tried his hand several times at playwriting and, although his various attempts in this literary genre were of modest stature, he was naturally inclined to work out his tales and some of his verse in terms of stage stylistics. He completed three very slight plays. *At Clancy's Wake* (1893) is a one-act sketch which brings to life the hilarious moments of an Irish wake in New York; *The Blood of the Martyr* (1898) satirizes in three brief acts German imperialistic policies in China. Another attempt at playwriting was his "Spanish-American War Play," unpublished in Crane's lifetime but included in *The War Dispatches of Stephen Crane* (1964): this two-act drama gives a mildly amusing but superficial picture of stereotyped national traits against the background of a real conflict that the author had seen at first hand. Only a fragment of the text of "The

Ghost" — his English play — has reached us so far and it is difficult to take seriously what was meant to be a mere Christmas
entertainment. All his other attempts at playwriting were abor-
tive.

What remains most striking in Crane's style considered as a
a whole is a concern for brevity and a constant use of irony which
serves a twofold purpose: it provides his best work with tightly
knit thematic structures and reveals his tacit belief in a rigid set
of values which condemns indifference and conformism, and ex-
tols moral courage and integrity.

Seen in the perspective of the years which have elapsed since
his death, Crane's work is surprisingly modern. His influence
on the war literature of the twentieth century in England and
America has been very significant. Many of Hemingway's novels
and short stories disclose a similar preoccupation with "the moral
problem of conduct" and obvious stylistic affinities; distinct
echoes of *The Red Badge* can be heard in *A Farewell to Arms.*
In England we could trace recurring correspondences in the work
of Joseph Conrad and Ford Madox Ford. Ford, like Conrad, had
been a good friend of Crane's during the last three years of his
life, and both defended his literary and moral reputation in magazine articles or prefaces after his death. The plight of the isolated hero, which became a favorite theme of Conrad's, stemmed
directly from *The Red Badge of Courage.* Obsession with the
fear of showing a white feather haunted the soul of the author of
Lord Jim as much as that of the creator of Henry Fleming. In
his own fiction Ford Madox Ford used complex techniques and
mixed many strands of life, but some of the most dramatic scenes
in *A Man Could Stand Up,* which are mere vignettes of life at
the front, remind us in their bare and rugged prose of deliberately unpoetic descriptions of war in *The Red Badge.* Like Crane,
Ford emphasized "the eternal waiting that is War" and the crip-
pling effects of noise on a battlefield. And, in order to describe the
subtle change taking place in a soldier's mind, he used almost
Cranean terms.

Among the pioneers of the "free-verse army" Crane is often neglected by anthologists or literary critics. Yet he gave to the poetry of his country the patterns and rhythms of an "exasperated prose" that foreshadows modern poetic expression.

Carl Van Doren wrote in 1924: "Modern American literature may be said, accurately enough, to have begun with Stephen Crane." This statement needs to be qualified, but Crane was one of the leading figures of protest of his generation and thus showed the way to American liberalism. His influence in the field of the novel has affected a mode of thought rather than literary techniques, if we leave aside his synaesthetic use of imagery which survives almost intact in F. Scott Fitzgerald. Crane's impact has been felt mostly in the genre of the short story, for which he displayed a personal preference. "The Blue Hotel," "The Bride Comes to Yellow Sky," and, above all, "The Open Boat" are some of the finest models of American literary achievement in this genre, and the greatest successes of Faulkner, Sherwood Anderson, Hemingway, Fitzgerald, and other modern American short-story writers hark back to these models. Accuracy in details, conciseness, and effective rendering, framed and supported by an ironic structure, are now frequently regarded as essential requirements by American practitioners of the short story.

Most of Crane's work could be explained in terms of his religious background and he always betrays, even in his most sportive mood, the serious preoccupations of the born moralist. However, his slum stories, instead of aiming to move the reader by exaggerated pathos and convert him to the cause of reform, wish to convert him to the cause of psychological truth; social implications are left for the reader to discover but are not explicitly stated. When dealing with his main theme, war, he gradually worked out a revolutionary stand, doing away with externals and reducing human conflict to a classic drama of internal forces struggling with elemental powers. From Henry Fleming in *The Red Badge* to Timothy Lean in the "Spitzbergen Tales" the itinerary of heroism evolves from a path sprinkled with doubtful victories to a road doggedly followed with a sturdy and silent acceptance of personal responsibility; diseased and action-hampering introspection eventually gives way to selfless and unassuming patterns of affirmation. "The Open Boat" contains a plea for human solidarity and *Wounds in the Rain,* in spite of a persistent and depressing background of military servitude, discreetly affirms the superiority of collective to individual prowess. A subtle feeling of warmth and brotherhood pervades the later studies of Crane on war; even "The Upturned Face," a macabre piece which describes a burial scene on the front line, places the reader in the midst of an ultimate manifestation of soldierly brotherhood.

It is in the novel of manners that Crane's achievement is at its lowest ebb. He did not try to study complex human relationships born of urban settings but dealt with a few basic themes, rivalries between lovers, or conflicts between generations and social classes. Often unable to provide his puppets with life, he proved his mastery in the art of reproducing informal dialogue. He experimented in the field of the picaresque novel — a medium he had already used in several short stories — but *The O'Ruddy* cannot be regarded as a genuine offspring of his mind since Robert Barr gave this novel its conclusion and ultimate form.

Crane's identity runs no risk of being drowned in a backflow of imitators, because his style remains his own. His unerring eye for color, his brilliant use of synaesthetic effects, his love for the potent metaphor made him controversially famous in his lifetime and now stamp him as a truly original artist. His sometimes erratic grammar no longer shocks us, while his cinematic techniques have come into their own.

It was his aim to underline elements of absurdity in human life, and his work contains disquieting overtones for sedate minds. His was a voice of dissent which rejected the ostensibly impregnable soundness of historical Christianity, the conventional vision of a well-ordered society, and that genteel tradition of culture which never left drawing rooms and libraries. Crane inherited the New England habit of individual assertion. He fits well into the American liberal tradition and can, in some respects, be regarded as a spiritual son of Emerson. Any form of dogmatism in any field of human life seemed to him both childish and harmful to what he valued above everything else, the integrity of the human soul. No problem could, according to him, ever find a definitive solution and he had certainly listened to Emerson's advice: "Congratulate yourself if you have done something strange and extravagant, and broken the monotony of a decorous age." This sentence adorned a beam in one of the studios of the old Art Students' League building in New York where Crane lived sporadically in 1893 and 1894. Above and beyond this cult of nonconformism is another idea of Emerson's which involves the deeper regions of the soul: "Always do what you are afraid to do." Crane put this motto into practice so consistently that he wrecked his health and seriously endangered his moral reputation in his own country.

His recent popularity, essentially due to a revival of critical interest during the 1950's, should help prepare the ground for a clearer assessment of Crane's achievement. To our generation he can still teach moral integrity, a revised conception of courage, and psychological truth, all the more effectively because he did not resort to traditional didactic devices. He can also show modern prose writers the flexibility of the English language and encourage them to make linguistic experiments and create a language free from any excessive tyranny of the past, perfectly in tune with the spirit of the age and yet retaining the robust vitality which is the trademark of the classic.

Gertrude Stein

A T LEAST three Gertrude Steins have been accounted for in modern criticism, biography, and gossip: the formidably gracious and effective matron of modern American letters, expatriate mistress of ceremonies; the theorist of language and literature and of their fusion in "composition as explanation" of the thing seen; and the artist, author of two or three distinguished books and of a dozen or more provocative and puzzling others. The first of these has been abundantly described, testified to, and in one sense or another exploited. From the time she agreed to separate from brother Leo (1912), to set up her own literary shop in Paris, her prestige as an informal arbiter of special tastes in the arts grew and flourished. She posed for the role, and having succeeded in carrying it off, became convinced of its genuineness and worth. Subsequently the roles of hostess and critic were combined, and in her triumphant tour of America (1934–35) she was known both as an engaging and intriguing personality and as a person who had many penetrating things to say. At times vague, often apparently naive, she was nevertheless appreciated by those who knew her and troubled themselves to read her work as a dedicated spirit, narrowly intent upon expanding and illustrating her original views of language and its literary function.

The woman who invited gossip, superficial interest in her eccentricities, laughter and even ridicule, was a part of the ceremony that was her work. That she was received with enthusiasm in the 1920's by many of the postwar generation of writers is a testimony to the fascination she exercised over young talents looking for new forms and manners. When she settled in Paris (1903), at 27, rue de Fleurus, she was unknown and unpublished. With her brother she began to purchase modern paintings (Picasso, Matisse, Cézanne, Braque) and to encourage the careers of several artists. Her talent for judging the art may have been debatable, but her skill in making the artist indebted to her was not; and in a few years her *salon* featured a variety of paintings, vying for the honor of a position on its walls. They were dominated by Picasso's portrait of her, which looked down upon its subject at her desk, a memorable testimony to the beginnings of twentieth-century experiment in the arts.

The response to Miss Stein was not always respectful. The very nature of her insistence upon divergent forms and practices puzzled many and made them shy away from what seemed to them a clever game or a play for notoriety. As a dominating woman, she inspired trust in many at the start, then offended that trust or seemed to exploit it too selfishly. The flowers of friendship often faded. The sponsors of "realistic decorum," who wanted their literature intelligible and overtly "purposeful," left her early; only *Three Lives* (1909) pleased them, and this not all. But even more tolerant contemporaries found her work wearisomely repetitious, formless, and offensively coy. While she seemed in the vanguard of the new literature and was for a time (in the 1920's especially) honored by its pundits and sponsors, her position as titular head of the *avant-garde* was often threatened and finally lost altogether. Harsh ridicule of her stubborn dowagership was not uncommon; and however simply honest and decorous her *ménage aux arts* proved actually to be, the spectacle of the mistress of ceremonies invited suspicion both of her motives and of the clarity of her intentions. Katherine Anne Porter, who on at least one other occasion had found her work formidably impressive, provided the most cleverly devastating of disparagements (in an essay, "The Wooden Umbrella," 1947). She described Miss Stein as "of the company of Amazons which nineteenth-century America produced among its many prodigies: not-men, not-women, answerable to no function in either sex, whose careers were carried on, and how successfully, in whatever field they chose: they were educators, writers, editors, politicians, artists, world travelers, and international hostesses, who lived in public and by the public and played out their self-assumed, self-created roles in such masterly freedom as only a few early medieval queens had equaled."

Miss Porter's suggestion of the female prodigy is not altogether unwise, though she does not appreciate sufficiently the facts of her subject's persistence and of her dedication to an art and the theory of an art. Gertrude Stein did not begin her career as a writer; when, after she had reached the age of fifteen and begun "to understand boredom" (as John Malcolm Brinnin puts it, in *The Third Rose*, 1959), she thought of the life of a scholar. At Radcliffe, which she entered in 1893, she had courses with George Santayana, Josiah Royce, William Vaughn Moody, and, most important, William James. Her first interest was experimental psychology, and with Leon Solomons she collaborated on a study of "Normal Motor Adjustment" (*Psychological Review*, September 1896). She then began a course in pre-medicine at the Johns Hopkins University, thinking that it would be the best preparation for the life of a psychologist.

The academic life did not last. In 1902, she and Leo traveled to England, where she sat for a while in the British Museum, "living continuously," as Brinnin says, "with the English language." In the next year, Leo found the Paris apartment where she was to live most of her life to the beginning of World War II. The years as a student, the time spent reading English classics, and the experiences of buying and defending contemporary art all fell quite neatly into the pattern that was her life and her career. She was very much the American artist; but, like many Americans of a later generation, she found Paris an ideal "second country" from which to observe and to describe her native land.

It almost seemed that Miss Stein's first years in Paris were intended as a way of preparing for modern literature. In *The Autobiography of Alice B. Toklas* (1933) she served as a historian of the new generation (or at least, an informal diarist of its affairs), but she was also actively engaged in sponsoring and directing its ambitions. Before World War I she was interested mostly in painting and, very much with Leo's help, learned to understand modernist painting and bought and displayed the new canvases; above all, she considered Cézanne and Picasso as closely identified with what she was trying to do in writing. When the younger generation of writers arrived from America (or stayed on, after the war), many of them headed for the rue de Fleurus and the author of *Three Lives* and *Tender Buttons* (1914). In the 1920's, she became the leader of an informal *salon*, in which she talked with and advised Hemingway, Fitzgerald, Sherwood Anderson, and scores of others, known and unknown, talented and mediocre. She shared this role of elder spokesman with another "pioneer expatriate," Ezra Pound (who was in Paris in the early 1920's), and with British poet and novelist Ford Madox Ford, who edited the *Transatlantic Review* in 1924–25.

Her career as sponsor of bright young men was not without its difficulties, many of them of her own making; but despite personal squabbles, her reputation as an informal critic grew and she was soon asked to explain her methods on more formal occasions. The most famous of these were the trip in 1925 to Oxford and Cambridge universities, where she delivered the lecture "Composition as Explanation," which remains the key discussion of her literary practice; and the months spent in America a decade later. From the latter excursion came *Narration* and *Lectures in America* (both 1935), which are elaborations upon her theory, and especially show her skill in handling the give-and-take of semiformal audiences. But she was best at the improvised personal discussion of writing and art, which she carried on over the years in

Paris with a succession of admirers and followers through the decades between the wars.

In 1937 Miss Stein moved to number 5, rue de Christine, also on the Left Bank; some years later, she and her companion Alice B. Toklas were caught in the confusions of World War II and remained in exile in Bilignin, in southern France; from the experiences there and with the liberation by American troops came *Wars I Have Seen* (1944) and *Brewsie and Willie* (1946). When she returned to Paris after the war, she became an informal hostess to scores of American soldiers, who counted a visit to her teas and her "evenings" at the top of the list of tourist attractions. In 1946, she suffered a decline in health and was admitted to the American Hospital in Paris; there, after a futile operation, she died on July 27. In her last moments she summoned energy enough to say "What is the answer?" and, failing to get a response, concluded her life with this, its companion query: "In that case, what is the question?" It was a most suitable conclusion of a life devoted to the major questions and answers that had puzzled herself and her contemporaries.

The truth is that Gertrude Stein was a nineteenth-century American with a difference. Born in 1874, she spent twenty-six years in the nineteenth century, forty-six in the twentieth. She herself claimed that, with Henry James, she had initiated in literature the "twentieth-century way" of knowing and of writing. Brinnin claims that "while she spent a lifetime trying to escape the nineteenth century, her career belongs to its sunset phase — to the era of William James and John Dewey, George Bernard Shaw and the science of economic reform, of the 'Boston marriage' and votes for women, of the incandescent lamp and the Michelson-Morley experiment." The idea is in part persuasive, and particularly the superficially startling suggestion of her belief in the "enlightened, the rational mind." It is only that she pushed the rational modes so far as to produce apparently irrational results. But, while the impetus of her literary practice was nineteenth century, she was right in maintaining that its result was wholly consonant with the twentieth-century scene and that she provided a remarkably acute sense of its intellectual decorum and habitude. She was if anything more "modern" than Eliot and Pound. What attracted such younger artists as Hemingway to her was her conviction not only that "the past did not matter" but that the present was overweeningly demanding and that its "spirit" and rhythms had to be continuously sustained in literature. Her primary contribution to twentieth-century literature was methodological. Except when she wrote reminiscences (and she did these superbly and with great popular success), her work was only indifferently related to context. Its major objective was to illustrate and to refine the manner of fusing the "seeing" and the re-creation of an importunate present moment.

This is both her major achievement and her principal concern. Her famous lecture "Composition as Explanation" (published as a book in 1926) contains the gist of her intention: "There is singularly nothing that makes a difference a difference in beginning and in the middle and in ending except that each generation has something different at which they are all looking. By this I mean so simply that anybody knows it that composition is the difference which makes each and all of them then different from other generations and this is what makes everything different otherwise they are all alike and everybody knows it because everybody says it." In her *Picasso* (1939) she remarks upon this — to her — essential truth again, but with a difference: "People really do not change from one generation to another . . . indeed nothing changes from one generation to another except the things seen and the things seen make that generation, that is to say nothing changes in people from one generation to another except the way of seeing and being seen . . ." Her lifework is a continuous illustration of this text, with many changes and variations, but with a remarkably dedicated consistency of attention to it.

It is a simple thesis, logical and rational, in the manner of Mr. Brinnin's nineteenth-century apostles of the rational: its very simplicity proved both its strength and its weakness. Miss Stein pushed it very far indeed. Her fight with the nineteenth century was motivated by a kind of subjectively classical dislike of "emotion"; to her the word meant *any* form of distracting implication that weakens the effectiveness of the conscious grasp of the thing seen at the moment in which it is seen.

In short, Miss Stein was engaged in an analysis of the mind in its precise function of apprehending and experiencing objects. Change for her was nuance, gradation, the gradual accretion of subtle qualifications of meaning. In literature, she was the sturdiest and the most persistent enemy of the "substantial" self (which is to say, the self independent and transcendent of conscious experience). For the initial push required of this task she was indebted primarily to William James, and especially to his *Principles of Psychology* (1890). As a student of James, she thought of herself for a while as a "scientist of the mind," but the practices and the methods were limited and fallible, and she herself was scarcely temperamentally suited to them. She was not to become a scientist; nor did she follow James beyond the implications of laboratory psychology and its rudimentary essays in definition. While she refers approvingly to such other James books as *The Will to Believe* (1897) and *The Varieties of Religious Experience* (1902), she was a faithful and on occasions a discerning pupil only of his exercises in practical and radical empiricism.

This is not to say that Miss Stein comprehended William James as a philosopher, or that she admired his later discussions of metaphysics and immortality. James's use of imagery was designed almost entirely to adorn a text or persuade a student. Language was to him necessarily precise, but not necessarily the substance of experience. In most respects, James was the nineteenth-century scientist who puzzled at times over the discouraging inferences he might make of his insights. He excited Miss Stein most when he discussed the nature and the limits of consciousness; but while he took pride in his discovery of the "flow" or "stream" of consciousness, which seemed at least to rescue it from an impasse, Miss Stein was much more interested in the fact of an *arrested* consciousness, apparently static and fixed and sacrificing motion or flow to precision. James saw consciousness as process, Miss Stein as a cube or form or shape, to which the resources of the arts must be applied for most effective definition.

Nevertheless, the essential doctrine was there, with all of its modest cautions. James denied the possibility of a "substantial" or a transcendent self, or at least maintained that psychology could not account for it. Psychology was after all a "natural science, an account of particular finite streams of thought, coexisting and succeeding in time" (*Principles of Psychology*). We can *know* only about a state of consciousness as a particular situation, though it is possible to infer from it both time and will. The irreducible minimum of the conscious ego in the *process of being conscious* is the focus of real knowledge. It exists instantaneously, is then superseded by another instant. Assuming the metaphor of the "flow," these instants cohere, and if we wish to explore the psychology of willed decision and choice, they have as well a structure that is self-determined. But in the severely controlled passages of his *Principles,* James was able to say (was even forced to admit) that "the only states of consciousness that we naturally deal with are found in personal consciousnesses, minds, selves, concrete particular I's and you's." The minutiae of self-identity are strictly of the occasion, but definition of them involves the use of relational and qualifying words: "There is not a conjunction or a preposition, and hardly an adverbial phrase, syntactic form, or inflection of voice . . . that does not express some shading or other of relation which we at some moment actually feel to exist between the larger objects of our thought."

Gertrude Stein was fascinated by the substance of these relations. To her, they seemed to have the virtues of solid reality, to exist in a more than linguistic or logical sense, to be hard and three-dimensional. They were geometric forms of thought, and they fixed the meaning of the thing seen in the focus of its actually existing *as a thing.* Experience for her, then, was objective to the point of being indistinguishable from reality. In this sense, she was radically different from the naturalist, who (like Dreiser and Norris) saw things primarily in massive and relentless sequence and structure. She was also sharply independent of the scrupulous realism of such a man as Flaubert; she sought not *le mot* but *l'objet juste.*

She did not ignore "flow," but found it very difficult to attend to, and dangerous as well, for attention to it ran the risk of losing the integrity and precision of the word-object nexus. She generally agreed with James's suggestion that "Resemblance among the parts of a continuum of feelings (especially bodily feelings) experienced along with things widely different in all other regards, thus constitutes the real and verifiable 'personal identity' which we feel." The procession of resemblances constituted movement for her; they were the means of progressing from one instant of consciousness to the next. But the reality lay not in the "flow" (which was incidental and awkward), but in the objective condition of the word-object relation in each instant.

Miss Stein's flirtations with contextuality can be illustrated in any number of passages, and especially well in one from the portrait of "Miss Furr and Miss Skeene" (in *Geography and Plays,* 1922). The rhythm moves gracefully enough in terms of central sounds and shades of meaning, circling about the focus, moving away and (with a slight variation) back toward it: "She was quite regularly gay. She told many then the way of being gay, she taught very many then little ways they could use in being gay. She was living very well, she was gay then, she went on living then, she was regular in being gay, she always was living very well and was gay very well and was telling about little ways one could be learning to use in being gay, and later was telling them quite often, telling them again and again."

The progress is discernible, but not prominent, and Miss Stein is concerned to preserve the essential experience from the accidents of flow. In another passage, this one from the more famous "Melanctha," the narrative progress is clear, and yet one has the impression that she is building solidly from center, that she is much more interested in determining a substance of character than in telling "what happened": "Jeff Campbell never knew very well these days what it was that was going on inside him. All he knew was, he was uneasy now always to be with Melanctha. All

he knew was, that he was always uneasy when he was with Melanctha, not the way he used to be from just not being very understanding, but now, because he never could be honest with her,
because he was now always feeling her strong suffering, in her, because he knew now he was having a straight, good feeling with
her, but she went so fast, and he was so slow to her; Jeff knew his
right feeling never got a chance to show itself as strong, to her."

William Carlos Williams, marveling at her skill, said that she
has "taken the words to her choice . . . to emphasize further what
she has in mind she has completely unlinked them from their former relationships to the sentence. . . . She has placed writing on a
plane where it may deal unhampered with its own affairs, unbur-
dened with scientific and philosophic lumber." She herself spoke
of the "feeling of words doing as they want to do and as they have
to do when they have to live . . ." (*Narration*). The danger is that
words, so scrupulously separated from familiar or suggestive contexts, come to have an abstract role and meaning, which they do
not vividly and recognizably describe. But this is not only a risk
Miss Stein is willing to take; it is substantially what she wants to
do. For objects, she says, do not present themselves manageably
to the consciousness in a riot of colorful detail; they are (as is experience) eligible to gradual change, in each successive detail
preserving what they have had before altering it slightly and in
minute degree. No more eloquent testimony of the shrewdness of
her energy of attention is available than the famous play upon
"pigeons" in *Four Saints in Three Acts*:

> Pigeons on the grass alas.
> Pigeons on the grass alas.
> Short longer grass longer longer shorter
> yellow grass. Pigeons large pigeons on
> the shorter longer yellow grass alas
> pigeons on the grass.
> If they were not pigeons what were they.

The risk of abstraction in this "ballet of words" is assumed in
the interests of what she calls (in *The Autobiography of Alice B.
Toklas*) her "pure passion for exactitude."

Miss Stein's fight against time, against the intrusions of the past
and of extra-situational meaning, is a similarly important concern. On the basis of the relation of experience to before, after,
and because, she judged it to be pure or adulterated. Being is not
remembering, she said in *What Are Masterpieces* (1940): "At any
moment when you are you you are you without the memory of
yourself because if you remember yourself while you are you you
are not for purposes of creating you." In *The Geographical History of America* (1936) she discussed a major distinction, which
was to recur again in later writings, that between human nature
and the human mind. The predominating characteristic of human nature is that it "clings to identity, its insistence on itself as
personality," and this effort to assert identity distracts from the
necessary, minimal function of the mind. The mind, however,
knows only in the process of its knowing; pure mind is not distracted into wishing to know who it is that is knowing and in
what sequence of remembering: "it knows what it knows and
knowing what it knows it has nothing to do with seeing what it
remembers. . . ."

The distinction is carried beyond these limits, into geography
and history. One of the reasons why America is above all of the
twentieth century, she said, is that there are larger spaces, much
flat land which "is connected with the human mind." In 1934–35,
when she traveled by plane for the first time, she saw how well
suited America was to the exercises of the human mind. Up there,
she said, there was no "remembering," the human mind worked
entirely without depending upon past, and the geometrically
"pure" landscape encouraged its functioning without interference
from time. All of this speculation is closely associated with Miss
Stein's views of identity. The reliance upon the clichés of tradition, the desire to have movement and progress in writing (a beginning, a middle, and an end whose relationships are obvious
and predictable) — these inhibit the successful analysis of consciousness as she assumed James had defined it. Because of its
geography, which did not encourage close, intimate "daily" living but instead suggested adventure, America was most properly

the country of the human mind, the most venturesome of all cultures, and the first to move into the twentieth century.

Spain also was appropriately landscaped; and Spain was quite naturally the birthplace of cubism, which was to Miss Stein the most important modern development in the visual arts to parallel hers in literature. In *The Geographical History of America* she had distinguished between the literary practices of "going on" and "staying inside," and had of course preferred the latter, for "there is not going on not in the human mind there is just staying within." The same distinction needs to be made in the other arts: in music, she was pleased only with the "ballet" repetition of sounds attached to words, like Virgil Thomson's score for her *Four Saints in Three Acts* (which she first published independently in *transition*, 1929); in painting, it was the fixed patterning of spatial relations, first of Cézanne and then of Picasso after the "Rose period." She had had many sittings for her portrait; then, when she went away, he had brushed in the face in a few hours. The lines and forms of the face are quite independently expressive of its objective nature; they mark an important break from color tones and representational sentimentalities that had characterized Picasso's painting to that time.

Three Lives was written from the dual incentives of Flaubert and Cézanne. As Elizabeth Sprigge puts it (in her *Gertrude Stein,* 1957): ". . . with Flaubert [of *Trois contes*] in the forefront of her mind and William James at the back of it, Cézanne before her eyes and Baltimore in memory, she began to write *Three Lives.*" With the exception of James, each of these associations is halfway to being traditional, closely tied to the nineteenth century, and an invitation to "remembering." She thus *identified* herself with her literary and actual past, though she went beyond it as well, to establish the beginnings of a technique of separation. Shortly after her first two published books, she dropped subject matter, or context as such, and moved on to explore the nature of language itself, separated from memory and time, in the manner of James's definition of pure consciousness in the *Principles.* The words related to each other as the lines did in Picasso's art. She wished to

make a space art out of an art that had been dominated by both
time and associative meanings. It was quite radically different
from Joyce's maneuverings of language, which were after all rich
in allusion and association, and dominated by a number of ambitious and brilliant forms of schematic interpretation. It was also
very different from the Proustian moment, rescued as that was
from the past but indispensably associated with the memory. Both
of these techniques assumed complex schemata of interrelation-
ships of past and present and relied absolutely upon them. The
Joycean epiphany, like the Proustian moment, gains its supreme
value from associations not directly a part of the particular experience but a "sentimental" or an erudite or a philosophic expansion of it.

Miss Stein was engaged in nothing less than nonrepresentational writing. Its root sources were American, as Picasso's were
Spanish. Both Spanish and American cultures, at least in her view,
were linked to the character of the landscape and to the manner
in which it encouraged a creative activity that was independent of
tradition and cultural "remembering." Just how genuine her "literary cubism" was it is difficult to say. The question of the deno-
tative and contextual values of words needs to be answered. She
maintained that both context and denotation were properties of
the moment of consciousness. As the architecture of Spain did not
need to obey an enforced, familiar context, neither did words have
to mean what they had meant before. Words in relation to each
other were also subject to the same independent usage; syntax
was a matter of much concern. She developed a form of criticism
that tried to protect usage from clichés and the risk of the
familiar.

In many ways Miss Stein's critical volumes (*Lectures in America*; *Narration*; *How to Write*, 1931; *Composition as Explanation*;
Picasso) have often been received with more charity than her creative work; but this is at least partly because in them she
explained what she was doing and there was (at least in many of
them) a discursive line that one might, with some effort, follow to

its conclusion. Her criticism is not distinct or separable from her other works; nor is it merely an explanation of what she does elsewhere. The two kinds of work are often interchangeable, and at any rate she did not contradict herself in the one in order to gain converts to the other.

Miss Stein was, first of all, a shrewd (though often an eccentric) observer of twentieth-century culture. *Lectures in America* contains many such deceptively simple observations of language and culture as these: "One century has words, another century chooses words; another century uses words and then another century using the words no longer has them"; ". . . in the nineteenth century what they thought was not what they said, but and this may sound like the same thing only it is not, they said what they thought and they were thinking what they thought." The essential difference between England and America is that because England is an island, there is always "daily living" and everything is therefore neatly put together and linked to precedent and custom and tradition. "Nothing is perplexing if there is an island," she said in *Geography and Plays*. "The special sign of this is in dusting." Americans, however, who live on a huge continent where there is much space separating persons, do not have this decorum of "daily living": "The American not living every minute of every day in a daily way does not make what he has to say to be soothing he wants what he has to say to be exciting" (*Narration*). The root meaning of this distinction has much to do with Miss Stein's central insistence upon the purely objective character of experiencing. Apparently, if one does have space, he is less likely to rely on precedent, tradition, the contrivances of "daily living," and is more inclined to take experience for what it is, even to venture into new experience. There is less search for "identity" in this case, less of what we have come to know in another context as "bad faith."

When Miss Stein defined the process of writing, she thought of it as a delicate balance of motion and form, the form providing the present context, the motion formally (and gracefully) described in terms of it. For Miss Stein was always striving for such balances, a balance such as is achieved in a ballet, where the dancer combines motion with the illusion of a fixed point within a formally described space. As she put it in *Lectures in America,* she was "achieving something that had neither the balance of a sentence nor the balance of a paragraph but a balance a new balance that had to do with a sense of movement of time included in a given space which as I have already said is a definitely American thing."

To perfect the balance of movement and form, there must be many repetitions, as there are for example in the play on "pigeons" and "grass" of *Four Saints in Three Acts.* Miss Stein set down as the second of her three "rules of composition" that to maintain a "continuous present" one must "begin again and again" (*Composition as Explanation*). Repetition is an essential strategy in composition; it guarantees similarity and forces the consciousness upon the nature of the thing seen while at the same time it provides the avenue along which movement and change may occur. Hence Miss Stein's writing is often accused of being monotonous and wearisomely repetitious; but it is deliberately so, to preserve it from being superficial. Deliberate simplicities ("a rose is a rose is a rose is a rose") are an important characteristic of modern prose style. They are as effectively a rendering of experience and a scenic reflectiveness in the writing of Hemingway, for example, as the syntactic effusions of Faulkner are a means of recording his sensibility in relation to his material. Miss Stein compared what she was doing to the cinema — not to what was happening in it but to the way in which images are persistently there in a scenic sense while they are also subject to modulations of quality and shifts of position: ". . . it was like a cinema picture made up of succession and each moment having its own emphasis that is its own difference and so there was the moving and the existence of each moment as it was in me" (*Lectures in America*).

This is, in a sense, a solution to the problem posed much earlier to Miss Stein of preserving the *integrity* of the scene while allowing for change within it, or admitting qualitative variants that exist within it: the difference between pigeons on the grass and large pigeons on the shorter yellow grass alas. Narration, therefore, is a succession of these minute, subtle gradations of change; the image is substantially what it has always been, but it admits slowly accretions of variant meaning. This is not progress so much as it is an enriching of process. Miss Stein is of course much concerned over the necessities posed by narration. Throughout her career she avoided committing herself to the representation of abrupt changes (except occasionally to shift radically from century to century when she felt the need to do so). Her "novels" have a static quality; sometimes they are empty of overtly significant movement, even of conventional content. Her characters endure experience more often than they initiate it. And the major signs of development within her fiction are an increasing complexity of attitude and a change of relational terms. The fiction "develops" by accretion in much the same way as sentences move into paragraphs — neither situation calls for much movement in either space or time.

One of her enigmatic "definitions" is relevant in this connection. In that difficult and puzzling book *How to Write,* she shows how the *nature* of a definition actually contains the character of the thing defined: "A narrative a narrative of one of that one having met to repeat that one of that one replace one one replace one one of that one two replace two of that one there never having been two of that one one of that one." This is virtually a synopsis of "plot"; it quite adequately describes the limited maneuverings (in "Melanctha," for example) of persons in space. Narrative, as distinguished from succession, shows a variation and shading of persons, not from one into another, but from an aspect of one to an aspect of another. In a sense which she herself appreciated, there is a valuable suggestion here of the line of narrative development from Henry James to Hemingway. In the matter of niceties of discrimination, granted that they live in very different worlds indeed and have rather importantly differing views of both moral and cultural proprieties, there is much to suggest of comparison in the basic technical maneuvers of James and Miss Stein. James's intense concentration upon the nuances and shades of meaning within a given moment of his novel has the quality of unique representation, of his having suspended context in a desire to operate imaginatively within a created convention. Miss Stein definitely set about at one time to emulate James, in a short novel written in 1903 but not published until 1951, *Things as They Are* (originally called *Quod Erat Demonstrandum*); and, while this conscious affectation of another writer's poses results in many dreary banalities, there are several characteristics of manner that the two writers have in common: a tendency to stay within the consciousnesses of the characters as they "consider" their situations; suspension of the narrative from any involvement in the particulars of a scene; lack of interest in documentation with respect to space and time; and a sense of the narrated experience as an imagined, aesthetically controlled "convention."

This parallel should not be pushed too far. It is really a question of what is made of consciousness in a work of art. Henry James remained within the world of appearances, and if his sense of place was not often specified in his fictions, it at any rate yielded many symbolic meanings and contrasts that are an essential part of their design. One may say that Miss Stein, who might conceivably have become a novelist like Henry James, did not because she lacked his interest in the design of conventions and moral forms that gives substance to his fiction. She preferred William to Henry; and, in her case, the line of descent in modern literature is from the psychologist rather than from the novelist. Because it was so, her role in modern literature is quite different.

Except for a group of novels in the 1880's, Henry James's work opposed rather than altered the naturalism which is a major trend in our literature. Miss Stein, however, in her role primarily of critic, made a larger contribution to the modification of naturalism. Her curious insistence upon what she called "science," which should "explain and include everything," made several changes possible in postwar naturalism: in the conception of time and movement of narrative; in the matter of purifying language, making it more "responsible" to the situations to which it addressed itself; in the process of simplifying syntax, making the sentence the key of narration and allowing succession a larger role in fiction; and finally in making a reliance upon what Hemingway called "spiritual faking" seem simply ridiculous. It seems not unreasonable to assume that the great difference between Dreiser's *An American Tragedy* (1925), with its clumsy locutions and absurd involutions, and Hemingway's *The Sun Also Rises* (1926) is not altogether unrelated to Gertrude Stein's influence upon the younger artist.

She limited herself deliberately in the matter of subject, having a distaste for "subjects" as such, and worked often within a "scientifically pure," an isolated, situation. The result was a method repeated and refined, almost obsessively practiced, but above all immune from the worst gaucheries of naive naturalism. Whatever of it Hemingway took to himself served him immensely well — even though, as may have been, he did it "without understanding it" (as Miss Stein claimed in *The Autobiography of Alice B. Toklas*). John Peale Bishop has said of Hemingway that he had an abundance of material but lacked the refinements of a method; but, as Bishop adds, he "had known in his own person an experience for which Gertrude Stein had vainly sought a substitute in words" ("Homage to Hemingway," 1936). Which is rather as much as to say that Hemingway had a subject but lacked a method and somehow managed to borrow it from her. Whatever this may mean, Hemingway's indebtedness to Miss Stein should be obvious enough. It is as if she were working to perfect techniques for his use; though it is mainly to *Three Lives* and *The Making of Americans* (1925) that he is indebted.

The debt consists roughly of these essentials: first, definitely a sense of looking at things in a "contemporary" way, working out a style consistent to "the thing seen"; a revision of time sense, so that (in the fiction of the 1920's at least) he avoided a simple chronological succession of events and paced his narrative, in a variation of her description of narrative progression, so that progress occurs in terms of clusters of personal relationships, considerably more complicated though no more sophisticated than those in "Melanctha"; a much more shrewd and accurate sense of movement and the exploitation of scene than the naturalists had, as though their crudities had been refined with her aid. In *Death in the Afternoon* (1932), Hemingway describes a literary style as "the sequence of motion and fact which made the emotion." It is true that Miss Stein would rather have inhibited the "motion" than not — she always objected to his obsession with violence; but the fundamental manner was there: of concentration upon the object at hand, attention to the precise language needed to make it come to life, a careful sense of timing and pacing, and a suppression of relational and qualifying words that may have been beyond his power to make genuinely expressive.

In many respects Miss Stein's concern over the limits of complication in writing seems overly anxious and fastidious. She cared little for punctuation of any kind, claimed that it interfered with the "going on"; a comma, for example, "by helping you along holding your coat for you and putting on your shoes keeps you from living your life as actively as you should lead it . . ." (*Lectures in America*). But she saved most of her attention for the risks a writer takes when he pushes beyond the securities of the sentence. She has rung many changes upon the famous remark "A sentence is not emotional, a paragraph is" (*How to Write*). When you push beyond the sentence, you also push beyond the genuine focus upon the object. Sequences of words and thought begin; movement begins. Paragraphs are threatened by the distractions of "beginning, middle, and end," and extraneous matter is bound to get into them. "A sentence has not really any beginning or middle or ending because each part is its part as its part," she said in *Narration*, "and so the whole exists within by the balance within but the paragraph exists not by a balance within but by a succession." A sentence is beautifully balanced (if it has the correct kinds of words within it): it is "inside itself by its internal balancing . . ." and gains its merit because of the tight, exact, clear interrelationship of parts. True knowledge, she maintained, depends upon an "immediate existing"; this is William James's pure sense of the "in-itself," beyond which he went a long way in both his psychology and his philosophy. Miss Stein did not follow him, but remained as if transfixed within the limits of "immediate existence." She deliberately wrenched words not only from familiar context but from almost any context at all. Yet the effects are intermittently extraordinary, though even the most dedicated follower at times admits to weariness.

Miss Stein was above all convinced that the twentieth century was interested, as she put it in *Lectures in America,* in *feeling a thing existing:* "we that is any human being living has inevitably to feel the thing anything being existing, but the name of that thing of that anything is no longer anything to thrill any one but children." And this leads us, finally, to her genuine value as a critic of modern literature: she is above all the most important sponsor of what we have called "presentational immediacy," of the integrity and the uniqueness of the "thing seen at the moment it is seen." Though she read widely and even exhaustively in the classics, they had no meaning for her except as they pointed to parallels with the present. Most importantly, it was the *visual* sense that intrigued her, the shape, color, depth, dimension, and texture of the thing seen. In the grain of that texture lie the differences from one generation to another. Her sense of time was limited to two things: the alterations (subtle as they may be) in the way of seeing things; the effect of force on surfaces. Of war she said that it speeds up change, that it makes spectacular differences not only in the arrangements of objects in space but also in the ways in which one "feels existence." In the case of World War II, which she described in *Wars I Have Seen* as an unheroic war, when the "nice heroic deeds" were no longer possible, it made a radical difference. In any case, the twentieth century was remarkably different from the nineteenth, and the difference simply emphasized the need for a radical change in sensibilities, so that it could be honestly and faithfully recorded.

The essential difference was fragmentation, or the separation of objects and persons from each other so that they could no longer feel securely dependent upon one another. This change the Americans understood far more clearly than the Europeans; Miss Stein was convinced that the twentieth century was American and that

Europe was able only after World War II to break from the nineteenth. Partly this was because the American space enabled Americans to see things in a "cubist way," and their speed of movement above or along the landscape made them see reality as a disembodied, geometrical series of forms. But it was mostly because of that remarkable convergence of self-consciousness and science, which nourished each other, the one forcing analysis, the other reducing it to a study of pure and impersonal forms.

Gertrude Stein offers a remarkably interesting series of observations; they are all in these volumes of criticism, all of them united in her single and singular preoccupation with the elements of consciousness, in her version of William James's *Principles.* The effect upon her literary practice was to reduce its scope and to introduce one after another kind of abstraction and attenuation. She set about deliberately eliminating time from human consideration, moving from the idea of "history as generations" of *The Making of Americans* to the pure stasis of her late plays. Having been left with space, she tried to purify it, holding it in the syntactic balance of the carefully limited sentence and protecting it from the threat of superficial and destructive motion. She worked hard at the task of reducing connotation to the bare minimum necessary to suggest a context of any kind. In consequence, she was left with a very much reduced field of deliberation: not surrealistic or impressionistic, not at all realistic, a world of concepts all but deprived of percepts, providing an intellectual music of successions and echolalic improvisations. The story of how she traveled this long road from *Three Lives* is a fascinating one, and it ought to be given at least in outline.

Miss Stein was obviously making a bow to the great French tradition when she wrote *Three Lives.* Her first title was *Three Histories,* and she says she had tried a translation of Flaubert's *Trois contes* at the time of composing her own book. The epigraph is from Jules Laforgue: "Donc je suis un malheureux et ce n'est ni ma faute ni celle de la vie" ("For I am an unhappy man, and it is neither my fault nor life's"). The book was published, at her expense, by the Grafton Press of New York in 1909. It had a long, slow struggle for success, but is the book to which almost all critics turn approvingly, no matter what they think of her other work.

It contains three "portraits," but they are narratives as well, two of them ("The Good Anna" and "The Gentle Lena") fairly simple and straightforward, the third ("Melanctha") a subtle analysis of the mind and temperament of its Negro heroine. Unlike *Things as They Are* (which preceded it by two years in date of composition), the major roles are taken by members of the servant or working class; Anna and Lena are German servants in upper-middle-class households, Melanctha a daughter of a Negro workingman. One of the major contributions of *Three Lives* to American literature was its clear proof that such characters are susceptible to the same kind of analysis as James had used with his characters of high degree and undoubtedly superior status. In fact, at least in the case of Melanctha, Miss Stein seems to have set out to prove that the quality and complexity of a consciousness depend not at all upon status, that they are there and differ only in degree and kind of articulateness from the others. It is true that Anna's concerns are with the several members of the households she serves, that her standards are fairly easy to define, and that her fidelity to them makes the diagramming of her career a fairly simple task. Yet "The Good Anna" is generously provided with niceties of observation. The simplicities of Anna are after all based upon a complex set of social manners, which are supported and made vividly real by emotional attachments and tensions. The simplicities of Miss Stein's manner are deceptive; Anna emerges as "good" but also complexly real. She is viewed in terms of her consciousness of place, manner, and code. The "goodness" of Anna appears often to be wasted on lazy mistresses, or to have the contrary effect of "spoiling" the men whom she favors as masters; but goodness is in itself a convention that has many particular forms of expression, and the values of Anna's goodness are realized with a full appreciation of their pathos, occasional eccentricity, and ultimate soundness. "The Gentle Lena" is almost pure pathos. She suffers experience without really understanding what is happening to her. The manners of her world require of her decisions that she is scarcely able to comprehend. In both of these *histoires* a basic convention (of the servant class, of the German household, of ranks and sexes) is assumed; the narrative functions in terms of it, and the quality of portrait is measured against the limits it sets up and determines.

Miss Stein's originality comes in part from her sense of intimate understanding; the two figures are seen "from the inside," and their sensibilities determine both the style of presentation and its meaning. But the two sketches are relatively simple, if only because the relationship between temperament and convention provides for a minimum of tension. For the most part, Anna is able to meet an emotional crisis by enclosing it within the social and domestic convention to which she has been in the manner bred. Lena's pathos comes from her immaturity, her inability to appreciate any crisis personally; she dies without really understanding why she has lived. She is passively a victim of the failure of persons to respond to a convention and to live within it. Melanctha Herbert is different in two ways from Lena, whom she otherwise superficially resembles: she actively pushes herself into the society, struggling to understand it; the convention in her case is more flexible and allows for more subtly interesting experiments in personal experience.

"Melanctha" is also stylistically more interesting than the other two; we find in it the beginnings of Miss Stein's distinctive manner. She herself recognized that fact and referred to it on a number of occasions in her critical writings. In 1925 she said that in "Melanctha" there was "a constant recurring and beginning there was a marked direction in the direction of being in the present although naturally I had been accustomed to past present and future, and why, because the composition forming around me was a prolonged present" (*Composition as Explanation*). "Melanctha" was her first full experiment in the use of a "continuous present." Though here there is a definite sense of narrative progress, the style moves from a succession of centers, linking them and giving them an appearance of unity and centrality. The effect is of a succession of consciously apprehended moments of experience, to each of which fully complex states of "present" emotion, temperament, and convention (as they are presently sensed and understood) adhere. But it is also significantly true that Miss Stein presents these states in the idiom and within the range of articulation of her characters; the words used are those that they would and should use. As Donald Sutherland has said, in the best critical study of Gertrude Stein so far published, ". . . the word had to have not its romantic or literary meaning but the immediate meaning it had to the contemporary using it, a literal axiomatic meaning confined to the simple situations of the average life" (*Gertrude Stein: A Biography of Her Work*, 1951).

"Melanctha" is an intricate pattern of human conflicts, moving forward and back with the heroine as she forces herself into experience, hesitates at the edge of understanding it, moves back toward its beginnings. It is, as Miss Stein has said of it, a pattern of "beginning again and again." Melanctha Herbert must move into the violent world, to test her desire and to reach "understanding." She was always "seeking rest and quiet, and always she could find new ways to be in trouble." Each of the significant phrases is repeated, again and again, in slightly new contexts, until one is aware of change within a central pattern of conscious experience. When her desire for experience leads to violence, she "discovers wisdom," though she "never did or meant anything that was wrong." She "wandered on the edge of wisdom." Wisdom in this sense means a fulfillment for which Melanctha understands that she is in some way responsible, above all one in which she has actively participated.

The heart of the narrative is Melanctha's complex relationship with Jefferson Campbell, "a serious, earnest, good young joyous doctor." He suggests the promise of a "more refined" adventure in "wisdom" than she has had so far. They alternately reach and withdraw from "understanding." As her more volatile and passionate nature pushes forward, he retreats; her "real strong feeling" excites and puzzles him. He must "go fast" with her, and he doesn't understand how he can explain to her what it is she should want him to want. The most brilliantly effective passages of the tale describe the torture of their trying to decide what they mean to each other and what they mean by meaning it and what they might have meant if they had not meant it at the beginning. The temperamental clashes are too much for both of them; they come near to understanding, but never quite go all the way, and the frustration is an agony to both of them.

When she has finally taught him to be in love with her, she loses interest in him. It is not what she has wanted at all, or rather the realization of what she has vaguely sought proves to be less in quality and intensity than she has wished it to be. "I ain't got certainly no hot passion any more now in me." The agony of not understanding what one is wanting — of not wanting it when one has it — affects both with equal intensity. Jeff Campbell's shame is a complex and powerful feeling of both frustration and fear: "Only sometimes he shivered hot with shame when he remembered some things he once had been feeling." When they move away from each other, and Melanctha once more searches for "wisdom," the tale is all but finished. It has revealed fully what it had started to say. Melanctha's subsequent adventures are unsuccessful, because she has not adjusted emotionally to the apparently contrary necessities to "go slow" and to "go fast" at the same time. She cannot break away from passion or adjust to human circumstance. The burden of trying to understand is really too much for her; though she never killed herself because she was blue, she often thought "this would really be the best way for her to do." Instead she fades away, dies in a home for poor consumptives. Her passion spent and dispersed, she is no longer "herself," or the person who vigorously tried to realize the wisdom of being what she wanted to be.

The progress from vague desires to initial experiments in satisfaction, to major crisis and failure, is brilliantly intricate. The burden of movement is assumed by words and phrases. Miss Stein "begins again and again," she "uses everything," she maintains a "continuous present." The pattern is that of a spiral moving within and beyond several levels and stages of passion and knowledge. The language changes and remains the same; slight additions and qualifications indicate advances and retreats, and Melanctha's progress in "wisdom" is shown in a successively sharpened emphasis in the language. Perhaps the key word is "trouble"; it suggests a commitment to experience without a full understanding of it. Trouble occurs when passion is forced beyond the comprehension of those involved in its expression. Jeff Campbell, for example, "had never yet in his life had real trouble." Melanctha always "could only find new ways to be in trouble." Because neither is able to redeem "wisdom" from the menace of "trouble," the relationship fails. Miss Stein is similarly masterly in her development of their uncertainties: Jeff is never really "very sure about her"; at the critical moment, "All he knew was he wanted Melanctha should be there beside him, and he wanted very badly, too, always to throw her from him"; he was always uneasy because "he knew now he had a good, straight, strong feeling of right loving for her, and yet he never could use it to be good and honest with her."

The style and substance are an immense advance beyond those of "The Good Anna" and "The Gentle Lena." The personal tensions are communicated naturally and easily, while in Miss Stein's first writing (*Things as They Are*), the language clumsily interferes and the conflicts are handled in an interplay of artificial and unreal poses. "Melanctha" strikes one as a peculiarly effective piece, whose place in modern literature is important in a wide variety of ways. It is, for one thing, a triumph of analysis of the kind that Henry James (who at the time of its writing was producing his most complex works) could never have achieved. This is in itself a fact of more than ordinary importance, since it suggests a broadening of perspective in the functions and uses of analysis. Its application to the minds of relatively "unlettered" persons pointed away from the clumsy assumptions of contemporary naturalists who seemed to think that subconsciously a person's emotional status was as complex as his background and social level dictated. It is infinitely superior, in analytic correctness and appropriateness at least, to Dreiser's fumbling attempts to define Sister Carrie's "vague yearnings for the ideal." Sherwood Anderson's sketches of lonely, inarticulate souls come closer both in type and in merit; but Anderson lacked Miss Stein's intensity, and his analyses often settled into formula characterizations.

"Melanctha" is also important in its relation to the Negro consciousness. Richard Wright said that reading it was one of the most important events of his career. Its importance has nothing to do with the Negro per se as belonging to a social or economic class; in fact, "Melanctha" succeeds in part because it assumes an equality that underlies social discrimination, an equality of feeling and emotion.

Finally, it has done much — much more than the early naturalists were able to do — by way of breaking down artificial barriers of class, manner, "culture." The "simple soul," the "peasant complex," the "servant's mind" are all ruled out. Miss Stein may be said here to have initiated or shown the possibilities of an entirely new type of "novel of manners." Partly this is because manners are in themselves surface indications of personality; they are a group's simplest ways of identifying itself and of measuring forms and degrees of compliance and conformity. But "manners" in another sense are the external sign of social articulation. They may be understood at any level and in any context of human relationships. Such words as "wisdom," "passion," and "trouble" are universals, to which "manners" adhere as particular social expressions. This fact, which seems extraordinarily simple at this remove of time, was not at all easy to grasp at the beginning of the century. Class distinctions have always been a difficulty in the struggle to set up and to maintain fictional structures. The trouble is seen in gaucheries of style that get in the way of an author's full grasp of his characters. In a sense, Miss Stein's desire to emulate Flaubert (however actual the relationship can be proved to be) was here more appropriate than her rather stubborn and awkward attempt to set up a "Jamesian shop" in *Things as They Are*. She did present a *type* of Emma Bovary in "Melanctha," but she did not borrow Flaubert's Normandy for backdrop. The pathos of unachieved "wisdom," of the failure to find unobtrusive settings for emotional drives, exists in both works; but they are each happily self-sufficient.

The link between *Three Lives* and *The Making of Americans* is at first rather difficult to see; the two are so different in scope and length that they would appear to have nothing at all in common. Yet there is a means of seeing the one as an outgrowth of the other that becomes more convincing the more one attends to it. Miss Stein has herself described *The Making of Americans* (which she wrote in 1906–8) as an outgrowth of her interest in experimental psychology. The experiments themselves taught her nothing, but they started several kinds of curiosity in human types. She became "enormously interested," she says in *Lectures in America*, "in the types of their characters that is what I even then thought of as the bottom nature of them . . ." The "bottom nature" was revealed, as it is in *The Making of Americans,* by the way in which "everybody said the same thing over and over again with infinite variations but over and over again until finally if you listened with great intensity you could hear it rise and fall and tell all that that there was inside them . . ." Here it was not so much the words but the movement of thought, the circling back, the going over the same ground, the alternation of particulars and generalities.

The Making of Americans is in a sense a book about time, about history, particularly about American history. But there are no events, in the ordinary sense; nor are there heroes such as we find in political and social histories. To begin, we must sense what Miss Stein means by history and time. Time is the passing of generations; the span from grandfather to grandson is a long one, and it comprehends a full measure of historical parallels and variation. The quality of Miss Stein's history is a quality of observations repeated from generation to generation, of the cumulative wisdom of domestic generalities as they meet and are modified by particular circumstances. The death of generations is as important as the living in which they acquire identity. Identity is in itself dependent upon one's being within a transition from death of the past generation to one's own death. Generations overlap, but they also succeed one another; and it is the repetition of "what they say," together with the variants upon "what has been said," that makes time and history. The true *modus operandi* of *The Making of Americans* is custom, as this is communicated from one generation to the next. So that what changes within a few months of the lifetime of Melanctha Herbert becomes in *The Making of Americans* a succession of family patterns. In the use of words, formulas, phrases, wisdom and its imperfect manifestations in human life are given form: "Nay they love to remember, and to tell it over, and most often to their children, what they have been and what they have done and how they themselves have made it all to be so different and how well it is for these children that they have had a strong father who knew how to do it so that youngsters could so have it."

The effect of this retelling and recasting of family wisdom is of course substantial and immense in the long account of the Herslands and the Dehnings, in a book of 925 closely printed pages. But it is not true, as B. L. Reid maintains (in *Art by Subtraction,* 1958), that the shorter version edited by Bernard Fay for Harcourt, Brace (1934) was better than the original and that Miss Stein had therefore no sense of proportion. In one sense at least the original is not long enough; it may be said that a "history" of this sort, to account for the minutiae of what people say when they seem to be repeating their father's saying it, must attend to infinitesimal variants. *The Making of Americans* is an "abstract" book, or it tends in the direction of abstractness; but this impression is only the result of its inital foundation in the scrutiny of types. Its primary effect is like that of the Old Testament, if the wars and the visitations were omitted. Generations follow one another without actually succeeding one another. They move in a stately procession of living and saying and believing and behaving, and they are concerned with specific variations of first and last things.

As in *Three Lives*, the style and movement rely upon the key of repetition. Repetition with variants upon text is the stylistic practice of all of Miss Stein's work. Here the pattern is set up to defeat the ordinary belief in time, to give time a Biblical dignity, and to remove persons as far as possible from the exigencies of clocks. "There are many ways of being a man," she says; "there are many millions of each kind of them, more and more in ones living they are there repeating themselves around one, every one of them in his own way being the kind of man he has in him, and there are always many millions made just like each of them." This brings the idea of individual differences down to a basic generality; the 900-odd pages are used to define the differences, and the eventual impression is to emphasize the sameness-in-difference. "Every one then has in their living repeating, repeating of every kind of thing in them, repeating of the kind of impatient feeling they have in them, of the anxious feeling almost every one has more or less always in them."

This repetition of characteristics makes for a constant intermingling of universal and particular. Miss Stein is convinced that the general is realized, if one will but look, in the particular manifestation of it; and, if one is satisfied that this is true, time will seem to be absorbed in the shifting and slow groupings of particulars in a set of principles. Persons become absorbed in types, particulars in generalities. The particular hides in the world, but it also hides from it; the conflict between the two, once formulated, is the most one can make of time and history: "Being important to one's self inside one. Being lonesome inside one. Making the world small to one to lose from one the lonesome feeling a big world feeling can make inside any one who has not it in them to feel themselves as big as any world can be around them."

Between *The Making of Americans* and her next important work, Miss Stein wrote "portraits." She had hoped to write, in *A Long Gay Book,* something as long and as ambitious as the *Americans* volume, but it did not turn out that way, so she turned then to short exercises, responses to persons in relation to her and to situations. They were to the general design of her work what Hemingway's "chapters" of *In Our Time* (1925) were to the major themes of his first two novels. But the portraits were also a step in the direction of greater abstractness and of freeing herself from time and from what she called "remembering." The portraits had the visual impact that the words of *Tender Buttons* were to have, in relation to the objects with which they were associated. As she said (in *Lectures in America*), "I had in hundreds of ways related words, then sentences then paragraphs to the thing at which I was looking." The portraits were not so complete a removal from representation as were the majority of *Tender Buttons* sketches. The titles always served to direct the manner of understanding the context, as in "sitwell Edith Sitwell" (1925) and "He and They, Hemingway" (1923); in the latter case the following lines illustrate the conjunction: "How do you do and good-bye. Good-bye and how do you do. Well and how do you do." There are links, however, between the earlier portraits and *Tender Buttons,* which suggest that they are a move away from the two major books and in the direction of greater abstractness and experimental "purity." *Tender Buttons* is called by John Malcolm Brinnin "thought-in-the-process-of-being-recorded." The language is truly a move away from the area of familiar denotation, and toward an absolute objectivity. The objects contained here are not named; seldom do the words used to respond to them suggest them. The passages are, instead, creations in themselves, independent existences. They are the moments of consciousness which William James discussed, but without his suggestion of continuity and references beyond themselves. Miss Stein's language tends to fix attention entirely upon itself, not upon her or upon what context it might allusively suggest. This is an extreme way of putting it, of course; Miss Stein did not always remain so objectively pure. "Celery," for example, retains much of what celery is known to be and taste: "Celery tastes tastes where in curled lashes and little bits and mostly in remains." The slicing of a roast is suggested as a family ceremony, in "Roastbeef": "All the time that there is use there is use and any time there is surface there is a surface, and every time there is an exception there is an exception and every time there is a division there is a dividing."

But *Tender Buttons* shows her well launched in the new style:

lean and abstract, playfully and eccentrically unconventional, erratic and unpredictable. Miss Stein's work following *Tender Buttons* can be seen in three classifications: the experimental works, in which attempts to create the greatest objectivity lead to usages and devices that are isolated from all traditional literature (there are plays, portraits, and novels in this group, each of them a radical departure from what its genre has customarily meant); the autobiographies, of which *The Autobiography of Alice B. Toklas* and *Everybody's Autobiography* (1937) are the major achievements; and "reflections," partly autobiographical and partly philosophical, in which her general stance as an unorthodox, unconventional writer is expanded to allow her to assume a position as commentator upon twentieth-century culture. All three of these classes are closely interrelated. Miss Stein the artist of the first group makes possible the "celebrity" Miss Stein of the autobiographies, who in turn is listened to (though not always respectfully) in relation to the third class of books. In addition, we have the figure of Miss Stein the literary theorist whom we have already considered in some detail.

With respect to the first of these classes, the principal examples are portraits and plays. In the former case, the portraits sometimes expanded into "novels," like the much-worked-over *Ida* (1941), and some of the posthumous works published by the Yale University Press. In these cases the novel is a development out of the focus of attitude and character found in the portrait, or an expansion of it. "Ada" is self-contained within a fixed context; *Ida* moves geographically but remains static as a personality. The novel is often a fuller rendering of surfaces. At times, as in *Mrs. Reynolds* (written in 1946), it resembles somewhat the kind of technique used in "The Good Anna." At other times, as in *Two: Gertrude Stein and Her Brother* (written in 1910–12), there is of course an autobiographical basis and the piece is an extended, a lengthened portrait. There are many suggestions of Miss Stein in all these works — of her at work, seated in her chair, of her dogs and her place; the place intrudes upon the consciousness but it does not therefore make the work autobiographical.

The most revealing examples of her experiments are the plays. There is a great difference between so simple an arrangement of phrases and "characters" as "A Curtain Raiser" (*Geography and Plays*) and the elaborate ballet of sounds and phrases in *Four Saints in Three Acts.* Yet the same conception of the drama is maintained. Again, as in her other works, Miss Stein adapts the play structure to her needs and to her conception of art. She said several times that there was something distressing about the pace of ordinary drama. Audiences were always being required to "catch up" emotionally to the play, and there was always a disturbing gap between them and it. As in her other work, she hoped to close this gap by putting audience and work on an equal footing, by removing the necessities of plot, movement, "remembering" from the play. Because she helped them less (that is, she did not "put them into" a situation to which they would have to adjust emotionally), she helped them more.

All of this meant that she would have to be arbitrary in her selection and arrangement of words and phrases. There are no discernible relationships between characters and phrasing; there are no characters really, in the conventional sense. There are only persons speaking words, and occasionally numbers. The plays have the same intransigently nonrepresentational quality as abstract painting. "A Curtain Raiser" is a good example:

> Six.
> Twenty.
> > Outrageous.
> Late.
> Weak.
> > Forty.
> More in any wetness.
> Sixty three certainly.
> Five.
> Sixteen.
> Seven.
> Three.
> More in orderly.   Seventy-five.

Even when there appears to be a conventional dialogue (as in

"Turkey and Bones and Eating and We Liked It," *Geography and Plays*), the dialogue is only apparently dramatic; it is actually static and has no relation to action real or imagined. As in her portraits-into-novels, the plays vary from simple structures of a few lines to elaborate interplays of sounds and words. "Not Sightly" (*Geography and Plays*) contains many Steinian plays upon sounds arranged in a form of order and structure that suggest the ballet rather than the drama: ". . . when similar and jointed and prized and quilted quietly quilted tights quietly quilted tight minds when three innerly expensive shrugs meant more . . ."

The most elaborate, and the most successful, of these experiments is *Four Saints in Three Acts*. The history of this play has to do with Miss Stein's love of Spain, with her having come upon a group of statuary in a Paris shop window, with her interest in "saintliness" as an especial maneuvering of the will and sensibility. It may be thought of as another "laboratory observation," though this time immensely expanded and lyrically enhanced by the use of some of her more tuneful juxtapositions of sounds and rhythms. Her saints are not religious in any theological sense. They are domestic and "living"; that is, they have the character of simple and unsophisticated souls engaged in an exchange of simple "beatitudes." Donald Sutherland has exceptionally well described Miss Stein's view of saints: they were "primarily useful to her as they afforded a stable metaphor on which to maintain her own generically poetic exaltation, her own vision of a world saturated with miracles." *Four Saints* lends itself especially well to the suggestion of music; her phrasing and repetitions are exceptionally "melodious," and they suggest as well the measures and pauses in music. She was interested in sounds, as she was in the visual impact of spaces; they were both necessary to the comprehension of the thing consciously apprehended. The play is a wonder of both sounds and meanings interwoven and in movement. None of these elements add up conventionally to a "plot"; nor is theology discussed. But the suggestion of the miraculous and of sanctity is nevertheless there. In the version with Virgil Thomson's music (first performed in Hartford, Connecticut, in 1934), it

acquired an additional dimension, though it is possible to suspect that this addition went far toward making it more of a "traditional" play than Miss Stein had intended.

Four Saints in Three Acts is a play upon the will toward saintliness, and upon the quality of saintliness as a human disposition
and temperament, as "Melanctha" was an analysis of passion in
its move toward social complication. It is, therefore, as a whole,
an aesthetic object without context except what the concept of
abstract disposition of saintliness can give it. It makes an elaborate design out of a possible and a probable form or type of human disposition. Since this disposition is saintliness and neither
passion nor convention, the effect is ceremonial and gay and colorful and — within Miss Stein's own scope of apprehension — be-
atific. These are all available to emotional response, but the play
lacks what she always regarded as an "audience trap," the building of suspense through plot, the directing of the audience's sense
of time and event, stimulating the need for the audience to recon-
struct themselves in terms of the drama that was unfolding.

One way of appraising Gertrude Stein's value in modern literature is to say that she was pre-eminently a theorist (a "scientist" of
sorts), who offered some illustrations of what she thought literature should be. It is true that we are always busy examining her
creative work as demonstration, to "see if composition comes out
as she says it should." There is no question of her value as a critic
whose primary function was to define language and to examine
its place in the work of art. Perhaps it is, after all, her main claim
to eminence. It would be a false reading of her work, however, to
say that it served only to validate her theory. The work often
stands by and for itself. It does not stand by itself in the manner
of other contemporary masterpieces, however. Its merits are essentially those of a work designed to break new experimental
ground. It is tendentious in the most useful and illuminating
sense that word might have. Its limitations are a result of her
virtues; one may truthfully say that the limitations are necessary
to the virtues.

Of the three major values I see in Miss Stein's contribution to modern literature, one is intrinsic and the other two "historical" in the sense of their affecting the nature of contemporary work. As for the intrinsic value, some of her writings remain as substantial masterpieces, though of two kinds: *Three Lives* is a minor masterpiece of great significance to modern writing because it is intrinsically good and impressive as literature and was received as such by many of her sensitive contemporaries; *The Making of Americans* cannot be so regarded, but must be thought of as the most elaborate of all demonstrations, intrinsically great but valuable because its merits come from its elaborate illustration of a theory of time and history; *Four Saints in Three Acts* is similarly beautifully successful but never truly separable from the variety of theoretical convictions from which it emerged. There are other pieces that move somewhere between the level of demonstration and the status of *sui generis* masterpiece. Some of these, like the novel *Ida*, the little books *Paris France* (1940) and *Picasso*, and *The Geographical History of America*, have frequently a strong and persuasive identity as books of unaffected wisdom; they are original and characteristic of their author, but they are also, in the sense in which she was capable of being so, profound.

Of the other two kinds of merit she has demonstrated, one must point to her role as an informal teacher, a guide and a leader in the "new literature." This aspect is difficult to see clearly because it is confused by gossip and claims and counterclaims. Nor is it possible to determine exactly *what* it was she was able to do for others. It is certainly *not* true that, as Brinnin claims, her influence "has been all but nil," though the sense in which he makes that claim has some merit. Her influence is very difficult to determine, and it is furthermore hard to separate it from the kind of influence a person like Sherwood Anderson had upon his contemporaries. The personal charm, the awesome regard in which many have seemed to hold her, the impact of her personality in the matter of making an idea "seem right" at the time she was considering it: these have all to be considered as variable and ultimately doubtful conditions. Those critics who were her personal friends seem to have come away more than convinced, often enthusiastically moved. But her personality is now receding; she is, after all, dead. And the work itself must ultimately become the test of influence. Any true measure is impossible, but it is not unlikely that such works as *Three Lives* and *The Making of Americans* have already served as "writer's texts" and will continue to do so. Above all, in many little ways, the "argument" of Miss Stein's criticism, which we have examined, seems very probably destined to have a major effect, not so much upon any specific author or text, but upon the writer who seeks a way out of naturalist impasses (naturalism is pervasive in modern literature, but it seems also destined to lead to impasses) and does not wish to exploit currently popular ideologies as a means.

This position, of Miss Stein as critic or theorist or both, is distinctive and yet an important part of modern criticism. Despite Miss Stein's overwhelming "presence" on the modern literary scene, she actually asks for and even demands an impersonal literature. It is true that many of her works are gratuitously personal, and that often she coyly peeps out at the reader from behind whatever large object conceals her. But unless we wish to assume that her critical discourses are merely self-ingratiating, the appeal in them is to a literature divested not only of specific autobiographical meaning but of the traditional structural implications of literature. These virtues are considerable because the limitations are so enthusiastically admitted and so significantly assumed. There is nothing specious about Gertrude Stein; to call her a supreme egotist does not convict her of simply posing before her Picassos for personal gain. She has had much to say, and she has often said it with a stubborn (perhaps a naively truculent) persistence. When her manner of saying it is penetrable, and it often is, the ideas are worth the value that she has been able to give them. She will, at any rate, merit a position in literary criticism as the person who carried as far as it might go William James's analysis of consciousness. Beyond that, she has stared hard at the prospect of an art objectively hard and autonomously real, using its instruments in strangely new but often startlingly effective ways. Much of what she has done to prove her theoretic convictions falls far short of enabling her to do so. She has had many failures, and in any case the perspective of an old-maid eccentric can scarcely be expected to yield large truths consistently. There is a wide margin between her profound insights and her more obvious and banal observations.

These conditions limit her usefulness, but they do not destroy it. She has the undoubted strength of the creative person who is able to call upon her powers of imagination to prove what literature might be. The true value of her criticism lies in its applicability to her work as creative artist, and by extension to the problems of those who are stimulated to follow its example. Her "modernity" is a necessary corrective of that of others, as theirs is needed to keep her distinction within reasonable limits.

◤ JULIAN MOYNAHAN

Vladimir Nabokov

◤ S INCE Proust we have accepted the view that memory is
an art, maybe the sole art to have survived God's death,
and that nostalgia may encapsulate a metaphysic. Until V. V.
Nabokov came to America in 1940 we Americans had no great
modern artist in nostalgia of our own, although F. Scott Fitzgerald strikes the authentic note when he imagines Nick Carraway observing Gatsby waiting for the green light in the closing
paragraphs of *The Great Gatsby*. Gatsby mistakes the past for the
future — the characteristic error of nostalgists — when he anticipates a reunion with Daisy, that shopworn Louisville Lolita,
which "was already behind him, somewhere back in that vast obscurity beyond the city, where the dark fields of the republic
rolled on under the night." And Fitzgerald's power of evocation
in this instance arises from the fact, tragic for his entire career,
that he too is a nostalgist, "borne back ceaselessly into the past,"
victim of a disposition and attitude he rarely was able to command for the servicing of his art.

"Nostalgist" is a graceless term. In *Pale Fire* Nabokov coins the
expression "preterist: one who collects cold nests" for the artist

162

who commands the past qua past, never confusing it with present and future although his created characters may do so, and drawing from this beguiling imaginative realm rich material for an art of memory which illuminates the whole range of time through which the artist has lived. Considering William Faulkner's obsession with lapsed time in his Yoknapatawpha County sequence we might think that he before Nabokov is the great American artist of preterism. Yet in Faulkner time is spatialized, into an echoing corridor where characters like Quentin Compson and Rosa Coldfield run furiously, doing battle with ghosts from Civil War times and earlier; or it is frozen into a hallucinatory instant when ghostly men-at-arms relive at close of day their moment of glorious risk under the rapt eye of a defeated eccentric like the Reverend Gail Hightower.

Preterist art, by contrast, works in a cooler, more classical fashion. Both Proust and Nabokov establish clear boundaries between past and present, provide elaborate and meticulously drafted maps for their realms of recollection, and carefully choose the grounds, or privileged moments, at which past and present will be allowed, briefly and dangerously, to meet and commingle. The goal of these artists is something more important than self-discovery or the discovery of cultural and regional identity. It is the discovery and definition of human consciousness, conceived as the master key to the riddle of reality, conceived also as providing limited, transitory glimpses of the realm of essence.

Neither Proust nor Nabokov permits this essentially metaphysical quest to sterilize his fictional art. Both remain great tragicomic novelists in close touch with the actualities of man in contemporary society and with central issues of modern history. Thirst for the eternal never alienates their loyalty to the human condition although it may constitute the deepest source of their great originality and power as stylists and fabulists. In the following pages I shall try to indicate the range, charm, and contemporary relevance of Nabokov's prose artistry without, I hope, ever quite losing sight of his cunning, wholly devoted pursuit of certain overwhelming questions which the publicists of the death of God once thought, mistakenly, to have put to death as well.

Nabokov was born in 1899 into a rich, accomplished, and socially enlightened St. Petersburg family which had given admirals,
scholars, and statesmen to the Russian nation over many generations. He enjoyed a privileged and secure boyhood, dividing his
time between the beautiful Nabokov country estate called Vyra
and a town house ample and elegant enough to accommodate under the Soviets a foreign diplomatic mission and later a school of
architecture. He attended an excellent and progressive school in
the city and spent his holidays at the country estate, where he
became an expert tennis player and amateur lepidopterist, and
on the French Riviera, to which the Nabokovs were accustomed
to travel annually by train to enjoy sea bathing and the sedate
life in luxurious hotels led by the high European bourgeoisie of
that vanished time.

This Edenic phase was abruptly terminated when Vladimir's
father, who had been a leading member of the Russian Constituent Assembly, took his family south to Yalta to avoid the Red
armies of the Bolshevik Revolution and, upon the collapse of
White military resistance in the Crimea, fled with them into exile
in Western Europe.

Between 1919 and 1922 Vladimir, who had learned English
thoroughly from governesses and tutors while a small child, studied modern languages and literature at Trinity College, Cambridge. After graduating with first-class honors he rejoined his
family in Berlin and set about launching a career as an émigré
poet, critic, and novelist. In 1922 his beloved and admired father
fell victim to a pair of Russian right-monarchist gunmen while
chairing a political meeting and Vladimir, the oldest son, became
head of a family for which the condition of exile from its native
country was destined to be permanent.

Throughout the 1920's and 1930's, writing in Russian under
the pen name V. Sirin and residing first in Berlin and then in
Paris, Nabokov produced a brilliant series of poems, stories, and
novels which established him as unquestionably the most gifted

Russian writer-in-exile of his generation. At the same time, his attitude toward the endless political intrigues, fantasies of imminent Romanov restoration, religious manias, and literary cabals of the Russian émigré circles centering on Berlin, Prague, and Paris remained detached, ironic, and independent. He suffered with his fellow Russians the inconvenience and indignity of the Nansen passport, issued by the League of Nations to stateless persons, and financial problems at times forced him into such temporary extraliterary expedients as coaching tennis, giving English-language lessons, and composing chess problems for magazines. But there was no extended period during the difficult first two decades of his career when he was deflected from his main task — the creation of a major literary oeuvre in Russian, culminating in *Dar* or *The Gift* (1938), a masterpiece of wit, poetic fantasy, and stylistic games which remains, in my opinion, one of his three finest novels as well as one of the great books of twentieth-century literature in any language.

In 1940 when Nabokov departed for America, accompanied by his wife Véra and young son Dmitri, a new twenty-year phase of his career opened. Begun in the distress and obscurity of a second exile during wartime, it was to turn, but not fully until after 1955 and the publication of *Lolita,* into an extraordinary, and perhaps peculiarly American, success story. As early as 1939, while still in France, he had begun to write in English, no doubt in wary anticipation of an impending move to England or America as Hitler's troops were massing to overrun Western Europe as far as the Atlantic. He settled first in the Boston area, taught Russian literature at Wellesley while simultaneously conducting scientific research in lepidopterology at the Harvard Entomological Museum, and brought out his first full-length literary work in English, the beguiling and melancholy *The Real Life of Sebastian Knight,* in 1941.

Over approximately the next decade and a half there occurred the amazing transformation of this middle-aged, twice-exiled European artist, scientist, and scholar into the great American author whom the world acknowledges today. His stories and verses and the chapters of his memoir about his Russian and European years appearing in the *New Yorker* during the late 1940's and early 1950's, which showed a constantly expanding command of English written style and its American vernacular adjuncts, established him with an American audience. At Cornell, where he taught Russian literature for some ten years after leaving Boston, he was able to pursue the nostalgic yet profound studies in Pushkin which culminated in his monumental four-volume translation of *Eugene Onegin* with commentaries (1964). Cornell also exposed him to the pleasures, pangs, pomps, and bizarreries of American academic life, an experience he would put richly to use in writing the comic and touching prose sketches that make up *Pnin* (1957) and the third of his three greatest books, *Pale Fire* (1962). Even the long American academic vacations made a signal contribution, for it was during summers away from Cornell, while traveling extensively through North America on butterfly-hunting expeditions, that he became familiar with the ambiance of highways and byways, the subculture of motels, filling stations, frazzled eateries, and bypassed, desperate resorts which contribute so sinister and pitiful a flavor to the imaginative environment of *Lolita*.

Publication of *Lolita*, the second of his triumvirate of master-pieces, in 1955, marks the full emergence of the butterfly from the chrysalis, the point at which Nabokov was able to come at long last into full control of his artistic destiny. The book's financial success permitted him to resign his Cornell post, and a much-enhanced interest in all aspects of Nabokov's work throughout the English-speaking world has led over the past decade to the publication in excellent English translations (most of them by his son Dmitri) of nearly all the novels and novellas he had brought out in Russian during the twenties and thirties. This important project, which is still under way, has won a magical second life for the work of Nabokov's pre-American career while simplifying the task of evaluating his total achievement in fiction and confirming his position in the forefront of modern writers.

Since 1960 Nabokov has lived abroad once again, in Montreux,

Switzerland. He remains an American citizen, revisits the United States frequently, and continues to affirm an affectionate attachment to this country in recent published interviews. Although he turned seventy in 1969 and was honored by a festschrift to which a wide international array of critics, scholars, and creative writers contributed, he is still in full career as a writer himself. In 1967 he brought out his own Russian translation of *Lolita* and 1969 saw publication of *Ada; or Ardor,* a quarter-million-word "family chronicle" novel in English, conceived in a rather baroque stylistic vein and containing some spectacular erotic episodes along with an elaborate plot, a stunningly original setting, and a lengthy terminal essay on the nature of time. Not now, and it is to be hoped, not for many years to come, can a critical commentator pretend to say the last word about this, as it were, amphibious Russian and American creative personality.

Speak, Memory (1951, revised edition 1966), called *Conclusive Evidence* in the British edition and *Drugiye Berega* (Other Shores) in a less well known and partly variant Russian version, is both an autobiography covering Nabokov's first forty-one years and a carefully shaped work of art devoted to the muse of memory, "Mnemosyne." For our purposes it provides a bridge between its author's lived experience and his re-creation of that experience in writing; and, not surprisingly, because it is a creative work of first rank, it reveals themes, conceptions, and images which one finds in various combinations and enlargements in his fiction proper.

It begins, rather like the famous first chapter of Dickens' *Great Expectations,* with an account of the infant child's awakening to consciousness. Awareness of self is born simultaneously with an awareness of an imprisonment in time, a time stranded between two eternities of darkness, all-past and all-future, a time defined as "walls . . . separating me and my bruised fists from the free world of timelessness," a prison that "is spherical and without exits." Rebellion against this tragic state of affairs is also born with consciousness of it and seeks in consciousness itself — in the

heightening of consciousness we call imagination — a way out.
There is no way out "short of suicide." This is surely one master
idea in all of Nabokov's work. Yet through consciousness, through
reflection on the riddling and cryptic appearances of the world,
both outer and inner, in which the prisoner finds himself im-
mured, he begins to discover or invent patterns, themes, repetitions, which hint at or gesture toward a possibility of transcendence into "the free world of timelessness" from which he has been
banished through the catastrophic accident of biologic birth. And
art, supremely, is the reflection of consciousness through which
these discoveries become possible.

If the world is made of cryptic and riddling appearances, what
can the prisoner discover, even through the agency of imagination, that amounts to more than deception piled on deception,
trompe l'oeil painting on a prison wall? In Chapter One of *Speak,
Memory* Nabokov tells of General Kuropatkin, a visitor to the St.
Petersburg house who amused the five-year-old Vladimir by arranging matches on the divan, first horizontally to form the sea in
calm weather and then zigzag to form a stormy sea. The matches
were scattered when the General, interrupted by an aide, rushed
off to take command of — and to lose! — Russia's war in the Far
East against Japan. Fifteen years later, when Nabokov's father
was fleeing to southern Russia, he encountered on a bridge a gray-
bearded peasant who asked him for a light. It was General Kuropatkin in disguise.

Here Nabokov remarks, "What pleases me is the evolution of
the match theme," and we shall not take his point at all if we take
the story altogether unseriously. The difference between the General, mocked by riddling destiny in the matter of matches, and
Nabokov, reflecting upon a "repetitional theme," is considerable.
Both the writer and the General are prisoners of contingency but
the latter abides in dungeon darkness while the former has found
a light by which he can see and reflect upon where and what he is.
Thus, at the beginning of *Drugiye Berega*, Nabokov can speak of
his autobiographical aim which is "to describe the past with utmost precision and to discover in it extraordinary outlines: namely,

the development and repetition of hidden themes in the midst of one's overt destiny"; and, near the beginning of *Speak, Memory,* he can mention "the anonymous roller that pressed upon my life a certain intricate watermark whose unique design becomes visible when the lamp of art is made to shine through life's foolscap." The artist is at least free to spy out and to pursue, in the light of art, patterns removed from the domain of the absurd and meaningless by virtue of the mere fact that they *are,* visibly, of a certain shape and design: "the following of such thematic designs through one's life should be . . . the true purpose of autobiography."

Nevertheless, the basic theme is imprisonment, and Nabokov's novels are full of characters like Humbert Humbert whose frenzied pursuit of a certain "thematic design" called nymphets serves only to confirm his squalid, pitiful, and pathological enslavement. If liberation into timelessness is a real goal then all this activity of hunting down and following up, this spying and descrying in the light of consciousness and conscious art, falls far short of a real attained freedom. On Nabokov's own terms, is not the distinction between the artist-autobiographer and the unfortunate General simply the difference between a prisoner who takes exercise by creeping along the walls of his cell, holding aloft a guttering candle or feeble battery flashlight, and one who stays still in darkness waiting for death? They are both serving a life sentence and who therefore is to say that the less active one has made the worse adjustment?

This conclusion ignores a second great resource of the artist and autobiographer blessed with the power of imaginative reflection — his gift for making images. Toward the end of *Speak, Memory* Nabokov gaily describes the impact of the writings of the youthful and brilliant V. Sirin on Russian readers raised "on the sturdy straightforwardness of Russian realism." These readers, who were not in on the secret that Sirin and Nabokov are the same person, "were impressed by the mirror-like angles of his clear but weirdly misleading sentences and by the fact that the real life of his books flowed in his figures of speech, which one critic has compared to 'windows giving upon a contiguous world . . . a rolling corollary, the shadow of a train of thought.' "

The anonymous critic, who is certainly Nabokov himself in still another playful disguise, points up with the first of his comparisons the transcendent function of aesthetic images in Nabokov's work. Images are openings. Made out of words and from the materials of contingent experience, they paradoxically and magically create apertures in the walls of imprisoning time, transparencies which let in light from the free world of timelessness. Nabokov says of his own early works that the best "are those in which he condemns his people to the solitary confinement of their own souls." Actually, it is a cruelly true remark about all of his best works. But there is a way out, or at least a way of seeing out, for those who have sufficient imagination to fashion or discover an opening into timelessness. A number of Nabokov's "people," early and late, are driven to madness and death through their devotion to false images. Yet these failures, which must be seen finally as failures of imagination, of the image-making function in a generic sense, are never meant to suggest that the pursuit of transcendence through imagination should be abandoned as a hopeless project. If, for Nabokov, man is in prison, and if even the true images that he may descry or invent through artful intensities of consciousness tend, as they do in Yeats's great meditation on image making, "Among School Children," to break the heart by mocking man's contingency, the images still remain the only clue to the only thing worth attending to — the nature of the reality that lies ouside the prison wall. The search for windows remains fundamental to Nabokov's powerfully imagistic art: there are really no alternatives, except a collapse of consciousness or the physical act of suicide.

Speak, Memory itself sumptuously and cunningly triumphs over lapsed time and uses the master image of apertures to do so. At the beginning the author sees "the awakening of consciousness as a series of spaced flashes, with the intervals between them gradually diminishing until bright blocks of perception are formed, affording memory a slippery hold." By the third chapter these perceptual blocks have stopped dancing and the author can refer, more straightforwardly, to "the act of vividly recalling a patch of the past." By now the method of the book, which is to deal in separate chapters with a single block, patch, image, or frame of recalled experience, has become clear. But method and content fuse as he recalls certain crucial early experiences and scenes involving windows and introduces the bright patches constituted by stained glass and butterfly specimens into the account of his growing up on the family estate. The train windows of the St. Petersburg to Paris Express dominate in the seventh chapter, and the vertiginous experience of glimpsing bright flashes of landscape outside the rushing train reinforces the original account of infant consciousness as a series of spaced flashes. Nabokov begins Chapter Eight by remarking casually that he is going to show a few "slides" and within the chapter manages to put together the account of an actual Magic-Lantern Projection evening arranged by his tutor with a recollection of his discovery of the beauty of glass slides seen in work with the microscope. The latter were "translucent miniatures, pocket wonderlands, neat little worlds of hushed luminous hues" where, while contemplating this particular form of bright patch, he found a "delicate meeting place between imagination and knowledge."

In the context of memory this delicate meeting place is what the whole book is exploring; and the possibility of such exploration depends on the imagery of bright patches framed in an aperture. Even the boldly colored comic strips brought to him from America by his uncle — characteristically he is more interested in the pointillist technique of their reproduction than in the story they tell — become part of the pattern; as does "one last little garden" he walked in with his wife and son at St. Nazaire, just before going on board ship to sail to America — a garden with "a geometrical design which no doubt I could easily fill in with the colors of plausible flowers."

What is most fascinating about the memory art of *Speak, Memory* is that things long dead and vanished in the past come fully to life precisely by being placed within a series of frames, by being "reduced" or "fixed" in a pattern, by being subdued to imagery and artifice. If memory speaks it speaks visually, beckoning through a window, and we are left in the face of this happy mystery to reflect that the charmed life possessed by objects, persons, and places that time has consumed owes nothing to the prison house of temporality and everything to the art by which they have been evoked out of the "contiguous world" that Nabokov has opened the windows of his figures and images upon.

Collectors — of butterflies and cold nests — are often solitary men. But *Speak, Memory*, established upon the intuition of man's ineluctable solitude, terminates, through a happy inconsistency, in communion. Its last chapter, addressed to Nabokov's own wife and recollecting the birth and infancy of Dmitri, celebrates nothing less than a happy marriage. This marriage is the single gift out of the past which needs no re-creation in art. Nabokov says, "I must know where I stand, where you and my son stand"; and where he stands, in the now of affectionate concern to which the book returns from its exploration of the past, is upon "mortal love." All or nearly all of Nabokov's books are dedicated to his wife Véra, whose name in Russian is also the word for faith, belief, religion, and trust. Let us turn now to his novels proper to see what happens to his intuition of man's imprisonment in consciousness and time, his theme of transcendence through image making, and his faith in mortal marital love as he creates over a period of more than forty years a body of work in fiction which is like no other writer's anywhere in our part of the twentieth century.

There are now available in English nine Nabokov novels originally composed in Russian and seven composed in English. Before giving extended consideration to four of these books — my choices reflect factors of personal taste, a sense of where the inner dialectic of Nabokov's artistic vision is most significantly at work, and a keen sense of space limits here — I have a particular point to make about all his novels that can best be clarified through briefer discussion of a fairly large number of them.

The point is this: Nabokov's novels are never direct imitations of life. Invariably, they are imitations of imitations of life. A Nabokov novel does not begin with or issue from a selection of experience with concomitant selection of a governing point of view. Rather, it issues from the deliberate selection of a formal narrative type or structure, occasionally from selection of nonfictional narrative forms such as the biography, and, just once, from selection of the non-narrative form of scholarly commentary and emendation. Nabokov is a spirited and learned parodist of prose forms accumulated through the evolution of literary history in the West, yet his impulses to parody are not pedantic or frivolous; nor do they constitute acts of aggression against either literary history or literary art. Rather, he has a sophisticated and true awareness of how forms of literary art and organization are forms of consciousness au fond, of how a given type of narrative frames a definite perspective on experience. One kind of narrative, to change the metaphor, fences out — in terms of characterization, angle of narration, the representation of place or of societal data, the ordering of events, the tone and pace of narration, and so forth — one entire set of human possibilities while fencing in some other set. To put this oversimply, a gothic romance will usually eschew a hard, dry narrative tone, while a novel cast in the form of a confession will not employ the viewpoint of omniscience. A crime novel will usually be more logically ordered with respect to plot than a metaphysical fantasy emphasizing enigmatic aspects of reality. A *Bildungsroman* will stress the accumulating experience and viewpoint of one central character over that of other characters, and a ghost story, unless it is merely a debunking of the supernatural, will use supernatural material as though apparitions are real.

Nabokov uses all the types I have mentioned and others as well with full awareness of what each ordinarily can and cannot be made to do. Precisely because he is so aware he often introduces twists and drastic modifications, even sometimes breeds type with type, working somewhat on the analogy of the gifted laboratory experimenter who moves out from the known to the unknown by viewing the materials of his experiment from unexpected angles and combining them in new ways. It is a highly conscious process. Nabokov has nothing but contempt for the concept of simple sincerity in art, which he equates with a fatuous willingness to pour old spoiled wine into leaky bottles. He is, for example, one of the great originators in contemporary letters of that fictional hybrid called black comedy. Black comedy in his hands is just such a product of scrupulously supervised crossbreeding as no artistic practice or critical method founded upon moralistic notions of the sincere in art could have created or predicted.

King, Queen, Knave (1928), second earliest of his novels to receive English translation, conforms to the fictional type that centers on a young man of humble provincial origins who seeks social and commercial advancement in the city, only to become corrupted there and lapse back into a deeper obscurity. An obvious exemplar, to which Nabokov obliquely refers in a foreword written for the English translation of 1968, is Dreiser's *An American Tragedy*; but Nabokov's detached, deliberately diagrammatic treatment of his central characters — Dreyer, a Berlin department store owner, Martha, his unfaithful and treacherous wife, and knavish Franz, his dull, gullible, and ultimately treacherous nephew — reduces the central intrigue, a scheme to murder Dreyer that is attempted and bungled by the wife and nephew, to a kind of puppet show acted out by mannequinlike creatures whose relationships and conflicts can be fully specified by the cipher language of a game of cards: K (unwittingly) against QKn with a mysterious trump card of accident introduced at the last moment to give the game to K. *King, Queen, Knave,* by taking the nature out of Dreiserian (and Flaubertian) naturalism, exposes the bare bones of naturalistic contrivance. It also exposes the emptiness and sterility of an "advanced" German bourgeois milieu where people live lives of blank desperation in houses designed, decorated, and furnished according to the rational, geometric canons of the Bauhaus and the Dutch *De Stijl* movements.

The Eye (1930) is a novella belonging to the category of ghost story. An unhappy, self-obsessed young Russian named Smurov shoots himself because he is unlucky in love, is uncertain of his true nature, and imagines himself despised by various Russian expatriates frequenting a certain lodging house in Berlin. He then returns as a ghostly spy and wanders through the minds of the people who had spurned him in life, taking note of the several wholly distinct and incompatible versions of his own identity which different minds go on entertaining. At the end it appears that he is not dead after all, nor is the original mystery about the nature of "the true Smurov" cleared up to either his or the reader's satisfaction. This abiding mystery is a lively and illuminating way of pointing to the problems of identity created by the stance of extreme self-consciousness. *The Eye* is, at once, a comic investigation of late adolescent self-concern, the portrait of a shy, autistic, and endearing young man who ought to take up writing as a strategy for self-encounter, a fable about the vocation of the imagining and remarking artist and the price he pays in isolation and self-effacement for his special kind of awareness, and, finally, perhaps an early self-portrait of the artist who wrote it.

The Defense (also 1930) is the first of several novels which invent extraordinary variations on the imaginary biography. When Nabokov has this type in hand his central character is always remarkable and usually a genius. Moreover, the author nearly always chooses to emphasize the deep solitude and the inevitable estrangement from other people that represent the price exacted by destiny for the gift of high imaginative or intellectual powers. Most of Nabokov's central characters are unrepentant individualists; his geniuses are merely the extreme limit of the general case.

Luzhin, the Russian-born hero of *The Defense*, is a forlorn, inarticulate, and physically graceless chess genius, a sort of *idiot savant* of the international tournament circuit. After a wretched boyhood and a lonely adult career it becomes his fate to fall in

love (with a good woman who loves him in return) when it is too
late, when his mind has been taken over by a paranoid affliction
which resolves the issues, projects, and challenges of his daily life
into a series of chess moves based upon an unwinnable defensive
strategy. What Nabokov calls "chess effects" are worked into the
narrative throughout, reaching a climax in the last scene — one
of the great tours de force in all of Nabokov's fiction. Here Luzhin, the king at check in his own apartment, the rooms and corridors of which appear to him under the aspect of the game he is
forced to play and cannot win, tries to break out of the entrap-
ment by bursting through the frosted white square of the bath-
room window. But he falls to his death into a chasm of "dark and
pale squares" which show him "exactly what kind of eternity was
obligingly and inexorably spread out before him."

Nabokov's preface to the English translation of *The Defense*,
published in 1964, appears to hint that Luzhin's losing moves are
based on an actual historic match, the "Immortal Game" played
between L. Kieseritsky and A. Anderssen during a London tournament of masters in 1851. Although in *Speak, Memory* he characterizes his hobby of composing chess problems as a "beautiful,
complex and sterile art" there is nothing bloodless about the
"combinational" artistry of *The Defense*, and Luzhin himself, in
his gentleness, profound introversion, and total incapacity for
coping with the "real world," remains one of Nabokov's most
touching and lovingly drawn characterizations. For Nabokov the
chessboard appears as "a system of stresses and abysses," possessed
of the same three-dimensional qualities and fatal choices as life
itself. By the same token, life in Nabokov's novels can sometimes
appear, as it certainly does in *The Defense*, to be a three-dimensional chess game the issue of which is clouded by a terrible, teas-
ing question: are men the players at the board or are they merely
the pawns and other pieces of the game? And if the latter, who
controls the play?

John Shade, the "preterist" poet in *Pale Fire*, opts for the second theory and finds solace in the notion that the life he does not

control becomes endurable through his contemplative appreciation of its intricate "web of sense":

> Yes! It sufficed that I in life could find
> Some kind of link-and-bobolink, some kind
> Of correlated pattern in the game,
> Plexed artistry, and something of the same
> Pleasure in it as they who played it found.

But it is doubtful that Shade could respond with unqualified appreciation to the sequence of "topsyturvical coincidence" that led to his own violent death, and there are Nabokov novels which address the clouded issue of human fate and freedom with anything but equanimity. Two of these are perhaps best treated in close proximity because they are both novels about "actual" imprisonment and oppression at the hands — under the heel rather — of political state power.

Invitation to a Beheading (1938) follows the fictional type of metaphysical fantasy with political overtones that we are familiar with from the works of Franz Kafka. One can believe Nabokov's disclaimer of any knowledge of Kafka at the time of its composition around 1934, and still remain free to surmise that the book does respond imaginatively to certain grotesque and awful features of modern totalitarianism that Kafka's fiction had prophetically anticipated. The hero, Cincinnatus C., is sequestered in a solitary cell within a castle fortress and awaits execution by beheading. His crime, called "gnostical turpitude" in the bill of indictment against him, is to have remained an individual, thinking his own thoughts and reflecting on the world in his own way. He has no ally within the prison, unless it is Emmie, the jailer's child, who appears mysteriously within his cell, shows him enigmatic stick drawings which appear to diagram an escape route, and leads him, as if in a cruelly deceptive dream, through a maze of corridors that return him finally to his own cell. He is tricked at every turn: the other "prisoner" who tunnels through his cell wall turns out to be his executioner; his unfaithful wife sides with his tormentors; even the window high on one wall through which he longs to look out upon the "Tamara Gardens," a paradisal place where "we used to roam and hide" in childhood, is a painted fake complete with a clockwork spider spinning a synthetic web.

What is demanded of Cincinnatus before his beheading is something even worse than his confession to crimes he has not committed. It is complete, self-degrading cooperation in his own undoing. The regime, farcical in its inefficiency and the downright clownishness of its officials, maintains itself on a single obscene and inhuman principle, that of collaboration. In securing Cincinnatus' conviction the defense attorney has collaborated with the prosecutor and the judge with both. At the ultimate reach of infamy the prisoner is expected to waltz with the jailer, compliment the prison governor on the excellence of the prison accommodation, admire the axman for his expertise, and post to his decapitation as if honored by an Invitation to the Dance. Declining the invitation, Cincinnatus resists quietly to the end. Yet it is just this bizarre feature of the wholly corrupt prison world of *Invitation* that evokes direct parallels with the actual history of modern totalitarian states. Whether we think of the ritualistic public confessions of the Moscow treason trials in the 1930's or of the Nazi death camps in the 1940's, where prisoners were encouraged to compete for the privilege of dying last by helping the guards to torture and kill their fellow prisoners, we are contemplating the same perversion of the collaborative principle.

Despite these historical parallels, *Invitation to a Beheading* is scarcely a work of fictional realism. The temporal setting is future — almost no — time; the fortress and the adjacent town, with its winding streets, public fountain and statues, the Tamara Gardens and the woodland beyond, seem to belong to the vaguely medieval world of central European folklore rather than to the world we know. By contrast, *Bend Sinister* (1947), characterized by Nabokov as having "stylistic links" to *Invitation*, comes much closer to the type of the overtly political novel. In 1947 the small nations of Eastern Europe were bending left under pressure from the U.S.S.R. *Bend Sinister*, for all its qualities of fantasy and its many passages which hint that the oppressions suffered by its main characters reflect universal conditions, depicts a turning away from individual freedoms toward an imposed collectivism that closely resembles what was happening in such countries as Poland, Bulgaria, Hungary, Rumania, and Czechoslovakia during the immediate postwar period.

Bend Sinister, written in English, is perhaps Nabokov's only morbid book. Its hero, Adam Krug, a distinguished philosopher and university professor in a nameless country whose inhabitants speak a Slavic language of sorts, sees his beloved wife succumb to illness within the first few pages. Better for Krug to have died with her in view of what is to come. The country has been taken over by a revolutionary clique preaching perfect equality but employing totalitarian methods of terror and under the control of a dictator called Paduk — the Toad. Paduk, who is an old schoolfellow of Krug's, the sadistic bully of the play yard, and whose name is a virtual anagram of the Russian *upadok*, signifying decay, decline, degeneration, wants Krug broken into conformity so that less prominent citizens of the country will not be inspired by Krug's notorious individualism to go on thinking thoughts of their own.

The means taken to break him are awful and yet perfectly familiar to anyone who has read the newspapers during the past three or four decades. Krug is summoned to a blandishing and threatening interview with the Toad himself, "clothed from carbuncle to bunion in field gray," his eyes those "of a fish in a neglected aquarium." When the tactic is unsuccessful, the state apparatus of terror takes over. Krug is driven from the university and subjected to harassment and spying by the police. His only son, David, upon whom Krug lavishes the affection of a grief-stricken widower as well as a doting father, is stolen from him, tortured, and then murdered. Finally, Krug is put into solitary confinement after having been shown on film the particulars of his son's fate.

Both *Invitation to a Beheading* and *Bend Sinister*, to the extent that they are concerned with politics and the society, reflect a bottomless pessimism about politics and the social process in

our time. While reading these books one keeps remembering that
their author was driven into exile and saw his father killed because of "politics" and that the absolute individualism of Nabokov's world view tends to deny him the consolation of belief that
any agency, operating in or beyond history, will eventually redeem the sufferings inflicted on innocent and decent people by
savage and incompetent ideologues and power brokers in this
century. Both books end with spectacular Nabokovian *coups de
théâtre* the significance of which remains perfectly equivocal. At
the moment of his beheading, Cincinnatus finds that he is on his
feet and walking freely through collapsing and disintegrating bits
of stage scenery, "in that direction where, to judge by the voices,
stood beings akin to him." And at the moment when Krug, in
prison, is about to awaken to the "hideous misfortune" of his lot,
Nabokov tells us *in propria persona* that "I felt a pang of pity for
Adam and slid towards him along an inclined beam of pale light
— causing instantaneous madness, but at least saving him from
the senseless agony of his logical fate." In each case, especially in
the second, the author plays God, arriving from beyond the pris-
oning "form" (logical and teleological) of the story to help the
helpless character. But there is nothing in Nabokov's sense of the
human plight as a whole to which these acts of compassionate
intervention provide an analogy. There is no God of compassion
or redemption in the universe at large who will do for "Adam"
what the author Nabokov does for his characters by means of a
merely ironic, and in some sense despairing, trick of fiction.

After thus illustrating my point about the way Nabokov em-
ploys, modifies, and reanimates various narrative structures or
types — the way in which his books are artful imitations of imitations — I want now to consider in more depth the several books
in the Nabokov canon of fiction to which one finds oneself returning frequently; the books which express most hauntingly and
richly his deepest sense of life; which in particular represent the
core of permanence in his work, or rather, the permanent addition he has made to the house of fiction in our time.

I have in mind four novels — two from the 1930's originally

written in Russian, two from the 1950's and 1960's originally written in English — which arrange themselves across the language barrier and the time gap as two related pairings. The first pair consists of *Kamera Obskura* (1933) — titled *Camera Obscura* in its first translated version (London, 1936) but retitled *Laughter in the Dark* in its revised American translation of 1938, which I am following here — and *Lolita* (1955). These are intimately related as melodramas of audacious metaphysical crime centering upon the theme of the "nymphet." The second pair consists of *Dar* (1938; 1952), translated as *The Gift* in 1963, and *Pale Fire* (1962). The first is a book about a young poet which uses the framing devices of imaginary biography and the *Künstlerroman* to explore the themes of poetic art, Russian literary culture, and young love. The second is a book about an old poet which uses the devices of scholarly commentary, imaginary autobiography, and poetry itself to explore the themes of poetic art, of the irredeemability of time past, and of human solitude in counterpoise with wedded love.

Laughter in the Dark and *Lolita* differ tremendously in nearly all respects, not least in the degree of self-awareness of their chief characters, the suggestively named Albinus and the self-designated "Humbert Humbert." Yet Albinus and Humbert stand closer together in a crucially important respect than any other two characters in Nabokov. Both are possessed by a thirst for the infinite, suffer from the metaphysical obsession traditionally named the "desire and pursuit of the whole." Further, both have received a true intuition that the route to the infinite is through attachment to an adorable image or eidolon, yet both blunder, perversely and fatally, by haplessly confounding the image with its illusory reflection or echo in the flesh of a child-woman. The consequence is that they fall, into an enslavement entailing their torture and mockery by demonic men, artists themselves, who as film makers are in the business of degrading images, who as nemeses raised by the obsessions of their victims have (and delight in) the task of punishing Albinus and Humbert for their idolatrous passions.

Literally, "camera obscura" means "dark chamber." More comprehensively, a camera obscura is any dark chamber including photographic cameras, darkened cinema palaces, a prison cell, and, for Nabokov, the cranial cell behind the eyes wherein imprisoned consciousness languishes, with a lens or opening through which an image may be projected in "natural" colors onto a receptive surface. Nabokov's choice of the camera obscura as a guiding metaphor in his account of Albinus' dismal fate becomes perfectly logical and appropriate, given his powerfully visual imagination, his notion of images as windows and apertures, his notion of man as a prisoner languishing within walls of time and contingency, and his conviction that imagination is the faculty of consciousness which attempts to spy beyond the prison walls through image making. Albinus, an art dealer and connoisseur, sins through the eyes, by entering a darkened motion picture house and glimpsing there something deeply illicit and corrupt which he mistakes for a vision of human felicity. He is led on and on into deeper and darker mistaking until he receives the appropriate punishment for his misuse of the faculty of vision. Physically blinded, morally degraded, mocked, confined, and at last murdered by his vicious young mistress, he is the object of that awful laughter in the dark made mention of in the American translation's title.

Laughter in the Dark makes darkly ironic play with the "optical" themes of art connoisseurship, painting and caricature, film making, life modeling, and film stardom in conjunction with a melodramatic plot recalling the famous German film *Die Blaue Engel* to suggest that, whereas true art is a way of seeing truly in darkness, attachment to false images leads only to a deeper benightedness and closer confinement.

Albinus, a prosperous Berlin art dealer possessed of a genuine "passion for art" and a bourgeois German "happy family," reaches that familiar critical point in early middle age when a man of his type may fall prey to a malaise of uneasiness and dissatisfaction whose causes are half spiritual and half sexual. He thinks of launching new art projects and dreams of amatory adventures with pretty young girls that would restore to his life a dimension of erotic intensity missing from his marriage. The new art project takes shape from an idle habit he has fallen into of "having this or that Old Master sign landscapes and faces which he, Albinus, came across in real life: it turned his existence into a fine picture gallery — delightful fakes, all of them." He is interested in the new popular art of the movies and conceives the clever, possibly profitable scheme of producing cartoons which will animate a famous painting by one of the Dutch Old Masters like Brueghel and give the figures in the static picture a continuing life through an entire episode. At the beginning it would be something simple, "a stained window coming to life," yet to begin at all he needs a collaborator combining knowledge of art with skill as an animated cartoonist. Unfortunately, the man for the job, one Axel Rex, a gifted graphic artist and caricaturist, is away in America drawing newspaper cartoons.

Albinus writes to Rex who warms to the scheme and asks for large advances of money to undertake the work. Meanwhile Albinus wanders one day into a movie house called the Argus and sees in the dark the outline of his fate: "the melting outline of a cheek which looked as though it were painted by a great artist against a rich dark background." The possessor of the cheek, an usherette named Margot Peters, who is about seventeen and looks even younger, responds to Albinus' tentative advances. He begins an affair with her that soon becomes wretchedly obsessive for him and that scandalizes his family and friends and leads to the break-up of his marriage.

To this point, we can say that Albinus has indeed confused the passions appropriate to art and to life and is punished for it. But the book to this point has barely begun and the aftermath has little relevance to this merely cautionary moral. In becoming involved with Margot and with Rex, Albinus has crossed an invisible line into an absolutely sinister world organized as a conspiracy against him, a world of complete deception where the animate images of art and pseudo-art are manipulated by a master craftsman in the art of evildoing. To begin with, Margot, the tough, amoral, mindless slum child, turns out to be entirely a creature of the camera-obscura world. She has been first an artist's model posing for life classes in an art school, next the model and mistress of Axel Rex before his American sojourn, and her career as usherette is intended to be merely a stopover on the way to becoming a screen star. In the end she indeed becomes as a motion picture actress that "silver ghost of romance" — impalpable, depthless, talentless, soulless, the net product of advertising, publicity, and opportunistic manipulation — and, ironically enough, the human creature redefined as sheer artful image that Albinus had gone seeking when he began to frequent movie houses and sign real faces with the signatures of Old Masters.

It is a shattering coincidence that Margot should have been connected with Axel even before Albinus met her, although it is no surprise that she joins forces with him to manipulate and then destroy Albinus after Axel's return. Nabokov invariably uses such coincidences, plays with such loaded dice, in order to draw the reader away from his "realistic" expectations and to introduce him to a world where fate has little to do with character and functions like a conspiracy whose ultimate aim, as in the delusional systems of paranoiacs, is never actually made clear. Axel is a real artist of considerable talent who has made a career of faking pictures and drawing vicious caricatures, and who believes "that everything . . . in the domain of art . . . was only a more or less clever trick." He is a real confidence man too, with the practical aim of separating Albinus from his money. But his taste for the confidence game goes far beyond the practical. He sees himself as a "stage manager" who can be counted on to arrange the "roaring comedy" of Albinus' miseries and the kind of manager he "had in view was an elusive, double, triple, self-reflecting magic Proteus of a phantom, the shadow of many-colored glass balls flying in a curve, the ghost of a juggler on a shimmering curtain."

Here the stage manager melts into the performer, with Margot also on stage (or screen) to assist the clever magician or evil Magus in his show. Throughout the book Margot has the particular assignment, after leading Albinus on, of closing him in. She is always shutting doors on him and eventually seals him into permanent blindness as the result of an auto accident for which she is actually responsible. The phantom role comes to full flower for Axel when Albinus, after he has been blinded, takes a house in Switzerland and lives there alone — he imagines — with his adored Margot. In fact Axel is also in the house, a silent presence, going naked and making love to Margot under Albinus' very nose. He likes to watch Margot make faces of "comic" disgust when Albinus, thinking they are alone, embraces the girl tenderly. He will touch the blind man gently with the tips of his bare toes and dissolves in silent laughter when Albinus assumes that it is Margot's caressing touch. And he will sit close to him for hours until the blind man, sensing a presence near him, reaches out, whereupon Axel gleefully moves back out of reach. At this time Albinus is a man in ruins with most of his money gone; so the impulse to mischief which continues to drive Axel and Margot really does constitute a "motiveless malignity." It is a "comic" performance by devils playing "disinterestedly," i.e., for love of their "art," to an audience of one who cannot see.

Eventually Albinus learns what has been going on from his decent brother-in-law, Paul. He takes refuge in Paul's Berlin house and on a certain day manages to entrap Margot in the drawing room of the old family apartment, which she is busily looting of the art objects he had collected during his career as a connoisseur. He is armed and tries to sense where she is so that he can kill her. Their grim struggle, conducted behind closed doors and for him wholly in darkness, results in his own death when Margot grabs the revolver and shoots him. The final paragraphs, written as directions for a film or stage scene, stress that the door of the drawing room is now open and "the door leading from the hall to the landing is wide open, too." As we have seen with *Invitation to a Beheading*, physical death is the opening into freedom for the doomed, betrayed prisoner, although neither book can follow the released man through that opening.

Much of *Laughter in the Dark* is composed in Nabokov's

sprightliest and most playful vein. But to complain of the author's apparent callousness to the sufferings of his central character is to miss the important point. Albinus' "passion for art" which betrays him into a realm of sexual and social pathology really does contain "immortal longings" with which the author has complete sympathy. But the author understands, as Albinus does not, that the beguiling images and forms beckoning in the murk of human reality are for seeing and not for possessing — an insight available to the true artist though not to the connoisseur with his checkbook and collections. "Albinus' specialty had been his passion for art; his most brilliant discovery had been Margot. But now . . . it was as though she had returned to the darkness of the little cinema from which he had once withdrawn her." On his way into the Argus Cinema Albinus had noticed a poster showing "a man looking up at a window framing a child in a nightshirt." This representation, which will reappear as an imagistic theme in *Lolita,* scrupulously balances an idea of aspiration toward something purely beautiful with the pathology of voyeurism and sexual perversion. It is also a warning which Albinus cannot read or heed because he is so mad for form that he will not distinguish between form and its replica or model: "Now, the vision of the promised kiss filled him with such ecstasy that it seemed hardly possible it could be still further intensified. And yet beyond it, down a vista of mirrors, there was still to be reached the dim white form of her body, that very form which art students had sketched so conscientiously and so badly."

Lolita's unique appropriation of the American landscape, its comic and sinister play with American social institutions and roles and their deep-lying anomie, the wit and beauty of its endlessly inventive narrative style, coming in the midst of a bad decade for American fiction, fell upon our literary scene like a small hurricane ("Hurricane Lolita"!). Fifteen years later criticism was just beginning to take the measure of the book. When the critical history of the American novel in the 1960's and 1970's is written, *Lolita*'s presence and influence in that history will be major and central. *Lolita* killed fictional naturalism, already moribund, with one merciful blow. More important, it nerved a new generation of writers to meet the drastic and fantastic realities of American life with a countering imaginative fierceness and boldness. Our most interesting recent writers, from Barth to Burroughs, from Thomas Berger to Thomas Pynchon, owe more to Nabokov, to the Nabokov of *Lolita* especially, than to any other contemporary figure, American or foreign.

In terms of Nabokov's own work *Lolita* has a similar centrality and prominence. In it he comes to final accommodation with the nymphet theme, which had been echoing and re-echoing in his work for decades, and links the theme lucidly to the master themes of nostalgia (or preterism) and of imagination which form the principal coordinates of his entire created world. Unlike Albinus, who never understands what he is doing, Humbert Humbert, conducting his own defense — "O ladies and gentlemen of the jury" — and, as critics often fail to note, his own prosecution, comes to know fully what he has done and is responsible for. He is in all of Nabokov's fiction the supremely conscious individualist, the wholly confident manipulator of the bewildering variety of his roles, and in this confidence reflects Nabokov's own masterly grasp of his most complex creation in character.

Nabokov has remarked of Humbert that although he went straight and properly to hell after the guards found him dead of a coronary in his cell, where he awaited trial for the slaying of Quilty, the man who had taken Lolita from him, Humbert may be allowed the privilege of returning to earth for one day each year. On that day one might expect him to haunt the environs of the little mining town in the American West, mentioned in the book's concluding pages, "that lay at my feet, in a fold of the valley," from which rose "the melody of children at play." Here it was that the bestial and enchanted hunter of nymphets rejoined the human race when he at last "knew that the hopelessly poignant thing was not Lolita's absence from my side, but the absence of her voice from that concord." And if we are inclined to suspect his sentiments here there is another late episode which indicates the same belated conversion. Lolita has written him after years of

silence and absence to say she is married, pregnant, and in need
of money. He finds her in a shack in "Coalmont," eight hundred
miles from New York City, big-bellied, worn out at seventeen,
and he wants to steal her away again or kill her if she will not
come. But then he realizes that he loves her *as she is,* not merely
as the echo or memory "of the nymphet I had rolled myself upon
with such cries in the past . . . Thank God it was not that echo
alone that I worshiped." The "echo" of course points to the
"eidolon" he had pursued lifelong, spying into "jewel-bright"
windows and depraving little girls because the print of sexual
characteristics was still so faintly impressed upon their childish
bodies that he could pretend when savaging them that he was
cleaving to a pure form and recapturing the lost Edenic time he
had spent in childhood with "Annabel Lee." Lolita is spectacularly and maturely pregnant, no longer the "Idolores" of his original quest. He earns his overnight pass from hell by loving her
and leaving her — several thousand dollars richer — going off to
hunt down and kill the "rival devil," Quilty, whose taste for sexual frolics with children, as with dwarfs, is an ordinary piece of
psychopathy lacking transcendental overtones.

But even at Coalmont Humbert does not relinquish his habit
of imaginary role playing. He casts the scene as Don José's final
confrontation with Carmen ("*Changeons de vie, ma Carmen,*"
etc.) and says goodbye to his "American sweet immortal dead
love," who has just made him understand for the first time that
"the past was the past," under the aspect of a fat tenor from
grand opera. One of the joys of *Lolita* is Humbert's role playing.
Just as the book as a whole encapsulates and parodies every literary confession of a great sinner from St. Augustine to Sade,
Rousseau, and Stavrogin, so do Humbert's roles introduce a rich
variety of imaginative frames and thematic aspects through which
the book's action may be viewed.

To touch very lightly on this matter, consider the following.
When Lolita is Bee or Beatrice, Humbert is Dante and the
evoked mode is an inversion of "divine comedy" (hellish comedy?). When she is "Dolores Disparu," Humbert is Proust's Marcel

lamenting the vanished Albertine and the mode is Proustian speculation about the enigmas of time and memory. When she is Vee (Virginia Clemm), Humbert is Edgar Allan Poe and the frame is artist's biography in the era of "romantic agony." When she merges with "Annabel" Humbert is the child narrator of Poe's famous poem. And when Humbert, fleeing the mysterious Aztec red convertible with Lolita through the American night, murmurs *"lente, lente, currite noctis equi,"* Humbert is Faustus, Lolita is both Helen and Gretchen, and the mode, if not the mood, is that of Marlowe's tragic morality play. Also there are Humbert's less literary roles, each played to the hilt: the spy and voyeur ("Humbert Humbert — two eyes burning in the dark"), the European gentleman with a "past," the family friend, the husband and mature lover, the "stepfather" concerned to guard his little charge safely through the toils of teendom, the private investigator, the madman, the devil slayer ("guilty of killing Quilty"), and, finally and throughout, the pleader-prosecutor at heaven's bar — "O winged gentlemen!"

Nabokov's own cryptic key to *Lolita* was given in a 1956 "Postscript" to the first American edition. There he said the idea came to him in Paris in 1938, during an attack of neuralgia and after reading a "pointless" newspaper story about a scientist who attempted to teach an ape to draw. The ape did produce a drawing, but it was only of the bars of its cage. Humbert, that greatly talented ape, attempts a break-out, an act of transcendence, through his mad and cruel pursuit of the eidolon, incarnate in little Dolores Haze, Lolita, but he merely succeeds in confirming his confinement in matter, in the grossly sensual self, in vice and in time. One can add to this very little, except perhaps — since *Lolita* is already an assured American classic — a suggestion of how the book reverberates through our specifically American historic culture.

The core element of Humbert's sexual perversity, arch-romanticism, and derangement is an attitude toward time which may remind us of other eccentric or deranged heroes of American fiction. Humbert is fixated on the past — on his childhood love affair with "Annabel Lee" — and his pursuit, seduction, and enslavement of Dolores Haze are an attempt to reinstate in the present and preserve into the future what was irretrievably lost in the past. The expensiveness of indulgence in this illusion is very great: it costs no less than the wrecking of a child's life, as Humbert finally admits after abandoning his corrupt rationalizations concerning the natural depravity and sexual precocity of American little girls. Humbert and his time problem are summed up on the final page of *The Great Gatsby*, from which I quoted at the onset of this essay, and in a number of other classic American texts.

But how can this vile European stand in for an archetypal American? There is really no problem. America, as a "brand new, mad new dream world where everything [is] permissible," is Europe's dream of itself according to the romantic error that past time is retrievable. Emerson, Whitman, and Hart Crane might have approved Humbert's thought, if not his exact words and their appalling application. We are all Europeans when we dream that dangerous, beguiling, ever-so-American dream.

These speculations can be pushed a bit further under the general rubric of fate, freedom, and America. *Lolita,* because it is heavy with fate, would seem to present a situation in which the margin of freedom which interests us in fictional characters, particularly in the characters appearing in modern books, has diminished virtually to nothing. For instance, Humbert is obsessed, Lolita is enslaved, Charlotte Haze is totally duped, and a character like Quilty is the slave of his sinister vices. Add in fate as the "synchronizing phantom" arranging happenstance and coincidence upon wholly mysterious principles and freedom disappears altogether from the book. From another angle, there is freedom in *Lolita* of a rather awful sort. Humbert is free, unencumbered with compunction before his "conversion." Through most of the book he has the freedom of his viciousness, as does Quilty. Humbert's actions take place at a point in history when traditional sanctions have lapsed or at least loosened, and there would be very little consensus of judgment against his deeds from the "enlightened" sector of the community, apart from agreement that he is psychologically "disturbed." This in effect forgives and forgets by understanding or claiming to.

Dolores Haze also is free in a sense, in that the nature of contemporary American "suburban" culture ties her to nothing, asks nothing of her, presents her with nothing. What is she? A junior consumer, of comic books and bubble gum, a "starlet" with a thirst for cheap films and Coke. There is a great vacancy in and around her, a voidness and loneliness only partly created by Humbert's machinations. This vacancy is cultural in the first instance, American.

For Europe, as first de Tocqueville and then D. H. Lawrence have expounded, America has figured as the place beyond cabined and confined traditions and sanctions. It has been the place where time itself might be redeemed, where the dream of a new Eden, of a second life, could be realized. Naturally, there has been a dark, pathological side to this. America has been the place indubitably attractive to great mischief makers, psychopaths, men on the run, unclubable and violent persons, con men. Humbert lives on the dark side of the American freedom I am describing. There is some truth in the statement that what drove Humbert to America was his vice and the hope of satisfying it in the land of opportunity. And there is also some truth in the idea that the history of Lolita, who died in childbed in a town of the "remotest Northwest" on her way to Alaska, the last American frontier, expresses the final decadence of that European myth which we call the American Dream.

Nabokov has called *The Gift* "the best, the most nostalgic of my Russian novels." It is also, even in the excellent English translation of 1963, the least accessible of Nabokov's major works to the general English-speaking reader. As a *Künstlerroman* celebrating the life of literature and the literary life it tells the story of a young Russian émigré poet and critic named Fyodor Godunov-Cherdyntsev discovering his artistic powers and finding love as well over a three-year period in Berlin during the mid-1920's. But *The Gift* is also a complex, playful, and creative work of

literary criticism oriented toward the pre-Soviet Russian cultural
tradition and aimed as a sidelong polemic against certain dubious
values obtaining among literary and cultural pundits of the
Russian émigré community in Western Europe. Lacking close
knowledge of the literally dozens of minor and major Russian
writers the book alludes to, and of the many issues and person-
alities from the expatriate cultural scene at which the book
takes a fling, the reader may well feel he should acquire, along
with a mastery of Russian literature, history, and the language,
that ideal insomnia which Joyce recommended to the ideal
reader of *Finnegans Wake.*

Nevertheless, the main focus of Nabokov's revaluation of tradition is quite clear. Centering his attack on the liberal and progressive critic and novelist N. G. Chernyshevski, he tasks the
progressive wing of nineteenth-century Russian culture, and by
implication the liberal wing of the émigré community, with a
confusion of values whereby "enlightened" writers of small talent
have been overpraised at the expense of better writers possessing
unacceptable social and political views. For Nabokov and for Fyodor, the great tradition begins in Pushkin and is passed down
through a select few poets and prose writers whose social views,
radical or conservative, are of no bearing whatsoever. It is a tradition and dialogue of artists constituting the supreme gift the
Russian literary genius and language have to offer, a gift which
Fyodor aspires to receive, through an utmost effort of critical understanding, to share in to the limit of his developing artistic
powers, and to pass on uncompromised whether or not he ever
has the good fortune to return to a Russia in which a poet like
himself can once again carry on serious work.

The Gift is arranged in five big chapters and each chapter advances Fyodor's personal history while simultaneously undertaking assessments and recapitulations of Russian art. In the early
chapters Fyodor works at his own poetry, finds ways of support-
ing himself in a city whose people and their civic ways interest
him not in the slightest, meets and begins courting a delightful
and sensitive Russian girl named Zina Mertz whose vulgar step-

father is Fyodor's landlord. A mysterious poet-critic named Kon-cheyev appears and disappears at intervals. In rapid, allusive dia-logue Fyodor and this imaginary alter ego, with whom Fyodor is always in essential agreement about artistic values, work out their aesthetic credo and dismiss from contention all those mystics, pro-gressives, and poetasters who, in their arrogantly youthful view, appear as excrescences on the brilliant surface of Russian litera-ture. Chapter Two, which might be called the book of the father, shows Fyodor absorbed in biographical and critical studies of his poetic master, Pushkin, while also collecting information about the career of his fleshly father, a great naturalist-scientist who had disappeared at the time of the Bolshevik Revolution on his way back from one of his long expeditions in Central Asia. Fyodor's largely fictional reconstructions of these journeys, written under the stylistic influence of Pushkin and filled with exotic yet scien-tifically exact descriptions of the plants, butterflies, and land-scapes encountered en route, form one of Nabokov's most marvel-ous achievements in prose.

In Chapter Three Fyodor explores deeper into questions of the creative process in poetry, works out the important connections between the art of Pushkin and what is worth cherishing in later Russian verse, and begins research and writing for a "critical" bi-ography of Chernyshevski. Chapter Four is in its entirety a very funny yet mainly accurate and learned short biography of Cher-nyshevski. It introduces an imaginary authority named Stranno-lyubski (Strangelove?) who reports that during Chernyshevski's Si-berian exile "once an eagle appeared in his yard . . . It had come to peck at his liver but did not recognize Prometheus in him." Nabokov's (and Fyodor's) purpose is to expose Chernyshevski as the false Prometheus of Russian tradition, a savant whose sincere good intentions and abundant sufferings in the cause of righteous-ness cannot excuse the dullness, dogmatism, and anti-aesthetic bias of his judgments and influence.

Chapter Four, which might be called the book of the false father, forms the polemical climax of *The Gift*. If one aim of the work has been to locate and consolidate the great tradition of

Russian writing the corollary aim has been to expose an anti-tra-
dition incarnate in social critics of the Chernyshevskian school
whom Nabokov insists on seeing not only as the promulgators of
a sound tradition of reformism and social concern but also as
responsible for their own and others' bad writing, for a misappro-
priation of the Russian Hegelian tradition leading to dogmatic
Marxist-Leninism, and finally, for the worst excesses of Soviet
philistinism in the cultural sphere.

Chapter Four gave great offense to critics and progressives of
the émigré world, so much so that it was not printed as part of the
book until 1952. Chapter Five, anticipating this reaction, presents
excerpts from imaginary book reviews of Chapter Four. Nabokov
faithfully renders the style and bias of numerous literary pundits,
including several who write from a politically reactionary or fa-
natically religious point of view. But the best review, a sympathetic one, is contributed by "Koncheyev," who reappears just
when he is needed to aid the beleaguered and beset Fyodor in his
"heretical" undertakings: "[Koncheyev] began by drawing a picture of flight during an invasion or an earthquake, when the es-
capers carry away with them everything that they can lay hands
on, someone being sure to burden himself with a large, framed
portrait of some longforgotten relatives. 'Just such a portrait,'
wrote Koncheyev, 'is for the Russian intelligentsia the image of
Chernyshevski, which was spontaneously but accidentally carried
away abroad by the émigrés, together with other, more useful
things . . . Somebody suddenly confiscated the portrait.' "

At the end of *The Gift* Fyodor has grown the wings of a true
poet, has drawn a luminous portrait of Russian literary art as he
understands it, is happily and reciprocally in love with Zina, who
is ready to go anywhere with him. Writing to his mother in Paris
he remarks that while it is sheer sentimentality to expect to return to Russia, he can live more easily outside of his native country than some because he has taken away "the keys to her" — of
language, art, and memory — and because some day "I shall live
there in my books." *The Gift*, which is Nabokov's happiest book,
is also his "goodbye to all that," the work in which he frees him-

your grandpa went in Arkansas / To purge the rheumatic guilt of beef and bourbon." The speaker is bemused by effects and his idea only just struggles through. Purity, desiderated, is "wordless," so the only way to salvation of any kind is through a submarine solitude: "the glaucous glimmer where no voice can visit." But, in the mailbox at home, letters wait; there is no escape, terrestrial or spiritual. All that is left is "Hope, whose eye is round and does not wink."

In another poem, "Bearded Oaks," the lovers lie together, "Twin atolls on a shelf of shade," hoping in vain for exemption from identity. Their hope, being futile, is hopeless, like the innocence and purity evoked in "Picnic Remembered" and again bathed in the amber marine light that connotes illusory safety.

There is no way back; and resolute attempts to forget ensure only that we remember. *Eleven Poems* describes a progress toward self-knowledge. First there is a fall from some blithe, cushioned state; then a traumatic first taste of separateness; and finally a resolve to trust vaguely in the larger hope of "love's grace" in a world that sees American volunteers killing now on one side, in Spain, now on another, in Finland. Aspiring man (Alexis Carrel with his test-tube heart) only discovers his limitations and is then tempted to abandon hope. Warren's principal method in these poems itself reflects his theme. He sets sharp, Auden-like vignettes of individuals against or amid a vague malaise that recalls the romantic discontent of all times ("What has availed / Or failed? / Or will avail? / Hawk's poise, / The boxer's stance, / The sail"). As if proving the shock of separateness, certain images leap out from their context: "And seek that face which, greasy, frost-breathed, in furs / Bends to the bomb-sight over bitter Helsingfors." So too, certain facile injunctions ("Go to the clinic") bark vainly against the pull of spiritual desolation. There are no bright and brisk correctives to the growing sense of guilt.

These poems reconnoiter until they bump against life where it will not yield. But not all the collisions determine, as they well might, the structure of the poems. Warren, always fond of long lines and willing to let adjectives crowd nouns, works regularly

into transitional passages in which, under the appearance of
motivic accumulation, he marks time while shuffling ideas, one
of which eventually gains purpose and urges the poem to its next
goal. Most of Warren's poems oscillate in this way at some point
or other, and only his over-all strength of purpose brings them to
a conclusion rather than merely stopping them. As a result, litter
lies by the way, colorful but otiose:

> The peacock screamed, and his feathered fury made
> Legend shake, all day, while the sky ran pale as milk;
> That night, all night, the buck rabbit stamped in
>   the moonlit glade,
> And the owl's brain glowed like a coal in the
>   grove's combustible dark.

This fondness for minor pageantry sometimes impedes the novels
too while the idea behind it all, like a snubbed survivor, waits at
a distance. Hence Warren's strength and weakness: he never neg-
lects the surfaces of life and he sometimes fails to retrieve his
interpretation or his point before it vanishes beneath a clutter of
instances.

Thirty-six Poems presents man's share in the world's evil
through images of decay, sequestered animals, and the division of
son from parents. The vision is not profound, but ecological and
domestic. *Eleven Poems,* a subtler collection by far, registers evil
in ways more massive, more sustained. The advance is from desultory studies to a polyptych of man bearing darkness within him
wherever he goes. An inclusive certainty of grasp succeeds the
previous grasshopper techniques, and a gathering sense of mystery informs and unites the eleven poems included. Gravid, slow-
moving, and enameled, they introduce religious terms only to
clinch an argument or, more often, to transfigure retrospectively a
succession of images.

Selected Poems, 1923–1943 (1944) gathers together most of the
poems from these preceding volumes and includes some new
pieces too. "Variation: Ode to Fear" with its refrain, *"Timor mor-
tis conturbat me,"* and its list of cumulative banal occasions
("When Focke-Wulf mounts, or Zero, / And my knees say I'm no

hero") is a mock-ode, intendedly brittle and grotesquely poignant. The speaker, nauseated by cant, routine, slogans, hypocrisy minor and major, skimped or flip comments on Jesus, Saint Joan, and Milton, by silly discord and jejune pursuits — in short by the ephemera that engross diurnal man — relates all to the fear of death. This underestimated poem exposes a world too complex for any romantic, homogeneous mood or any sublime posture.

So too "Mexico Is a Foreign Country: Five Studies in Naturalism" includes a much wider array of emotions than the earlier poems. Gritty, facetious, sly, and willfully vulgar, the five parts introduce a Warren less resolutely grandiloquent, who now imports undignified objects and unprofound views into his lines:

> If only Ernest now were here
> To praise the bull, deride the steer,
> And anatomize for chillier chumps
> The local beauties' grinds and bumps . . .

It is not satire but a pert way of documenting the near-Dadaistic side of intelligent distress: ". . . here even the bladder achieves Nirvana, / And so I sit and think, 'mañana.' "

If such verse is destructive it also instructs. The poet's jaundiced review of the trivialities that survive all great ideas and noble motives attends a deeper, unshifting perception. All passes: "Viene galopando," says the old Mexican, "el mundo." This time round, the poet is willing to notice anything; nothing is excluded or lost, and the gain is a more complex view, all antinomies and incongruity:

> I do not know the mango's crime
> In its far place and different time,
> Nor does it know mine committed in a
> frostier clime . . .

It is God, the archetypal parent, who has now to be forgiven; and not only for the guilt man feels but also for making the world as harsh in meaningless contrasts as it is, and for conferring such delusive ideas as those of peace and innocence. Man and mango have to work out their respective salvations alone: "In separateness only does love learn definition." And the disquiet that pervades Warren's poems must finally, to any sensitive reader, seem a form of anger at causation. It is one thing to note that "Because he had spoken harshly to his mother, / The day became astonishingly bright," but quite another thing to confront the guilt consequent on having been born at all. Warren often degrades intermediate causes, relegating love ("Fellow, you tupped her years ago / That tonight my boots might crunch the snow") to animal level, man's nature to happenstance, and human intimacy to frantic parasitism.

These themes and motifs reappear full-scale in "The Ballad of Billie Potts." The prodigal son returns home and is murdered by parents who fail to recognize him. Warren handles this folktale from western Kentucky through alternating narrative and commentary, the one rich and awkward with doggerel sounds and Kentucky speech mannerisms, the other lofty, meditative, and often diffuse. A bizarre poem, it approaches caricature and cartoon, yet the moral — the wasted chance of trust — comes through unspoiled and, if anything, sharpened and straitened through contrast. Such a moral could hardly be exaggerated; it gains strength through being given such a hard time technically. Billie's father is an innkeeper who ambushes solitary travelers, each time doing violence to the recurring possibility of man's being a brother to man. Each time he attacks he destroys a chance of human community which, merely by doing nothing, he could preserve. He has free choice in this, but interferes with an established and maintainable peace until he causes the death of his own son. The point is that when Billie returns, rich and looking it, Billie too is a stranger who fits a stereotype, innocently counting on the absence of ill-will as all men must if they are not to become either paralyzed with fear or brutish through distrust. But his father "set the hatchet in his head," wrecking both the occasion for charity and the paternal-filial bond.

The father works by a defective ethic, regretting not the act of murder but his choice of victim. He regrets for immoral reasons, and Warren thus proves that an impersonal reflex of charity is superior to emotions that are merely partial. The world is full of strangers; therefore man must devise and uphold a code that gives each new relationship a chance to flourish. Whatever Billie's delusions about himself, he is entitled to human rights; but he loses more as a human than he could gain as a known son. And life's grand design is poorer far for his death than his parents are in bereavement. Special criteria, such as Billie's birthmark which the parents find when they dig up his body, are beside the point; it is the commonplace that counts in the arithmetic of goodwill.

If "Billie Potts" is blasphemous, it blasphemes as only the poem of a believer can. If Billie's father is God, striking categorically down irrespective of identity or age, then Warren has fixed on the harshness of mortality to make one point: trust in the long run is inevitable, whether it amounts to ignorance or fatalism. The only virtue in learning from experience is that life goes on, perpetually offering new chances against the old, depressing background:

> (There is always another country and always
> another place.
> There is always another name and another face.
> And the name and the face are you, and you
> The name and the face . . .)

Innocence cannot be retrieved, but it can be created out of evil: a man's children always start clean, and all the father can do is be humble before life's incessant renewals and seek to know himself, and his kind, better. For knowledge can sometimes improve man or help him to adjust, even if it can never perfect or redeem the defective, coiling human heritage: ". . . water is water and it flows, / Under the image on the water the water coils and goes / And its own beginning and its end only the water knows."

It is this concern that shapes Warren's outlook: the effort toward self-knowledge and responsible identity amidst the inscrutable flux. This is why, for ten years, away in a sense like Billie Potts, he deserted poetry for fiction. He could best express his main obsessions in narrative. He required space, sheer length, and mere succession to demonstrate his views on time's "brumal deeps" and "the great unsolsticed coil" of human destiny. Poems, distilling and compressing, present conclusions but not the dullness, the tedium, the *longueurs* of life. Proof sooner or later has to be made through accumulation, through a mass of "circumstantial texture" presented in full. The poems are points of light above the hubbub of the novels, but always related to that hubbub — its violence and eventfulness — through deploying the same view of history and guilt.

Already he had published *Night Rider* and *At Heaven's Gate*, experimenting in both novels with forms of commentary. The hand of the novelist shows intermittently in "Billie Potts," and it is no surprise to learn that, around 1944, when *Selected Poems* came out, Warren toyed with the idea of a novel about another ax-murder, this of a Negro slave by the nephews of Thomas Jefferson. But eventually, because the narrative required too much commentary, Warren decided against a novel and instead drafted a stage version with Jefferson as a chorus, along the lines of "Proud Flesh," an unpublished play he wrote in 1939, which later became the novel *All the King's Men*. What finally evolved was not a play but a dramatic poem enabling Warren to "get out of the box of mere chronology, and of incidental circumstantiality."

Between *Selected Poems* and this dramatic poem, *Brother to Dragons: A Tale in Verse and Voices* (1953), came the Pulitzer Prize-winning *All the King's Men* (1946), the long story *Blackberry Winter* (1946), a collection of short stories titled *Circus in the Attic* (1948), and "A Romantic Novel," *World Enough and Time* (1950). It was this period which fixed Warren's literary stance, claimed him for the novel, and settled in his own mind the criteria by which, ever the reticent moralist, he would select the matter to build his fiction from. It is only fair to trace his poetry and dramatic verse across this gap in time, for *Brother to Dragons* follows naturally from "Billie Potts" and the first two novels contain much that the poetry, seen whole, helps to clarify at once, the tropes and anagoges of the one genre helping to unite in the mind the more pedestrian and enumerative figures diffused through the other.

Brother to Dragons, meticulously and fluently written, has little of the stilted, air-beating rhetoric ("But I do not cuddle the hope that even your words could revoke the seminal assurance of time") that disfigures "Proud Flesh." The ax-slaying of a Negro by the sons of Jefferson's sister in 1811 generates a vivid, lavish parable in which the poet, as "R. P. W.," is a twentieth-century "interlocutor" desperately involved in the problem of evil versus aspiration. There is no direct action; the poem consists of events recapitulated during lunges of wide-ranging commentary, and traces Jefferson's advance from the ashamed bitterness of the disillusioned idealist to an attitude of skeptical pragmatism. Other characters — including Lilburn Lewis, the mother-fixated murderer, Meriwether Lewis, falsely accused of embezzlement, and Lucy, Lilburn's mother, who returns to win justice for her son — join as vocal and disputatious revenants in R. P. W.'s historic interview.

As Warren explains in his foreword, "historical sense and poetic sense" complement each other, the one a reminder of "the big myth we live," the other of "the little myth we make." History dwarfs and baffles; poetry augments and illumines. In a sense, the characters, far from antagonistic to one another, are dispersed segments of a compound ghost all sociably pursuing an identical comfort. They are less themselves than they are epitomes of prevalent human attitudes engaged in what Warren, in an address at Columbia University, called "continual and intimate interpenetration, an inevitable osmosis of being." R. P. W. puts it this way: "the Victim is Victor . . . because the Victim is lover of injustice." And one's reluctance to give intellectual attention to such wordplay is essential to Warren's success. We suspect paradox because if offers an unpalatable or preposterous dogma and shocks us with the long view from an opposite, complementary position such as history's. The result is to increase our sense of contiguity and of life's indivisibility.

Warren proves that only a synthesis of perspectives can teach us to live responsibly, while the verse itself — now a bemused liturgy of country detail, now a terse report of bloodletting, now a pattern of abstract nouns that reads like a denouement — embodies this diversity, increasing the centrifugal pull but motioning at the center. One of Warren's most powerful works, this colloquial catechism is as far as he could go without imposing the methods of the novelist on the poet's habitual shorthand. It ends with R. P. W. leaving "that perfect friendship" on the headland to rejoin his father who is dozing in the car. He takes with him something "Sweeter than hope," a prelude to a peace which nevertheless cannot come easily.

In *Promises: Poems 1954–1956*, which won Warren his second Pulitzer Prize when it appeared in 1957, he specifies his something "Sweeter than hope" in genealogies and modest proposals for his son and daughter. (He had married writer Eleanor Clark in 1950.) The father has given them the past and a future; he knows who they are historically, what they will be if they allow themselves only the right illusions. A neighbor's lovely child dismays him because, whatever parents think, beauty itself is only a promise, not an amulet. Rosanna, Warren's daughter, is safe in the sunlight of her laughter, but only while a child; and already much has happened to her that she still cannot know about. The son, Gabriel, gets sterner treatment as Warren sifts the past and separates the possibilities that died from the facts that are. Accident, he says, is relentlessly successful. The idea of family predominates, and even families are accidental stabilities based on an ineluctable past. Warren states the details with tender, unstraining empathy:

> What was the promise when, after the last
>   light had died,
> Children gravely, down walks, in spring dark,
>   under maples, drew
> Trains of shoe boxes, empty, with windows,
>   with candles inside,
> Going *chuck-chuck*, and blowing for crossings,
>   lonely, *oo-oo*?

He sees through the paraphernalia of these ingenuous rehearsals; sees through the ground itself to where "Side by side, Ruth and Robert," his own parents, lie forever. Their repose seems to guar-

antee the children's future, and he tells Gabriel about his own
boyhood, similarly guaranteed by a vision or hallucination of one
"old, rough-grizzled, and spent" who asked "Caint you let a man
lay!" and then moves on "in joy past contumely of stars or inso-
lent indifference of the dark air."

These lovely poems show Warren at his most relaxed, addressing the children on a storytelling, game-playing level while, in his
mind's eye, he sets them against vast landscapes and exigent in-
heritances. Musing on forefathers, he realizes where his power
ends and invokes "the light of humanness . . . under the shadow
of God's closing hand." The hand *will* close; the thing to worry
about is when. Of all the poems, perhaps "Infant Boy at Mid-
century" says most for all three, the father and his two, through
admitting so much of the world, and so much of his world-nur-
tured apprehension, into the presence of an almost overwhelming tenderness: on the one hand there are ticking clocks, "stew
and stink," "the barracks bath," and "Praetorian brutes"; on the
other, the time when

> . . . on a strange shore, an old man, toothless
>   and through,
> Groped hand from the lattice of personal disaster,
>   to touch you.
> He sat on the sand for an hour; said *ciao, bello,*
>   as evening fell.

Warren's basic wish in these poems begins with a toughminded
aphorism that sums up all his work: "the heart most mourns its
own infidelity," and in a series of fervent imperatives makes
Browning points: "Enfranchise the human possibility"; "Grace
undreamed is grace forgone." How fitting that the clearest account of his religious sense should entail this paternal assembly
of generations tapering down into the irrevocable existence of
two children.

The next book, *You, Emperors, and Others: Poems 1957–1960*
(1961), was disappointing. A few poems apart, the tone is captious
and weary, the mockery is routine ("In the age of denture and reduced alcoholic intake"), and the lyrical gestures are vapid

("Sleep, my dear, whatever your name is"). There is something
acerb here that detests but obsessively records the modern scene.
The best poems, such as "The Letter about Money, Love, or
Other Comfort, If Any," "Prognosis," and "Ballad: Between the
Box Cars," are narrative parables which, like the long-winded
titles, the long lines, the showy epigraphs, and the Byronic
rhymes ("Jantzen" and "pants on"), betray the presence of a novelist who resembles a rogue elephant in shoving aside or tram-
pling the finicking perfectionism of the poem-maker.

The book has a prelude in "Original Sin," a poem whose me-
ticulous, rhyming stanzas luridly relate an impersonal "you" to
the omnipresence of horror: "The nightmare stumbles past, and
you have heard / It fumble your door before it whimpers and is
gone." This poem — like *Brother to Dragons* a key to the whole
of Warren — illuminates the jumpiness which dominates *You,
Emperors, and Others.* A profound dislike of human nature is
what finally relates the poems to the fiction and gives dimension
to Warren's equally profound dismay with himself. The "you"-
figure is not so much a mask as a mirror that won't answer back
when something "Sweeter than hope" is betrayed. As Tobias Sears
says in *Band of Angels,* "it's so hard right in the middle of things
to remember that the power of soul must work through matter,
that even the filthiness of things is part of what Mr. Emerson calls
the perennial miracle the soul worketh, that matter often retains
something of its original tarnishment." Much of Warren's restlessness comes from his discovering that hard truths, even when
swallowed repeatedly, do not soften. Hence too some of his almost
gloating fascination with "the filthiness of things," even things
we are used to.

In his introduction to the Modern Library edition of Conrad's
Nostromo Warren takes pains to define "the philosophical novelist" as one "for whom the documentation of the world is constantly striving to rise to the level of generalization about values,
for whom the image strives to rise to symbol, for whom images always fall into a dialetical configuration, for whom the urgency of

experience, no matter how vividly and strongly experience may enchant, is the urgency to know the meaning of experience." In its voluminous and emphatic way this sheds light on Warren himself.

We have only to read a random page of Warren's prose to see that experience "enchants" him in the same measure as his desire to find meanings is urgent. Warren the sophisticated, highly educated teacher and penetrating critic has had to compete with Warren the pageant-loving southerner whose gift for exact lyrical abandon shows on every page. His progress and his upsets are the natural outcome of that conflict — not just because philosophy curtails angels' wings or because sensual delight saps analytical intellect, but because Warren has always been intellectually ambitious as well as a natural respecter of natural forces. Take the definition quoted above: it is a clever, persuasive denial of the creative artist's willpower. The "documentation," notice, does its own striving; so does the "image." It is as if Warren, reluctant to announce the passion to interpret as a feat of the mind, disguises it as a natural process that goes on independently of, perhaps even in spite of, the writer himself. Hence his vision:

> . . . every act is Janus-faced and double,
> And every act to become an act must resolve
> The essential polarity of possibility.
> Thus though the act is life and without action
> There is no life, yet action is a constant withering
> Of possibility, and hence of life.
> So by the act we live, and in action die.

Put like this, in *Brother to Dragons*, Warren's existential perplexity seems ambiguous. Compelled to engage in acts of will, men almost always find compensation in the pleasures of the senses: "I have a romantic kind of interest," he admitted in a *Paris Review* interview, "in the objects of American history: saddles, shoes, figures of speech, rifles, etc. They're worth a lot. Help you focus." And, for him, the complications of living and writing come about through "the anguish of option" — that between taking phenomena for their own sake and trying to interpret them.

The option is national. American society, as Warren says, came into being suddenly, and intelligent Americans are still grappling with the suddenness, the improvised nature, of it all. Warren pores over the nation's history, trying to decide how free and how determined the individual is. The War between the States was a second, hurried attempt at clarity; and the southerner, as he points out in *Segregation*, has a unique knowledge of what moral identity means on both the national and personal levels. In fact man's ability to analyze relates him even more subtly to history: to think about life is to become even more intimately enmeshed in it. Reflection proves that we carry the burden for much we are not responsible for and that, all the same, we have no genuine identity until we assume responsibilities unique to ourselves.

To attempt such a theme is no minor undertaking, and Warren's own attempts have not always been successful. The technical problems alone are immense; they involve him in his own theme. For example, writing on Katherine Anne Porter, he says that "the thematic considerations must, as it were, be validated in terms of circumstance and experience, and never be resolved in the poverty of statement." The truly philosophical novelist finds the work beginning to do itself, whereas another kind of novelist (Warren's type) has to keep making the thinker in him be a novelist.

His first published novel, *Night Rider* (1939), deals with the Kentucky tobacco wars of 1905–8 in which the growers organized themselves against the big buyers. But the literally benighted development of Perse Munn, the central character, has an allegorical force transcending the regional interest. (Warren printed an introductory note warning that *Night Rider* was not intended as a historical novel.) Munn travels erratically backwards through a self-imposed dark night of the soul, and the narrative is less documentary in impact than metaphorical. Munn covets power, espouses the cause of the Association of Growers of Dark Fired Tobacco, and gradually comes to enjoy his involvement with mobs: they give him a sense of dynamic immersion as well as the identity of a firm role. Demagoguery is both his narcotic and his undoing; he not only takes more than he gives but loses private tenacity of spirit the more his public power grows. He worries how to define "the true and unmoved center of his being" and becomes involved in violence, but involved like a sleepwalker, losing through self-destruction all he gains through being self-assertive.

Things move too fast for him. His marriage degenerates, the Association splits, illegal night-riding becomes a common terror, defection and dissension increase, and he yearns for a boyhood world where, as in the stereopticon, things stand still when you want them to. Imponderables multiply beyond his capacity to control and order them. He cannot, like Ianthe Sprague, the only relative he could turn to in Philadelphia while studying law, adapt himself: Ianthe liked to have the newspaper read to her at disjunctive random. To her neither order nor, therefore, chaos mattered. Brutalities and burnings, losses and accusations pile up until Munn has to escape to the rural retreat of Willie Proudfit, a man who has come through and who tells Munn about his own share of the American dream — open spaces, buffalo, gunfights, and eventual return to Kentucky. By now Munn has lost everything except the passion to vindicate his emptiness; he decides to kill Senator Tolliver, the father-figure who deserted the growers' cause and whom he hates for involving him (as he thinks) in the whole mess. Yet, as he tells Tolliver, his motive is not "because you are filthy, but for myself. To know what I am." Munn's last act embodies the only wisdom left to him: for so long one of the living dead, he eliminates paradox by attracting the fire of state troops who have been following him.

Night Rider is full of violent events counterpointed by Munn's self-probings. It is an exciting, thought-compelling book, but somehow lacks a dimension. All Warren's favorite concepts — will, identity, time, power, violence, escapism, guilt, and responsibility — get their turn in a vivid demonstration; but Willie Proudfit, as an instance of self-rehabilitation, seems ancillary and rudely imported. His self-communing pales beside the spectacular action, depriving the reader of the full meditative torment which brought such a character as Munn into being. Here Warren fights shy of "poverty of statement" and one misses what one gets from Malraux's *Man's Hope*, another novel about the mishaps of collective endeavor; and that is a sense of the novelist's undivided involvement in the theme he picks.

The next novel, *At Heaven's Gate* (1943), takes the theme further, once again offering characters who define themselves at the expense of natural order (just as Munn callously exploits everything, everyone, to hand), but also diagnosing their spiritual emptiness exhaustively. Again, too, there is an interpolated backwoods character who, like Willie Proudfit, has redeemed himself through homage to the source of his being: nature, family, tradition. Ashby Wyndham has sinned against his brother but atones in some degree through honest self-appraisal. And where Proudfit seems perfunctorily hauled in, Ashby Wyndham is there from the start, in jail, and he occupies alternate chapters as a grumbling integer in a novel conceived on lines both Dante-like and contrapuntal. Warren had already advanced a long way in ability to manipulate and interweave large, contrasting masses of experience.

Sue Murdock, defying the suave tyranny of her financier father, vents Warren's usual question: "Oh, what am I?" She deserts the man she loves, Jerry Calhoun, for being a mere carbon copy of her father, joins the retinue of bohemians run by Slim Sarrett, a homosexual poet-boxer, and becomes his mistress. Sue in the lower depths ("that dim, subaqueous world") is like Munn at Proudfit's home ("a submarine depth"). She too is capable of cruel outbursts. Munn works cruelty into his matrimonial lovemaking and she forces Jerry to take her physically in the room beneath her father's. They both rage against the outrage they think done to them, but impotently so.

Sue, moving from man to man, reveals the futility of defining oneself through others: if the effort succeeds, the self-definer only exhausts his host; if it fails, he uses the intimacy for a self-asserting revenge. The benighted and baffled despoil the best — those who in Slim's words "manage to maintain some shreds of reality and humanity." The agonizing thing is that the unstable person such as Sue cannot let those she clings to be anything but imper-

vious: she requires a monolith and construes all tenderness as
weakness, all confessed diffidence as failure. She punishes her own
faults in others at the same time as she repudiates her father, the
one man who meets her needs, for his tyranny.

Bogan Murdock, ruthlessly foreclosing homesteads, is the public's creature as well as his own man. He associates himself with
the dashing audacity of such as Andrew Jackson, but his panache
is grounded in insensitivity. He is a born survivor, "a great big
wonderful dream" (as one character describes him) sanctioned by
those he exploits. His is the image of the utter stranger, the man
too weak deep down to know what part weakness plays in being
truly human. If his daughter is asking for the moon (for a relationship that does not modify the other person) then he is a creature of lunar coldness, grandly asking nothing but power.

Yet both, simple in their wrongness, create enormous complexities in the lives of others; Warren uses them to compound further
the complexity he finds here, as always, ready-made in history
(Murdock has much in him of Luke Lea, the sometime United
States senator and convicted swindler from Tennessee). Warren's
over-all view is of the incalculable, unpredictable repercussions
our least endeavors provoke. Identity, in particular, is not a fixity
but a studiously maintained transaction with other people. The
means of self-establishment is also the prime agency of confusion,
especially for those who want perfection and utter consistency.

This is what Jack Burden discovers in *All the King's Men*
(1946) when he becomes involved with Governor Willie Stark's
political party machine. To him Stark is not so much a tyrant as
a divinely appointed savior; not an idealist but a practical, misunderstood redeemer of Louisiana. And it is from this opinion
that Burden, with his Ph.D. thesis in history following him around
in a parcel, advances to learn about the corruption that binds all
men together. He digs up facts that Stark can use against people
in his campaigns and thus brings about the suicide of Judge Irwin, who he then discovers is his own father, rather than Ellis
Burden, "the Scholarly Attorney," who had been his mother's
husband at the time of his birth. History's cupboards sometimes

ought to be left closed. He now has to reappraise the past in the light and horror of this knowledge. Burden's Landing, his birthplace, is not simply a backwater where his mother and former friends have obliviously sustained an outmoded, questionable way of life; it is a symbol of the incompleteness of modern man's knowledge. Where, previously, visiting the Landing he felt "sad and embarrassed and, somehow, defrauded," he learns to say "I could now accept the past which I had before felt was tainted and horrible." The Landing, although embarrassing Jack with its obsolescence and phoney consistency, possesses part of him forever, and he has to accept this fact in order to live.

A double standard emerges. Stark, ruthlessly pursuing the public good, succeeds by using the past to smear members of the present, but only until a modern idealist, Adam Stanton, shoots him for treating people as things. Stark knows that man is indivisible from history (though he denies it publicly); Burden tries to persuade himself of the contrary. Stark is right but uses his knowledge perniciously, dehumanizing both history and the living. Burden, wrong but tentative and therefore impressionable, acquiesces because he cannot respect history or its share in what individual people are. He learns the truth only when Stark's dispassionate policy and his own misapplied expertise bring ruin to Judge Irwin and, in so doing, expose the true ancestry of Jack Burden. The past endures.

So, through an example of personal shock demolishing inhuman abstractness, Warren condemns unspiritual secularism. Stark, like Bogan Murdock, wields power that derives from the fact that he can "vicariously fulfill certain secret needs of people about him"; but the people, whatever the demagogue says, cannot be separated from their own history any more than the demagogue can from his. The blandishments made possible through a booming technology may fool the people some of the time, but not all of them all of the time. Adam Stanton denounces Stark's six-million-dollar hospital as political window dressing and then, trapped in his own geometry, eventually accepts the directorship. Even the rampant idealist must finally admit the power and insidiousness of context, the glutinous hold of the social fabric. Stark tries to unravel the corrupt web of his life until, by interfering, he dooms his own son to an early death; Stanton, idealist too frequent, is killed in assassinating Willie. The repercussions of their conduct have already proliferated in countless, irrevocable ways; and Jack Burden, man of ideas, has to ponder the remnants, conscious always of how the idealists (Stanton, John Brown, Jefferson) match the pragmatists in callousness. What defeats them all is mere contingency: "I eat a persimmon," Burden thinks, "and the teeth of a tinker in Tibet are put on edge."

Part of the meaning of *All the King's Men* is that none of the evils totalitarianism claims to remedy is worse than totalitarianism itself. The same point occurs in "Proud Flesh" (in which the central character is called Talos instead of Stark). Later versions are the two stage adaptations of the novel and the motion-picture script. Understandably, Warren has been unable to leave the theme alone, not only assisting in adaptations but footnoting it in various essays.

Most of all, he has been careful to separate Willie Stark and his "state" from their matrices, Huey Long and Louisiana. The novel, he explains, grew from an experience of two worlds: factual and mythical. In the first a debilitated craving for elegance matched "drool-jawed grab and arrogant criminality" — a world that reminded him of "the airs and aspirations" attributed to Von Ribbentrop the ex-champagne salesman and to the clique around Edda Ciano. "For," as he says, "in Louisiana, in the 1930's, you felt somehow that you were living in the great world, or at least in a microcosm with all the forces and fatalities faithfully, if sometimes comically, drawn to scale." The other world, that of folklore and fabliau violence, included the glamour that gathered about Long's name and doings, refracting and inflating his image until it seemed a monstrous, sly outcrop from the Louisiana magma itself, mocking and outdoing the cypress swamps, the hovels of the mosspickers, the arsenical green of water the sun never touches, cottonmouth moccasins, and clicking, buzzing insects.

It is significant that Warren's first attempt to draw the "iron-groom" figure of Talos-Stark-Long was the verse drama begun in 1938 "in the shade of an olive tree by a wheat field near Perugia." He began with the myth: popular imagination improvised because it did not know, any more than Warren did, what the private Huey Long was like. And his continuing preoccupation with this demagogue-figure is as much mythological as reportorial; for all his profuse, complicated circumstantial evidence, his accounts have the impact of a folk ritual prepared by a poet who responds intensely to the organic power of "the dark and bloody ground" (the Indian name for Kentucky). His own summation is worth noting: denying he "was" Jack Burden, or Jack Burden only, he says he was all the characters and remains inextricably absorbed in them. "However important for my novel was the protracted dialectic between 'Huey' on the one side, and me on the other, it was far less important, in the end, than that deeper and darker dialectic for which the images and actions of a novel are the only language."

The theme is man, earthbound, earth-held, not one with nature but licensed by nature and obliged, always, to subject his aspirations to his religious sense: that is, to his sense of being indivisible from an organic whole he has not himself created. This essential derivedness and rootedness of man appears in Warren's note on the hitchhiker he picked up while driving to North Louisiana in 1934: he was "a country man, the kind you call a red-neck or a wool-hat, aging, aimless, nondescript, beat up by life and hard times and bad luck." Warren goes on to build a vision that tells us much about his way of apprehending a world in which people, as well as vegetation, provide the humus in which initiative grows and sometimes runs wild: "He was the god on the battlement, dimly perceived above the darkling tumult and the steaming carnage of the political struggle. He was a voice, a portent, and a natural force like the Mississippi River getting set to bust a levee. . . . it is certain that the rutted back roads and slab-side shacks that had spawned my nameless old hitchhiker . . . had, by that fall of 1934, made possible the rise of 'Huey.' My nameless hitchhiker was, mythologically speaking, Long's *sine qua non*."

For each of his tawdry Olympians Warren provides this kind of underworld; it remains when the Olympian has gone. Perse Munn, Bogan Murdock, and Willie Stark are consumed by the element that spawned them, and that element includes the re-treated and revulsed characters such as Willie Proudfit, Ashby Wyndham, and Jack Burden. In the long run, Warren's contrasts and probings must be read as examples only and not imputed back to him. As he told Ralph Ellison in the interview for the *Paris Review*, the writer's business is "not to illustrate virtue but to show how a fellow may move toward it — or away from it." In short, a field study, not a sermon.

At its most complete and cogent the field study amounts to Coleridge's inexhaustible repercussion. In shooting the albatross the Ancient Mariner tries to cancel the soul's relationship to the universe; but he is finally convinced by his imagination that such canceling is impossible and must yield to what Warren, writing on Melville, calls a "solution achieved in terms of . . . exercise of will." Violence rarely solves anything, although it seems to abolish a physical hindrance.

Imagination has two uses: popular and private. The first can produce and sanction monsters; the second can induce private nightmare. Bogan Murdock, like Willie Stark, is something the people thought up; Perse Munn is his own monster, spawned in his own whirling head at night. But there are virtuous uses too: rare for the popular imagination because massive numbers entail simplification and formulas, but fairly common for such as Coleridge's mariner and, in, say, *At Heaven's Gate* alone, Uncle Lew with the clubfoot, Duckfoot Blake, the maladroit Mr. Calhoun, Aunt Ursula the paralyzed, Private Porsum, and even Ashby Wyndham.

They all avoid abstraction: it stunts the reality of other people and warps the abstractor. Willie Stark, on the other hand, can be just as abstract-minded as Cass Mastern, Burden's Civil War an-cestor. Man, says Willie, "is conceived in sin and born in corruption and he passeth from the stink of the didie to the stench of the shroud." It is a blank and bland formulation, just as jejune as Mastern's weird assertion that "It is human defect — to try to know oneself by the self of another. One can only know oneself in God and in His great eye." Cass is the well-meaning man who releases his Mississippi slaves but only to even worse hardship in the North. He feels strongly that he cannot control the consequences of his actions, but dies believing that "it may be that only by the suffering of the innocent does God affirm that men are brothers." Thus, both Stark and Mastern, in the end, learn truth when it is too late to reform things but not to accept them.

Jack Burden, reflecting on persimmon and the Tibetan tinker, comes to a similar conclusion in the end. His Great Sleep and Great Twitch were mere behaviorism. Yet the casuistries that kept him deludedly serene were hardly more specious than the Scholarly Attorney's unscholarly formulations about the cosmos: "Separateness is identity and the only way for God to create, truly create, man was to make him separate from God Himself, and to be separate from God is sinful." Humanity is a congeries of clinging separate entities, and the only truth is in an independent, imaginative response to the knowable. Such is Warren's advice, and such his main fictional concealment of himself.

A single volume, *The Circus in the Attic* (1948), contains all of Warren's short stories, of which *Blackberry Winter*, published separately in 1946, is outstanding in the history of the genre as well as the most compact epitome of Warren's output. A man in his early forties recalls his initiation into manhood and the ways of nature. When a city-clad stranger comes to work on the farm during a time of storm and flood (like December 1811 in *Brother to Dragons*) the boy, little apprehending the devastation and stoicism evident everywhere, fastens to him and thus vicariously "goes away." This symbolic infidelity the adult narrator has come to regret; like the speaker in several of Warren's early poems he is saddened that as a boy he responded poorly to the beleaguered devotion of his parents. Guilt, ever-present in Warren's writings, dogs him until like old Jebb in the story he realizes the past is as unalterable as a ruined crop. Moreover, as if perfidy were not enough, it was perfidy at the wrong time: "blackberry winter" is when the genial spring unnaturally regresses and turns its back, reneging, just like the boy.

Once again Warren explores man and his relationship to the land. Neither is wholly predictable: the Negro maid uncharacteristically strikes her child; the river floods. There are no absolutes, but only risky combinations of transient circumstances, And the boy responds to the disorder of the time by holding to what is newest. "I did follow him, all the years," the narrator says remorsefully, stressing "did" to evoke the ghost of a foregone alternative.

Nothing of Warren's more convincingly demonstrates how complex his traditionalism is. The inevitability of change is a southern fact too, even though, as he is always saying, the supposed and usually mythical stability of the past is succeeded only by the instability of an unknown future. Man makes uneasy truces with nature which is reliable only because, in the mass, it never dies.

Predictably, then, Warren's favorite images express both an entranced horror with nature and horrified relief at man's power to control. Submerged in nature, man can know a vegetable peace; against it he can achieve a sterile safety. But he cannot safely ally himself with it, for it is inscrutable. Images of flood depict the odds. In "History among the Rocks" it is "a creek in flood" which will tumble and turn "a body, naked and lean." In *Brother to Dragons* R. P. W. speaks of "that deep flood that is our history," exemplifying "the drowned cow, swollen," while *Blackberry Winter* presents another cow "rolling and roiling down the creek." A poem in *Promises* tells how "A drowned cow bobbled down the creek" and a novel Warren published in 1964 is itself called *Flood.* Man cannot flood out the flood of history and time. On the other hand he can create roads, imaging the direct-mindedness of efficient modernity and facilitating the hectic placelessness to which the nation turns in escape. Only history has unlimited accommodations, and Warren's vision of America, a land cut

cleanly across by numbered highways, is ironical: man applies
Mercator to things fluid, aiding navigators but dominating nothing. *All the King's Men* opens with Jack Burden going on Highway 58 "northeast out of the city"; it is a straight, white-shimmer-
ing highway with a water mirage forever ahead — "that bright,
flooded place." *Flood* opens with a highway and stays on it for
several pages; and nothing could be clearer than this from
Brother to Dragons:

> Up Highway 109 from Hopkinsville,
> To Dawson Springs, then west on 62,
> Across Kentucky at the narrow neck,
> Two hours now, not more, for the road's fair.
> We ripped the July dazzle on the slab . . .

"Mexico Is a Foreign Country" makes its point with sinister
levity: "The highways are scenic, like destiny marked in red"; and
Segregation commemorates Highway 61 cutting south from Mem-
phis, "straight as a knife edge through the sad and baleful beauty
of the Delta country." *Flood* ends with "the chrome and safety
glass of cars passing on the new highway, yonder across the lake."
New mastodons for old.

Such images, recurring, evoke one another and crystallize Warren's feeling that man can best nature only by cutting across, by
disregarding and dividing, never by eliciting secrets from within.
The highway, symbol of initiative, speed, and control, is sterile,
plagued by fatigue, mirages, boredom, advertising, and death.
The flood, symbol of revenge, impersonality, and accident, is the
element that contains the highways. And, just as no road ever
conquers what it cuts through, so no neat network of ideas can
open up history; such is the gist of Warren's treatment of his intellectual characters. But men who live close to nature achieve understanding, inchoate as it is. They accept earth as their element
and source, privilege and torment.

Most of Warren's best stories are painful, guilt-ridden com-
memorations of some young person's rites of passage. Grandfather
Barden in "When the Light Gets Green" waits four years for
death and love. But his grandson, prey to familiar Warren inca-

pacities, cannot love: he lies, feels guilty, and, grown adult, feels even guiltier for still being unable to comprehend his deficiency. It is, probably, an unexpressed resolve to submit as little as necessary to the processes of mortality. Another boy, in "Christmas Gift," is similarly confounded by premature difficulties; but he copes by exchanging tokens with the doctor: candy for the chance to roll a cigarette. The boy in "Testament of Flood" does all his growing up in one instant of recognition. And, just as the young take their stand, gropingly or with unpracticed severity, so do those who have no future at all. Like Grandfather Barden, Viola the Negro cook in "Her Own People" lies in bed; discharged, she has nowhere to go, only death to look forward to. So she creates guilt all around her, exposing the spiritual debility of those who, like her employers, dare not love or live.

These are the problems of home, of growth within the tribe: having home, leaving it, aching to return, and being unable to dismiss intervening years. Home is also to be defined unsentimentally as any available intimate basis. For young and old alike, there must be a rock to build on even if it is only being unloved or unloving. The professor in "The Unvexed Isles" discovers how much of an unsophisticated, homesick midwesterner he is, but in re-establishing his marriage on this admitted truth cannot be wrong. Home is where candor sites it. So too the gelid marriage in "The Love of Elsie Barton: A Chronicle" stabilizes itself on bleak habit. Warren presents a choice: return to the source of one's being, like Billie Potts, or found a new home in maturity. All men crave the place where they are not naked or totally vulnerable. Bolton, the muted hero of "Circus in the Attic," is a case in point. He has repudiated his ancestors and must therefore find something to cleave to: his soft-pine circuses carved in secret, his draftee stepson, or writing his desultory, halfhearted history of the county.

Yet the longed-for world of home remains a terra incognita, less welcoming than present adversity. The reason is that childhood identity begins with the search for freely chosen, as distinct from inherited, attachments — and the guilt of cutting free. Warren's best stories prove the search a new imprisonment; his least successful posit odd, fey ironies on situations not evaluated by characters who are themselves inscrutable.

Warren, like Bolton's father, has become increasingly "aware of the powerful, vibrating, multitudinous web of life which binds the woman and child together, victor and victim." The search for new complicities returns man to old paradoxes. Life's patterns vary little; only private, poetic truth is abundantly various; historical and cosmic truth is infinitely monotonous — something to hold to but also something aloof.

Such acknowledgments and bafflements underlie the complications of *World Enough and Time* (1950), Warren's most mandarin performance. Based initially on a pamphlet, *The Confession of Jereboam O. Beauchamp* (1826), it has an epigraph from Spenser's *Faerie Queene* and takes its title from Marvell. Jerry Beaumont, self-appointed knight-errant of the night, is a latterday Artegall who ingenuously becomes his own victim, and Warren himself, for all the elaborate counterpoint of his narrative method and his intense preoccupation with identity ("Myself, oh, what am I?" asks Beaumont), lapses into the amenities of costume romance, a genre he condemns but likes to write in. The novel has a dazzling, intricate surface pitted with masterfully distanced dialogue; and nothing could be more to Warren's point. Surfaces can be recaptured but motives and inspirations cannot. "Their lips move but you do not hear the words . . . Nor hear the rustle of the heart," as he says in "Billie Potts."

Beaumont, trained as a lawyer, is drawn into state politics and, like most of Warren's idea-men, yearns to "define" himself through spectacular action. The yearning is Byronic as well as Spenserian. Beaumont, romantically assuming the cause of the supposedly dishonored Rachel Jordan, sets out to kill Cassius Fort, her former lover and his own mentor and backer. The rationale, or excuse, for this is dangerously abstract: "Could a man," he asks, "not come to some moment when, all dross and meanness of life consumed, he could live in the pure idea? If only for a moment?" Like Willie Stark he wants to force glory

from "the filth we strew"; but it is the same longing as the disillusioned Jefferson describes in *Brother to Dragons*:

> ... the sad child's play
> And old charade where man puts down the bad
> and then feels good.
> It is the sadistic farce by which the world is cleansed.
> And is not cleansed, for in the deep
> Hovel of the heart that Thing lies
> That will never unkennel himself to the
> contemptible steel ...

No man effaces nature. A yearning for purity is laudable but
belongs to adolescence, to the world of Warren's early poems. Human glory has to flourish in the daily world somewhere between
purity and filth; and romanticized violence, like the murderous
sadism of Lilburn Lewis, condemns itself. So at first sight does
Beaumont, terrified of drowning in history; but he is trapped.
His aspiration is too great for the conditions of man's life, yet
where else can he pursue it? His crime and penance, "being a man
and living in the world of men," coincide exactly, as for Jack
Burden. Small wonder that frustration so often in Warren's
writings erupts into violence, out of which a little comes — of
catharsis or satiety, but little enough when pitted against the
world and time.

Beaumont, an Adam Stanton brought to judgment, is hard to
decipher: is he coy martyr or glorious fake? The double narrative
— an impersonal historian documenting without passion and
Jerry himself venting his untidy soul — clouds everything. He is,
basically, as unknowable as John Brown. Between the historian's
confessed inadequacy and Beaumont's love of melodrama there is
no choosing. There is no adding the two together either: massed
data are useless when some areas remain blank. And Beaumont's
escape with Rachel into the fetid Eden of the swamp is another
of Warren's submarine-uterine removals. Beaumont deserts ideas
for the Great Sleep and thus, unlike Beauchamp in the original
document, has time to brood. Warren postpones his death until
he has had time to admit things to himself about the impossi-

bility of identity in isolation (to be unborn again), the impossibility of self-cleansing through condemning others (like Perse Munn), the superiority of truth to innocence and peace, the self-indictment that transcends codified justice, and the spectrum between law as a public absolute and law as a private appointment.

The novel is overwhelming. A galaxy of theatrically casuistical quandaries, it seems more complicated and less assimilable than life itself. Nothing becomes clear without generating tangential problems that are then added to what is central. The narrative merges into its theme, not so much defining complexity as increasing it through irrelevance. In such a context even the commonplace abruptness of death seems more enigmatic than usual. Warren never reduces the pressure and yet, wasting nothing, gains nothing he could not have gained less voluminously. It is as if, despairing of making sense out of so much complexity, he piled up data to overwhelm the reader too. Bewilderment is the novel's theme and, oddly enough, in view of all the oratorical intelligence on show, the only experience of which it ultimately extends our knowledge.

The same problem reappears in *Band of Angels* (1955). Continually drawn to questions of identity and motive Warren has Amantha Starr open the novel with "Oh, who am I?" Brought up on a Kentucky plantation and then sent north to school, she discovers on her father's death that she is half Negro. After being sold into slavery she is bought by Hamish Bond who becomes her lover and brings her momentary peace, or surcease, at any rate. But Bond is an impostor; his real name is Alec Hinks, and this revelation sets Amantha questioning everything, especially names, signs, appearances, tokens — in short, all the means of communication and identification. Warren's divided account of Beaumont has a parallel in this divided girl. Product of miscegenation, she is also the articulate, self-pitying victim of such as Bond (who profits through her confusing freedom with not being a slave), Seth Parton, the self-apotheosized rustic from Oberlin (she and he expect too much pain from piety), Tobias Sears the transcendentalist she marries, and Rau-Ru, Bond's colored henchman who eventually acquires an alias of his own — "Lt. Oliver Cromwell Jones." After much social and political upset in which individual rights and concerns disintegrate, Amantha and Tobias move to St. Louis and thence to Kansas where Tobias, who used to think (like Beaumont the knight-errant) of "dying into the undefiled whiteness of some self-image," begins to accept life and himself. Amantha, inspirited by his example, undertakes a similar self-revision and sheds the self-pity that made her more the victim of herself than of anyone else. She comes through, learning at last that identity depends on accepting one's separateness: "Don't ever call me poor little Manty again!" she tells Tobias, and the novel ends with her overwhelmed by the "awfulness of joy" and "all the old shadows" of their lives, as she says, "canceled in joy" too.

Amantha donnishly voices one of Warren's principal worries. "You do not live your life," she says, "but somehow, your life lives you, and you are, therefore, only what History does to you." Finally, however, she repudiates such self-excusing and realizes she cannot honestly attribute her rape to events at Harpers Ferry. And Warren himself insists that self-definition to counter incessant "osmosis of being" is as much a Christian duty as a Christian privilege. He will not countenance organized security or any imposed direction for the soul. But surely there is a point at which legislated security, especially in the South, gives the soul what it needs to work in: freedom from persecution, a civil right less fascinating than self-definition and for that reason often ignored in favor of metaphysical and religious bagatelles.

In *The Cave* (1959) Jasper Harrick, a Korean veteran who has failed to find himself even in combat, returns home to Tennessee and takes to exploring caves, reassuring his mother that "in the ground at least a fellow has a chance of knowing who he is." When Jasper is trapped underground his supposed friend, Isaac Sumpter, delays the rescue in order to turn it into a publicity stunt. And after Jasper dies the gathered crowd embark on a crazed orgy: "Thousands of people, he didn't know how many, had come here because a poor boy had got caught in the ground, and had lain there dying. They had wept, and prayed, and boozed, and sung and fought, and fornicated, and in all ways possible had striven to break through to the heart of the mystery which was themselves." Major and minor characters alike find Jasper's entombment catalytic in resolving their own lives. They explore and rediscover themselves and one another, seeking the temporary oblivions of violence or love, but seeking also, through such self-venting and self-exposure, to make themselves firm.

The novel depicts a hillbilly auto-da-fé in which the loud-speakers, television cameras, prayers, spotlights, songs, chants, and slogans travestying the subterranean doom of Jasper yet consti-tute the only means of making it meaningful to others and mak-ing those others articulate to themselves. The story advances through a series of colliding, related dilemmas, and Warren for once leaves the irony to reveal itself. Isaac Sumpter, deep in the spiritual dark of being technically a murderer, goes off to a career in the dud Samarkand of "Big Media"; but he reaches his point of departure only after a long, comprehensible, and wholly convincing elenchus of a kind unusual in Warren. And those other "strange prisoners" — Jack Harrick, the life-devouring brawler and womanizer, now dying; Nick the mis-married restau-rant-owner haunted by a corrupting image of Jean Harlow; Timothy Bingham the bank manager living by rote, not by the heart — come to developing, palpable life in a prose which, stop-ping just short of caricature, is as earthy, dynamic, and viscid as anything Warren has written. Those who gather at the cave find a meaning for their lives and not, like Amantha Starr invoking Harpers Ferry, an excuse.

Logically the next stage in Warren's demonstration — after Amantha's excuses and the crowd's voluptuous empathy in *The Cave* — should have been a homage to communal piety; and this is roughly what *Wilderness* (1961), in its perfunctory, mannered way, supplies. Adam Rosenzweig, clubfooted son of a Jewish Ba-varian poet and liberal, comes to America during the Civil War in search of justice and freedom. In various ways, through blood-shed, mob violence, and commonplace compassion, he enters into a new community whose least aggressive impulse is stated by Mose the illiterate ex-slave after he has watched someone dying: "I would'n keer, not if 'twas me. Layen thar bleeden." Also with Adam and Mose is a brutal planter, Jed Hawksworth, who has been run out of his native North Carolina. The three of them, becoming themselves in the "wilderness" of carnage and verminous mistrust created by the war, might have come out of Stephen Crane. The badge of *their* courage is that of a harshly tested identity. Adam kills a man and, after accounting to himself, undertakes a laconic dialectic that finally reconciles him to being involved, however grievously, with other men. *"We always do what we intend,"* he begins, at first impressed and awed by what he has done; but suddenly a sense of guilt desolates him. Then *"What I have done . . . I did for freedom"* yields to *"I did nothing I did not have to do."* After a recrudescence of his "if only" mood of remorse, he decides that every man is "a sacrifice for every other man." Everyone has betrayed him, including even his own father. But in this moment of clear sight he realizes too something like joy: *"Ah,* he thought, *this is it!* He felt the exaltation of one who discovers the great secret." And, dizzy with new power — even more elated than when, caught up in a mob, he almost stabbed a captured Negro — he steals a boot from the dead man and puts it on. Another rite has been staged.

A novel of short sentences and long meditations, *Wilderness* is terse, bleak, and disturbing not least because the three men, traveling as sutlers to the Federal Army, distract us little from the relentless simplicity of the plot and Adam's inevitable apocalypse. In *Flood* (1964), however, Warren resumes and raises to a beautiful symphonic level the same allegorical method, this time combining his profound concern for the past with the problems of durable identity. Two men, Brad Tolliver, native son who has been too long away, and Yasha Jones, guilt-haunted movie director, arrive in Fiddlersburg, Tennessee, to make a film about the town before it is evacuated for the building of a new dam. They stay with Brad's sister, whose husband is serving a life sentence in the jail nearby, and gradually come to know Fiddlers-

burg, past and present, with an intimacy they find both useful
and upsetting.

The whole book is rich with interacting, wholly functional patterns that complement one another: history's flood with flood
man-made; Brad's involvement with Fiddlersburg through memory and suffering; Jones's involvement through response to novelty and his search for integrity within himself; the flood that
ends one era but begins another; the preternatural vigor of the
town's last days contrasted with the inertia of the past and of
the unknown future. Brother Potts, dying, tries to hang on long
enough to conduct a memorial service, and Frog Eye, the swamp
rat, endures as a walking elegy of the almost forgotten past's survival.

Much intelligence and compassion underlie this assured novel.
Warren seems to have got himself more evenly, more compli-
catedly distributed among the characters than before. So the "argument" proceeds in concert (as in *Brother to Dragons*) and not
through one mind alone. Brad, like Jack Burden, goes home,
learns, but cannot stay; Jones, homesick but for nowhere in particular, goes off to happiness with Brad's sister, having asked
Brad, "How can one really define an accident . . . Unless . . . we
have already defined it?" Will and choice are resurgent, and Brad
reconciles himself to searching out — creating if necessary — "the
human necessity," a choice that enfranchises to the full "the human possibility." Something like hope obstinately perpetuates
itself.

No sharp-edged dogma emerges from these learned lessons. That
is not Warren's way. He remains true to his dictum that "the poet
wishes to indicate his vision has been earned" and that it "can
survive reference to the complexities and contradictions of experience." He often tangles his notions on ancestry, history, childhood, identity, will, violence, and grace into an opaque concep-
tual thicket. But he does make us think and he does undertake all the intellectual formulations that Hemingway avoids and
Faulkner turns into verbal skywriting. That is enough because
he also gives us action and the same stoical sense of doom as

they do. He knows life, is agonizedly involved in it, and his versatile searchings must strike a chord in every thoughtful reader. His dives into the dirt are more than an eccentric penance; they remind him, against all his hoping, of what is there: grief, wrath, injustice, blood, and evil. But, as he says in "Late Subterfuge," "Our grief can be endured" and "we have faith from evil bloometh good."

"There is no *you*," runs one sentence in *Flood*, "except in relation to all that unthinkableness that the world is." Warren shows what mind and heart can do with the unthinkable and, without pretending to understand, makes it thinkable-about, daring and exhorting others to approach it. That is the self-expending generosity of his achievement, the grandeur of its indignant impersonality, and also, in two senses, its only hope.

Norman Mailer

▼ W HEN Norman Mailer's *The Naked and the Dead* was published in 1948 it was all but universally acclaimed as a major novel marking the appearance of a new American writer destined for greatness. During the succeeding years, however, though Mailer had some warm defenders, the negative judgments among critics substantially outnumbered the positive as book after book appeared: novels, a play, collections of stories and poems, and gatherings of essays and other fugitive pieces. And yet, unlike most of his generation of novelists — the "war novelists" and the urban Jewish writers — Mailer continued to pursue a course of individualistic development and change which increasingly commanded the attention of peers, critics, and public; if his readers were sometimes baffled and frequently hostile they grew ever more interested. To use a somewhat Maileresque analogy, Mailer somewhat resembled, during his first twenty-five years as a professional writer, an overmatched boxer who, floored in the second round, springs back and sustains the fight far beyond expectations through variety and inventiveness of footwork and temporizing punches.

The match is still not decided. But however it finally comes out, there can be no doubt that the overmatched boxer will at the very least be remembered for his remarkable performance. Mailer's adversary during the 1950's and 1960's was that plodding but powerful opponent of idiosyncrasy and innovation which Eliot long ago dubbed "the tradition." Mailer had won his first round with a skillful and moving but conventional novel in the realist-naturalist mode. But most of his work since *The Naked and the Dead*, with the exception of a handful of stories from the late forties and early fifties, had been radically innovative in both substance and essential form without satisfying prevailing current conceptions of what constituted serious literary experimentation.

It was Mailer's apparent lack of artistic "seriousness" that troubled his serious critics most. When they were not either ridiculing or dismissing him, their main cry was the lamentation that a major talent was being wasted on trivial material or debased by sloppy craftsmanship. F. Scott Fitzgerald, whose work and career were in many ways similar to Mailer's, was criticized during his lifetime on much the same grounds. But what needed to be stressed in Mailer's case, as in Fitzgerald's, was that he was indeed a serious "experimentalist" writer, though an experimentalist of a different order than his moment in the history of "the tradition" allowed his public easily to recognize, accept, and understand.

James Joyce was the kind of experimentalist who applied innovative techniques to conventionally "realistic" fictional material. He sought out and found new routes to the old novelistic destinations. D. H. Lawrence, on the other hand, was the kind of writer who discovered new destinations — new materials and knowledge, and thus new obligations for fiction. His technical innovations, always less sophisticated, formal, and predominant than Joyce's, were functional consequences and by-products of what can only be called an experimentalist approach to the *subject matter* of fiction. In the course of writing *The Rainbow* and *Women in Love* Lawrence discovered, as he told Edward Garnett, that his subject

was no longer "the old stable *ego*" of human character, no longer
the "diamond" but rather the "carbon" which is the diamond's
elemental substance: "There is another *ego*, according to whose
action the individual is unrecognisable, and passes through, as it
were, allotropic states which it needs a deeper sense than any
we've been used to exercise, to discover are states of the same single
radically unchanged element. . . . Again I say, don't look for the
development of the novel to follow the lines of certain characters:
the characters fall into the form of some other rhythmic form, as
when one draws a fiddle-bow across a fine tray delicately sanded,
the sand takes lines unknown."

These metaphors describing the substantive nature of Lawrence's experimentation with both matter and form after *Sons
and Lovers* might as easily apply to Mailer, whose work after *The
Naked and the Dead* was similarly concerned with the "allotropy"
— the changing "rhythmic form" and "lines unknown" — of the
"carbon" of human character under complex stress. And like
Lawrence, Mailer seems to have become aware of his new departure only after standing away from the new work in hand to see
what he was doing and why he was doing it. While working on
Barbary Shore, he recalled in an interview, he found his Marxist
intellectual convictions continually distracted by compulsive preoccupations with "murder, suicide, orgy, psychosis." "I always
felt as if I were not writing the book myself." Other statements
by Mailer indicate that much the same creative pathology also
ruled the composition of *The Deer Park,* his third novel. The
personal stresses and anxieties that underlay the writing of these
two novels, and the stories that were spun off from them, found
confessional expression in Mailer's fourth book, a compilation of
fiction and nonfiction pieces with unifying connective additions
called *Advertisements for Myself,* which is the author's intense,
immediate, and unabashedly public reappraisal of himself, in
1959, as both artist and human being. Anxiety, compulsion, and
hints of psychosis had been the disruptive and only half-conscious
creative causes behind *Barbary Shore* and *The Deer Park.* Following the purgation and illumination represented by *Advertise-*

ments they become, in the later novels *An American Dream* and *Why Are We in Vietnam?* and the related volumes of nonfiction, the consciously molded substance of Mailer's hypertrophic images of life in America at mid-century.

A detailed account of this course of change and growth must be left for later. The important fact is that after several more books, plus a string of other accomplishments — including play producing, movie making, a fling at architectural design, and a great deal of moral, social, and political punditing, both on paper and on the hoof — the author of *The Naked and the Dead* emerged in the mid-sixties, despite his still uncertain reputation among serious literary people, as decidedly the most active and vivid public figure on the American literary scene.

Like his first published novel and stories, Mailer's early life was at least conventional enough not to foreshadow with any definiteness the panoply of idiosyncrasy that was to come later. Born January 31, 1923, in Long Branch, New Jersey, to Isaac and Fanny Mailer, Norman Mailer was raised and schooled in Brooklyn, graduating from Boys High School in 1939. While at Harvard, where he earned a B.S. degree in aeronautical engineering in 1943, Mailer began writing in earnest, contributing to the *Advocate*, working at his first two (and still unpublished) novels, and winning in 1941 *Story* magazine's annual college fiction contest. In 1944 he married his first wife and was drafted into the army, serving in the Pacific Theater until 1946. During the next year and a half, part of which was spent in Europe, where he was enrolled as a student at the Sorbonne, Mailer wrote *The Naked and the Dead*, which was published with immediate and dramatic success. The public purchased it in such numbers that it held at the top of the best seller lists for nearly three months. A movie contract was soon in the works; Lillian Hellman was slated to adapt it for the stage; and Sinclair Lewis was moved to dub Mailer "the greatest writer to come out of his generation."

Though Mailer himself once half-dismissed his first novel as a "conventional war novel," and though it was conceived and composed in a manner that Mailer was not to use again in a major

work, *The Naked and the Dead* is much more than a "war novel."
In the year of its publication Mailer put on record his view
that *The Naked and the Dead,* though cast in realist mold, is
"symbolic," expressive of "death and man's creative urge, fate,
man's desire to conquer the elements — all kinds of things you
never dream of separating and stating so baldly." And there is
no mistaking that the island itself, and the mountain at its center which Sergeant Croft commits himself and his platoon to con-
quering, acquire an almost Conradian symbolic significance in
the eyes of their chief beholders. Here is the soldiers' vision of
the setting of their destruction:

> It was a sensual isle, a Biblical land of ruby wines and golden
> sands and indigo trees. The men stared and stared. The island
> hovered before them like an Oriental monarch's conception of
> heaven, and they responded to it with an acute and terrible long-
> ing. It was a vision of all the beauty for which they had ever
> yearned, all the ecstasy they had ever sought. For a few minutes
> it dissolved the long dreary passage of the mute months in the
> jungle, without hope, without pride. If they had been alone
> they might have stretched out their arms to it.
> It could not last. Slowly, inevitably, the beach began to dissolve
> in the encompassing night. The golden sands grew faint, became
> gray-green, and darkened. The island sank into the water, and
> the tide of night washed over the rose and lavender hills. After a
> little while, there was only the gray-black ocean, the darkened sky,
> and the evil churning of the gray-white wake. Bits of phosphor-
> escence swirled in the foam. The black dead ocean looked like a
> mirror of the night; it was cold, implicit with dread and death.
> The men felt it absorb them in a silent pervasive terror. They
> turned back to their cots, settled down for the night, and shud-
> dered for a long while in their blankets.

In an interview three years later, just after completing *Barbary
Shore,* Mailer made this interesting disclosure about *The Naked
and the Dead*: "I don't think of myself as a realist. That terrible
word 'naturalism.' It was my literary heritage — the things I
learned from Dos Passos and Farrell. I took naturally to it, that's
the way one wrote a book. But I really was off on a mystic kick.
Actually — a funny thing — the biggest influence on *Naked* was

Moby Dick. . . . I was sure everyone would know. I had Ahab in it, and I suppose the mountain was Moby Dick. Of course, I also think the book will stand or fall as a realistic novel." This last qualification would also apply, of course, to *Moby Dick.* For Melville saw in the actual hazard and struggle of whaling, as Mailer did in war, the revealed pattern of the grandeur and tragedy of the whole human enterprise. Combat, for Mailer, is the chief means by which the higher laws of life become incarnate in human experience. War is his external subject matter in *The Naked and the Dead*; but his internal theme is the "crisis in human values" — identity, humanity, man, and the nature of their enemies in our time.

With war as the background typification of generalized external crisis, Mailer develops his internal themes by two principal means: first, extensively, through a number of Dos Passos-like diagnostic biographical portraits of a cross section of the fighting men; and second, intensively, through the protracted psychic struggle of mind and personality that takes place between Major General Cummings, the crypto-fascist commanding officer of the invading American forces, and his aide, a questioning liberal named Hearn. Both men have been shaped, though in opposite ways, by reaction against the privileged sterility of their midwestern bourgeois backgrounds. Cummings is the self-created prophet of a new totalitarianism who commands, in the name of his faith in order and authority, the breaking of men's spirits and the destruction of their wills. Hearn, bitter in his discontent, by nature a loner and yet tenderly humane in his half-guilty identification with the men he commands, is the uncertain voice of the liberal ideal of free man. Most of the fighting men are portrayed as already deprived, twisted, or stunted by the disintegrative and totalitarian forces and counterforces at work in their world, the forces whose contention has culminated in the war which now envelops them all. These men are the data of the dialectical contest which is taking place between Cummings and Hearn. That contest, the original of similar recurring patterns of individual contest, including sexual, in most of the rest of Mailer's work,

ends in a kind of draw. Hearn and his convictions are wasted
when he dies as a casual accident of war on an irrelevant mission.
And though the campaign is won, Cummings is in essence defeated because the agency of victory is not his active military
intelligence but rather a chain of chance accidents beyond his
control.

One notices not only that a true hero is lacking from the novel's epiclike action, but that his opposite, a forceful antagonist, is
lacking too. And yet a large enveloping energy has gathered,
thrust forward, and come through to significant issue. A great
spasm of nature, an inevitable motion of history, has superseded
the efficacies of individual men in a world that has begun to move
across Yeats's threshold of apocalypse where "the best lack all conviction" and "the worst / Are full of passionate intensity."

But at the core of this vast action, his presence stressing the
hero's absence, is Sergeant Croft. After the death of Hearn, he
leads the platoon on its doomed assault upon the mountain, dominating his men by the sheer intensity of his undefined "hunger"
for the mastery of life. A rough prototype of D. J. Jethroe of
Why Are We in Vietnam?, Croft has been sired by a tough Texas
dirt-farmer on a woman conventionally "weak . . . sweet and
mild." His father encourages in him a predator's taste for hunting, and he is by nature "mean." Why? "Oh, there are answers.
He is that way because of the corruption-of-the-society. He is that
way because the devil has claimed him for one of his own. It is
because he is a Texan; it is because he has renounced God." The
author interprets Croft in an aside as follows: "*He hated weakness and he loved practically nothing. There was a crude un-
formed vision in his soul but he was rarely conscious of it.*" This
embryonic "vision" is different from Hearn's superannuated liberalism and Cummings' authoritarian calculus because it is an
animal thing — an energy with fierce tendencies but no "form."
Croft represents the kinetic life-substance upon which such alternative ideologies as those of Hearn and Cummings must depend
for their unforeseeable realizations. In his irrational will and
passion, he is the human microcosm of the vast upsurge of in-

human forces in history which express themselves in the ironic irresolutions of the total action of *The Naked and the Dead.*

The Naked and the Dead, then, even if substantially conventional in form and style, is neveretheless one with the rest of Mailer's work in the apocalyptic energies of its vision. Those energies begin to find their requisite new form, and with that a new sort of voice, in the first of Mailer's "experimental" novels, *Barbary Shore,* published in 1951. *Barbary Shore* was the product, as Mailer has written in retrospect, of the author's "intense political preoccupation and a voyage in political affairs which began with the Progressive Party and has ended in the *cul-de-sac* (at least so far as action is concerned) of [his] being an anti-Stalinist Marxist who feels that war is probably inevitable." The omniscient authorial point of view of *The Naked and the Dead* is abandoned in *Barbary Shore* for first-person narrative, which is to continue as the preferred narrative form for Mailer's books thereafter. ("Memory is the seed of narrative, yeah," says D. J. Jethroe, narrator of *Why Are We in Vietnam?*) The book becomes, thus, an adaptation of *Bildungsroman*; its narrative substance is the hero's education for life in our time — or re-education, since he is suffering from amnesia somewhat inexplicitly induced by war and the breakdown of traditional political idealism. The setting is a Brooklyn rooming house operated by a sexually promiscuous and morally neuter proprietress named, with an irony appropriate to her role as life's presiding norm, Guinevere. In this setting, the case histories of three roomers are presented: an impotent, betrayed, and self-betraying idealist of the old revolutionary left; his demon, a stolid and perverted interrogator for the rightist "totalitarian" establishment; and a mad Cassandra-like girl whose derangement is a consequence and expression of history, and whom, as an exacerbated mirroring of his own distressed psyche, the hero half loves.

The heaviness and inertia of the novel — its garrulous expositions of ideological conflict and the dazed passivity and blankness of Lovett, the hero-narrator, before all he sees and hears — is only a little relieved when at the end he sprints into an inchoate future with a mysterious small object entrusted to his keeping by the failed leftist before his death. The precise nature of the object, which is hotly coveted by the furies of the right, is never specified. But what it means is perfectly clear. It is a symbol or talisman of the sacred idea of man free and whole; and in the moment of the narrator's active commitment to it in the face of the terrible odds and enemies ranged against it, and now against him as well, we are meant to feel that it has taken on the existential power of life itself.

Even this early in his career — after only two novels — it was clear that Mailer's imagination, unique in his generation, was cast in the epic mold. As bard and prophet to an age in which history is at odds with nature or "destiny," he was telling in a fevered voice of the permutations of the heroic imperative in a post-heroic world. His theme was the struggle of life and form against death and chaos. But his subject matter was history. And as he pursued the theme of the ideal through the matter of the actual he made a discovery: in our time the sources and resources of life have shifted, to use the shorthand of Mailer's own symbology, from "God" to "the devil." The vision of life at stalemate in *The Naked and the Dead* and *Barbary Shore* is explained by this discovery, a discovery whose fullness of realization in a changed imaginative vision comes clear in *The Deer Park*, published in 1955.

Desert D'Or, a resort of the rich and powerful modeled on Palm Springs, is the principal setting of *The Deer Park*. It is a denatured interior world of concrete and plastic, of harsh light and blinding shadow, thrown up in defiance of the encircling desert outside. This pattern of division between natural and unnatural that is established in the setting extends also to the characters, in whom desire and will, feeling and thought, the wellsprings of motive and motive's fulfillment in action, have been stricken apart. The natural current of the life-force has somehow been broken. And the inhabitants of this world of trauma and aftermath constitute a gallery of parodies of the human image ranging from the absurd to the piteous to the monstrous. They are,

as Mailer wrote in a note to his adaptation of *The Deer Park* for
the stage, "in hell."

Sergius O'Shaugnessy, the hero-narrator of *The Deer Park*, is
both an orphan and, like Lovett of *Barbary Shore*, a symbolic
waif of historical disaster. His surrogate home in the air force
and fulfillment in the exercise of the war pilot's impersonal skills
of destruction have been snatched from him in a sudden accidental revelation that he is a killer: "I realized that . . . I had
been busy setting fire to a dozen people, or two dozen, or had it
been a hundred?" In recoil from such horrors of the "real world"
he suffers a breakdown, is discharged, and on the winnings from
a prodigiously lucky gambling venture, he comes to Desert D'Or,
retreat of the gods of the "imaginary world," to rest, drift, gaze,
and spend. A blank slate to be written on, an empty vessel to be
filled, and — his vision of the burned flesh of his victims having
rendered him sexually impotent — a low flame needing fuel, Sergius O'Shaugnessy is the framing consciousness of an ample world
crowded with people exhibiting versions of his own predicament.
Among the most important of these are Charles Francis Eitel, a
gifted and formerly powerful Hollywood director, and Marion
Faye, dope pusher, impressario of call girls, and connoisseur of
the moral nuances of sadism. Both of these men become friends
of O'Shaugnessy and objects of his studious moral attention.

Eitel has had a golden age, a brief heroic period in the thirties
when as a true artist he made courageous movies on contemporary social themes, and when as a man of integrity he put his
life on the line in behalf of the fated struggle for democracy in
Spain. In reflexive response to the corruption of integrity which
has overtaken his art as he has risen to power in Hollywood,
Eitel rebuffs a congressional investigating committee seeking
from him incriminating political testimony against his colleagues.
In consequence, the industry blackballs him; and his loss of power
and identity in the "imaginary" world is measured in personal
terms by his loss of potency as both artist and lover. This sequen-
tial pattern of aspiration, action, corruption, moral illumination,
renunciation, exile, and impotence precisely parallels the pattern

of Sergius' life. Eitel is the distillate of the best values of the past
by which Sergius has been fathered and orphaned, and for Sergius, consequently, the question of Eitel's destiny — the question
of his potential for rebirth and self-renewal — has crucial moral
significance.

Eitel stumbles upon a "second chance" in the form of Elena
Esposito, and he muffs it. Another man's castoff, she is soiled, tawdry, and simple. She is a poor dancer and a worse actress, and her
manners are absurd. And yet she has the dignity and courage, and
finally the beauty, of a being wholly natural. Eitel's affair with
her becomes the nourishing ground of a new life for him. His
sexual potency is restored, and with it his creative potency as he
begins to work on a script which he imagines will be the redemption of his integrity as artist and man. But this new access of life
fills him with fear; it is the stirring in him of the heroic imperative, with its attendant commitments to solitary battle, lonely
journeyings in the unknown, and the risks of failure and defeat.
The doors of Hollywood begin to open again, and the thrones
and dominations of the "imaginary" world solicit his return: all
he must do is confess and recant before the committee, and he
may pass back through those doors. Half because of fear, half because of old habit, Eitel takes the easy way of surrender, shunning
the hazardous alternatives (as Elena, significantly, does not) represented by those dark angels of life and truth, Don Beda, high
priest of satyrism and orgy, and Marion Faye, the hipster prophet
of criminal idealism. His harvest is the life-in-death of security
through compromise, the corruption of his script and his talent,
and eventual marriage to a broken and exhausted Elena, which is
possible now that they are no longer "wedded" in a sacramental
sense.

Elena is a noble figure — defeated, but honorably so, in her
fated but heroic contest with time and what Hardy calls "crass
casualty." Eitel's enemies have been lesser ones — history and social circumstance — and his defeat is pitiful rather than noble,
because he has "sold out." But he has at least the saving grace of
his ironic intelligence, which enables him to understand, when

she proudly refuses his first offer of marriage, the principle of Elena's nobility: "the essence of spirit . . . was to choose the thing which did not better one's position but made it more perilous." Later on, when she has no more resources of refusal and he nourishes upon her defeat by "sacrificing" himself in marrying her, he understands his own corresponding cowardice: "there was that law of life so cruel and so just which demanded that one must grow or else pay more for remaining the same."

Eitel is Mailer's version of the traditional hero in his last historical incarnation. Vision, passion, and courage have dwindled in Eitel to intelligence, compassion, and guilt — the "cement" of the world, as Marion Faye contemptuously labels the last two, which binds men, enfeebles them, and turns them into spiritual "slobs." Eitel's very strengths are weaknesses, his virtues are faults, in a world where the apocalyptic beasts of anxiety and dread are raging in prisons of compromise and falsehood. And as the novel draws to its close and Eitel begins to fade into the penumbra of Sergius O'Shaugnessy's memorializing imagination, we are aware that the passing of the man is also the passing of the values he represented. Flanked by comic Lulu Meyers, a movie sex goddess who on impulse marries for "love" rather than career, and by tragic Marion Faye whose anarch's code of black moral reason leads him behind prison bars, the now enlightened Sergius is the chief chalice-bearer of new human values. He becomes a bullfighter, stud, and teacher of both arts. And he begins to write, his books presumably fired by the existential perils and ecstasies of combat and sexuality. Though the novel ends on a cheerful note of metaphysical exhilaration, Sergius, both as a character and as an archetype of new styles of human value, is vague and inchoate as well as faintly absurd. Sergius has survived all sorts of traumas and temptations and come through to freedom, but he is not very much more fully realized as an exemplar of new values in action than was his predecessor, Lovett. He has come to terms with the world that has wounded him, and like the good Emersonian "fatalists" that all such Mailer heroes are, he affirms it as his destined inheritance from nature and history. But neither he nor his author has yet found the requisite life-style, the new heroic mold through which to turn understanding and affirmation into creative, perhaps redemptive action.

Life threatened in our time by the forces of death is Mailer's subject everywhere. When he writes as a realist, as in *The Naked and the Dead*, life is stalemated and defeated by the forces of death. In the next two novels the intensities of anxiety and dread underlying Mailer's subject matter begin to dominate the rational, circumjacent forms of the realist, distorting them in the direction of the expressionistic and the surreal. And with this modification of form comes a coordinate modification of the heroes in whom the issue of the life-death struggle is finally centered. The narrator-hero of *Barbary Shore*, for whom the action encompassed by his consciousness is an elaborately instructive morality play, in the end escapes paralysis and spiritual death. The similarly educated narrator-hero of *The Deer Park* not only escapes but, as he bids fond farewell to the memories of the defeated and destroyed, discerns in the very chemistry of the disease and decomposition all around him the flicker and spur of new possibilities for life. "Think of Sex as Time," says "God" in a final dialogue with Sergius, "and Time as the connection of new circuits."

Barbary Shore and *The Deer Park*, both of them fictional investigations of the operative laws of death and endings, are novels that end with beginnings. Mailer's next novel, *An American Dream*, published in 1965, is in every way an extension and intensification of the manner and substance of its two predecessors. It begins, significantly, with an ending: the hero saves himself from spiritual death by committing a murder that restores him to life, action, growth. Seen in relation to *An American Dream*, the two preceding novels have the look of a single imaginative action of a precursory nature: a complex psycho-dramatic "sloughing-off," to use Lawrence's terms in *Studies in Classic American Literature*, of the "old consciousness" of an outworn idealistic humanism in preparation for a "new consciousness" requisite for survival and significant life in a psychotic world bordering on apocalypse and yearning toward death. The experiential educations of Mikey Lovett and Sergius O'Shaugnessy in *Barbary Shore* and *The Deer Park* are preparations of this "new consciousness" for active engagement with the world. Steve Rojack and D. J. Jethroe — respectively heroes of *An American Dream* and *Why Are We in Vietnam?* — are the beneficiaries of this process. Rojack, in a moment of freeing impulse, murders his rich, preternaturally domineering, death-threatening wife Deborah, a "bitch-goddess" of American power, and the summation of the death-force of historical fate. The charge of this self-galvanizing destruction of his immediate enemy propels him into action, turning fear, fatigue, and despair into a redemptive energy of desperation. With a courage nourished on the ultimate dread, the dread of death, he runs a varied course of triumphs — besting the sexual enmity of a cold nymphomaniac, the hunting wile of the police, the competition of a Negro stud of legendary sexual prowess, and an engulfing sea of guilt and self-doubt summoned by Deborah's father, Barney Kelly. He even finds love along the way, with a tender, used, and charming cabaret singer named Cherry. A composite of American realities like Deborah, she is Deborah's opposite and complement, a plucky victim of the forces of which Deborah is the emblematic goddess and proprietress. At the end Rojack is still running — his roles and costumes of war hero, congressman, professor, television personality, and husband of a socialite left far behind — now toward the darker and simpler challenges of the jungles of Guatemala and Yucatán.

In *Why Are We in Vietnam?* (1967), D. J. Jethroe has already reached his Guatemala and Yucatán. High on pot, the prose of the Marquis de Sade and William Burroughs, and the cheerfully psychotic inspiration that he may be the voice of a "Harlem spade" imprisoned in the body of the son of a white Dallas tycoon, he tells the story of how he got that way. It is an initiation story (new style) as *An American Dream* was a new-style story of sacrifice and redemption. The initiation, product of a hunting "safari" to Alaska with his father Rusty, D. J.'s best friend Tex, and assorted guides and associates, has two phases, both of them

involving radical divestments and ultimate tests of courage. In
the first phase, D. J. breaks spiritually with his father when, out
of habits of competitive vanity and self-justification, his father
claims the grizzly bear that D. J. has mortally wounded, violating
not only the father-son bond as reinforced by the hunt (stalking
their dangerous quarry D. J. sees himself and his father as "war
buddies") but also the sacred blood bond between killer and
prey. Thinks D. J., "Final end of love of one son for one father."
The second phase of the initiation, fruit of the alienation and
frustration sown by the first, is the twenty-four-hour northward
foray of D. J. and Tex, alone and without guns or instruments,
into the wild heart of the Brooks Range. In an ecstasy of fear and
trembling they witness a pageant of savageries — wolf, eagle, bear,
caribou, and moose, the figments of natural life locked in struggle
with death — culminating in a cosmic eruption of the Northern
Lights that is so magnificent and intense as to bring them to the
border of orgy and fratricide: "they were twins, never to be as
lovers again, but killer brothers, armed by something, prince of
darkness, lord of light, they did not know." They make a bond
in an exchange of blood, "the deep beast whispering, Fulfill my
will, go forth and kill." At the end, D. J., now eighteen, looks
beyond the Brooks Range of his initiatory "Guatemala and Yucatán" toward his mature destiny: "Hot damn, Vietnam."

    D. J. is the voice of the anxieties and compulsions that have
accumulated beneath the patterns of America's history and exploded at last in the manifest violence and chaos of its present.
In the electric North, which is the voltaic pile of a continent's
repressed, distorted, and perverted life-energies, he has faced
Demogorgon, and he comes back metamorphosed, a rudely
American voice of bardic ecstasy and prophecy. Completing the
journey of transformation only begun by Lovett and Sergius
O'Shaugnessy, D. J. and Steve Rojack have successfully tracked
the power of life, thieved by a conspiracy of history with nature
from its traditional home in the light, to its new home in darkness. In accomplishing this, they become exemplars of that "new

consciousness" requisite to continuing life's ancient battle against death in a psychotic world bordering on apocalyptic crisis.

Richard Poirier, identifying Mailer with Eliot's vision, sees him as similarly spurred by the "de-creative" aspects of creation. But if this is true, Mailer is even more closely related to Lawrence, who in the voice of Rupert Birkin of *Women in Love* discerned among the "marsh-flowers" of "destructive creation" certain blossoms that while they were spawned by the all-enveloping historical process of "universal dissolution" were not *"fleurs du mal,"* but rather "roses, warm and flamy." Lawrence himself was one of these exotic exceptions. And so is Mailer. If the roots of both writers necessarily nourish upon the food of darkness, the blossoms produced are bright with the warm colors of life, and grow toward the light. In Lawrence the blossom is the "man who has come through," the separate natural self released through the death of the conventional social self into a living and changing "star-equilibrium" with the otherness of nature and woman. In Mailer it is all this and a bit more: history, impelled by the American dream turned to nightmare, is a third constituent of the otherness, and the reborn self becomes an "existential hero."

Advertisements for Myself (1959) and *The Presidential Papers* (1963) are large and various but nevertheless unified collections of pieces, mostly nonfiction, written during the dozen years following Mailer's tentative effort and partial failure to achieve a new form in *Barbary Shore.* As books principally about their author, *Advertisements for Myself* and *The Presidential Papers* taken together have the shape, like *Barbary Shore* and *The Deer Park,* of a single action, the complex and difficult action of "sloughing off" the "old consciousness." "The existential hero," first coming to full life in *An American Dream* and *Why Are We in Vietnam?,* is Mailer's realization of this new style of consciousness. And *Advertisements for Myself* and *The Presidential Papers* are the record of its gestation in the mind of its creator, and of the large and small deaths prerequisite to its coming to birth.

Mailer uses his own "personality," he tells us, as the "armature" of *Advertisements* — an image aptly descriptive of both its

form and its impact. The reciprocal emotions of dread and determination whirl at the center of the book, as its author frankly
appraises, at mid-career, his qualified victories and larger defeats
during more than a decade of trying to live up to his potentials
and ambitions as a man and writer. The pieces collected in *Advertisements* — stories, essays, and poems; polemics, meditations,
and interviews; fragments of plays-in-progress and novels-to-be —
are the measure of the worth of the life being lived, the substance
of the tale being told. It is a tale, like Fitzgerald's in "The Crack-
Up" essays, of early success, subsequent failure and demoraliza-
tion, and the reflexive counterthrust of self-regeneration and re-
creation. *The Naked and the Dead*, which catapulted him to sudden and youthful fame, had, as he tells us in *Advertisements*, been
"easy to write." But nothing would be so easy again, for this
success was the beginning of his "existentialism," which was
"forced upon [him]," as he says, by his finding himself "prominent and empty," a "personage," at twenty-five. He must justify
the prominence and fill the emptiness. With such heroic models
before him as the life-style of Hemingway and the oeuvre of
Malraux, he thrusts experimentally into new territory with *Barbary Shore*, "the first of the existentialist novels in America." The
hostility and ridicule with which it is greeted in 1951 knock
him down. Deflated, ill, and anxious, he turns to writing "respectable" short stories in the earlier manner and jaunty socio-political
polemics for such magazines as *Partisan Review* and *Dissent* (of
which he also becomes an editor). All this is a sort of distraction
and temporizing in the face of the big comeback, the planned co-
lossal counterpunch which might dazzle the world with a star-
fall and revelations: a projected eight-volume novel of cosmic
proportions whose framing consciousness, a minor man and an
artist *manqué* named Sam Slovoda, has an alter ego dream-hero
named Sergius O'Shaugnessy. The great work hovering in the
wings refuses to emerge. But two related fragments appear, both
of them again in the new manner: the story "The Man Who
Loved Yoga," which is to be the great work's prologue, and a

protracted but relevant detour from the main route, a novel called *The Deer Park*.

The story of the vicissitudes accompanying *The Deer Park*'s publication and reception, most of it recounted in *Advertisements*, could itself be the stuff of a novel. The bad reception of *Barbary Shore* in 1951 and Mailer's divorce in 1952 are elements of a continuing pattern of gathering personal distress which characterize the years of *The Deer Park*'s composition. These distresses reach a penultimate crisis when *The Deer Park*, already in page proof, is suddenly held up by its publisher: Stanley Rinehart finds in it something unacceptably obscene. Just recently Mailer has accepted the challenge of writing an essay called "The Homosexual Villain" at the invitation of the magazine *One*, an undertaking which has blown up a "log jam of accumulated timidities and restraints" in him. Partially as a consequence, he refuses to make the change in *The Deer Park* for Rinehart, and the deal is off. The next ten weeks, at the end of which *The Deer Park* will be accepted by Putnam after refusal by several other houses, is a time of crisis for Mailer. He has undergone another death — the death of certain illusions about himself as "a figure in the landscape," and about the "honor" of publishers and writers in the American present — and feels himself becoming a "psychic outlaw."

Drawing his powers now from forays into the worlds of jazz, Harlem, and marijuana, he sees that the style of *The Deer Park* is wrong for the narrator he wants to create — it is too poetic, in the vein of Fitzgerald's Nick Carraway. He begins to rewrite from page proof, thirsting for the kind of self-redemptive success which would change the world a little, and at the same time dreading the possibility of a bad reception and low sales. The revised *The Deer Park*, once published, is only a "middling success." And Mailer measures the quality of its success not only by sales and reviews but by the glimpses of possibility that have begun to emerge for the harried author with his last-minute impetus to rewrite it. Though tentative and incomplete, the accomplished changes adumbrate a new hero: the tender, wounded, and de-

tached observer of the earlier version has begun to turn into a
Sergius O'Shaugnessy who is not only "good" but also "ambitious"; a Sergius who, instead of virtuously spurning Hollywood's
offer to film his life, might have taken the bait in a spirit of adventure and run it to some perilous triumph. The published
book, its author laments, is but a hint of what might have been:
the masterpiece in Mailer's generation equivalent to *The Sun
Also Rises* in Hemingway's. As a "middling success," *The Deer
Park* represents to its author his gross failure to bid on "the biggest hand" he had ever held, and a discovery that after all he
hadn't the magic to "hasten the time of apocalypse."

But even so, this fumble, this failure, is no dead end. Like the
emptiness of his success with *The Naked and the Dead,* and the
fullness of his failure with *Barbary Shore,* it is a threshold to possibility. He has a vision, now, of what he must try to be and do
as a writer, and of how considerable are the odds ranged
against him. And like Sergius, who takes up bullfighting at the
end of *The Deer Park,* he moves directly into the arena of the
world's action as a matador of existential polemics — a rebel general of "Hip" — in the pages of *The Village Voice,* which he
helped found in 1955. Though a fresh excursion into novel writing is delayed by these side trips into journalism, *The Village
Voice* pieces are important as snapshots of the "new" Mailer soon
fully to emerge as exemplar and spokesman of the needed "new
consciousness." His first important effort in the new mode is the
essay *The White Negro,* written in 1957 and first published, by
City Lights, in 1958 (it was reprinted in *Advertisements*).

A speculative psycho-cultural essay on the modern predicament, *The White Negro* is a paradigm of the vision, the ideas, the
motifs and symbols that will shape all of Mailer's future work in
whatever form. The Hipster refuses to capitulate to the repressive
denaturing, dehumanizing death-force of a "totalitarian" society.
But because he is active — unlike the bourgeois "beat" who with-
draws and passively sublimates in the surrogate quasi-life of song,
flowers, meditation, hallucinogens, and "love" — he is confronted
by the immediate dangers of physical violence and death. Like

the black he is an *uncitizen* (hence the label "white Negro") and danger is the medium of his life. Pleasure is his end; energy, courage, and wile are his means. The dynamic poise of his life-style implies the constitution, in microcosm, of a whole culture: decorums of manners, dress, language; an ethic; an aesthetic; even, finally, a metaphysic and a theology. The philosophy of the Hip, Mailer reflects, is the formed insight of a "radical humanist" "brooding" on the energizing phenomenon of the black revolution in contemporary America.

The Hipster is, of course, only one of many possible realizations of the "new consciousness" of which Mailer is the prophet. He is but one version of the idea of the existential hero, whose incarnation not only *may* but *must* be limitless and unpredictable. For the existential hero is the Dostoevskian underground man come aboveground into the Tolstoian mainstream of history. It is not known what he will be there, only that he will *do* — his being a function of his acting, rather than the other way around. He is a Sisyphus released from the stone of his dogged abstract commitment, a Hemingway galvanized into new life by the very terrors that threaten paralysis and death. Evading the fateful impasse between heroic "intactness" and human "completeness" that destroyed Fitzgerald's Dick Diver, he is a vital synthesis of the polar values of self-control and spontaneity represented in *The Deer Park* by Marion Faye, the black Puritan of moral scruple, and Don Beda, the rosy orgiast of the senses. Extensively educated in anguish, division, and impotence, Sergius O'Shaugnessy has just touched the regenerative power of that synthesis when the book of his salvation closes. The same efflorescence in his creator, which achieves full bloom in *The Presidential Papers*, seems to have been nourished by a similar curriculum, as recounted in *Advertisements*, of prior defeats and despairs. *Advertisements*, in contrast to its successor, *The Presidential Papers*, is a book in the mode of elegy, recording in lyric regret and anger the difficult passing of romantic idealism and the death of youth's illusions. But *Advertisements* also has elegy's *dramatic* mode, being shaped as a total action embodying patterns of divestment and purgation which yield up at last a clear prospect of fresh possibilities: "Tomorrow to fresh woods, and pastures new." *The White Negro*, which Mailer tells us was written in the depths of "fear that I was no longer a writer," turns out to be the bright and central song of a "man who has come through." It is after all, he sees, one of his "best things." In it, and in the pair of stories in the "existential" mode, "The Time of Her Time" and "Advertisements for Myself on the Way Out," published at the close of *Advertisements*, can be found, as he says, "the real end of this muted autobiography of the near-beat adventurer who was myself."

The end of a life, whether well or badly lived, Mailer writes in *Advertisements*, is "seed." The "seed" of the agonies survived by the hero of *Advertisements* is *The Presidential Papers*, in which the author steps forth, re-created as public man and existentialist prophet, to address America and its leaders on the exigent realities of the age.

The "armature" of this book is not the author's personality in crisis, but rather an *idea* — the idea of "existential politics": "Existential politics is simple. It has a basic argument: if there is a strong ineradicable strain in human nature, one must not try to suppress it or anomaly, cancer and plague will follow. Instead one must find an art into which it can grow." In *The Presidential Papers* the pattern of personal crisis and salvation of self traced in *Advertisements* has been transmuted, by the chemistry of analogy so characteristic of Mailer's imagination, into the public terms of politics and history. But though the drama is now public rather than private, Mailer's self is no less central to the action. In the preface to *The Presidential Papers* he defines his role: to infuse John F. Kennedy, whose glamour and magnetism give him the potential of an "existential hero" in the arena of politics, with the requisite "existential" political consciousness. Mailer's commitment here is to steal back, for the languishing forces of "God," some of the energies of life which have passed over to the forces of darkness. But because history has moved so far on the downward path of de-creation, he must do it as a kind of un-

dercover agent: he must perforce speak as a "devil." His first success as a metaphysical Robin Hood is his brilliant *Esquire* piece
on Kennedy's nomination by the 1960 Democratic convention,
which was written, despite his candidate's moribund "liberal"
program, for the purpose of getting this rare man, so blessed
"with a face," elected. (For it was Mailer's belief that this essay,
a product of his "Faustian" pact with "Mephisto," was the gen-
erative cause of Kennedy's small plurality over Nixon in the
election.) The rest of *The Presidential Papers* is a contemporaneous critique (with the blood, sweat, and tears of immediate response staining the pages) of "the Kennedy years," that ambiguous and perhaps despair-making historical return on its author's
original existential wager.

Of all the fine pieces following, perhaps the most memorable
is the essay on the Patterson-Liston fight, subtitled "Death." This
essay is many things: It is a skillful piece of evocative journalism
about an actual event; a symbolist's reading of the forces at war
in the submerged psyche of America; a strange, oblique prophecy,
through a poet's analysis of the attrition and inevitable doom of
the spirit of American liberal idealism, of Kennedy's assassina-
tion. It is also a gaily profound exploration of the absurdity, and
perhaps the peril, awaiting the writer as performing tragic-
comedian whose ambition is to ride at the same time both bright
Pegasus and the dark horses of wrath. But if the end — or "seed" —
of life is life itself, then that effort must be made in spite of all
hazard: "To believe the impossible may be won," Mailer writes
elsewhere in *The Presidential Papers*, "creates a strength from
which the impossible may be attacked." And in our time, though
the memory of "God" and the light may shape ultimate heroic
purpose, the hero draws nourishment for his "humanism" (a favorite recurring word of Mailer's) from the devil's realm, ventur-
ing ever more deeply — as Mailer does in the barbarous poems
and scatological dialogues collected in *Cannibals and Christians*
— into the territories of darkness.

Cannibals and Christians, published in 1966, is not so good a
book as its two omnibus predecessors, though it has its bright

spots, such as the piece on Goldwater's nomination and the temptation it wakens in its author to ride this newest bandwagon of the devil. The drama of self-discovery and re-creation, which gave unity to the brilliance and variety of *Advertisements* and *Papers,* is slowed and muffled in *Cannibals* by the didactic accents of the guru who gazes upon a vision that is cooling toward dogma and repetition. But it is perhaps understandable that the imaginative breakthrough represented by *An American Dream* should be followed by a somewhat studious contemplation of the truths revealed, for something more than half of the stuff of *Cannibals* was written shortly after *Dream.* Mailer himself seems to be aware of the condition. Written in a time of "plague" and under a lurid cloud of apocalyptic expectations, the collection is concerned with themes, he says, more appropriate to a novel. He feels again the impulse to "go back to that long novel," announced several years back but still unwritten. *Cannibals,* he reflects, may be the last such collection for a while. Of course, it was not the last.

After *Cannibals,* in addition to publishing *Why Are We in Vietnam?* Mailer produced off Broadway his dramatization of *The Deer Park,* a crisply successful play in which a much clearer and more effective Sergius O'Shaugnessy was purchased at the expense of the novel's richly internal realization of Eitel and Elena. He also directed, produced, and starred in three full-length "existential" films of his own conceiving. The requisite honors began, belatedly, to come his way: in 1967 he was elected to the National Institute of Arts and Letters. And in October of the same year, this author of twelve books, father of six children, and veteran of four wives — "heroines all," he once gallantly affirmed — proved his continued interest in the public life of his time by getting himself arrested, jailed, and fined for an act of civil disobedience in the great Washington demonstrations against the war in Vietnam.

The immediate result of this experience was *The Armies of the Night,* published in the spring of 1968, a kind of autobiographical novel with a protagonist called "Mailer" who is at once an absurd citizen of "technology-land" in crisis and a bard of the bright dream that lies behind the thickening miasmas of the be-

trayed and perishing republic. It is unquestionably one of Mailer's best books — passionate, humorous, acutely intelligent, and as always, eloquent in its empathy with the drift of history. It has new riches in it, too, of a more incidental kind, such as a gallery of sharply intimate verbal cartoons, highlighted with the reflected pigments of Mailer's own uniquely anxious self-image, of such primary men of the 1960's as Robert Lowell, Dwight Macdonald, and Paul Goodman. But most striking of all are its undercurrents of a softer emotion, a new tenderness for life that lets the author muse warmly along the way on his troubled love for his wife, his children, his mythic America. There is even a touch of nostalgic religious craving in it, a small recurring thirst for "Christ." But though the texture of feeling is more varied, the old Mailer, familiarly gravid with the epic furies and ambitions of a diminutive Brooklyn Achilles, still prevails:

Mailer, looking back, thought bitter words he would not say: "You, Lowell, beloved poet of many, what do you know of the dirt and the dark deliveries of the necessary? What do you know of dignity hard-achieved, and dignity lost through innocence, and dignity lost by sacrifice for a cause one cannot name. What do you know about getting fat against your will, and turning into a clown of an arriviste baron when you would rather be an eagle or a count, or rarest of all, some natural aristocrat from these damned democratic states? No, the only subject we share, you and I, is that species of perception which shows that if we are not very loyal to our unendurable and most exigent inner light, then some day we may burn. How dare you condemn me! . . . How dare you scorn the explosive I employ?"

Lowell falls backward at this moment in the narrative, a noble Hector going bump on his head, as if toppled by the lightning bolt of his adversary's thought. Though *The Armies of the Night* is tempered with new softnesses and warmths, such passages would deter one from concluding too easily that Mailer might have been getting ready to write his hymn of reconciliation — his *Tempest* or "Lapis Lazuli," his *Billy Budd* or *Old Man and the Sea.*

Good as *The Armies of the Night* is, and prolific in a variety of

media as Mailer has been since its publication, the great opus so long ago announced remains unachieved. Were such varied and frequent detours from the high road of novel writing threatening, at this prime of his creative life, the ultimate dissipation of Mailer's talent as a major writer? This already familiar question was raised yet again by an interviewer in *Playboy* for January 1968. Mailer answered that the pattern of his career was dictated by his instinctive feeling that "the best way to grow was not to write one novel after another but to move from activity to activity, a notion that began with Renaissance man." He did not mention the example of Milton, but he might as well have. Then, coming down off the high horse of the moment's rhetoric, he added genially, "It's not my idea, after all."

He was, of course, right both about himself and about "the tradition." With the romantic movement the imaginative writer became alienated from public life. Next, under the neoclassical reactive pressure of modernist formalism, he became in a sense alienated even from his work — which was not to be an utterance but an object, a product of the "impersonal" operations of imagination. With this background in view, it is clear that Mailer's uniqueness as a mid-century writer lay in his conscious cultivation, in the manner of Yeats, of a dynamic interrelation between his art and his life-style. Intensely himself, he was nevertheless the writer reborn in the dimension of public man. Engorged with the inclusive themes of his age and his nation, his work has been nevertheless deeply personal. "I've been working on one book most of my life," he told the *Playboy* interviewer. "Probably since I started with *Barbary Shore*, certainly with and since *The Deer Park*, I've been working on one book." As he tells us in the introduction to *Cannibals and Christians*, he is, like Lawrence, Henry Miller, and Hemingway, writing "one continuing book . . . of [his] life and the vision of [his] existence." He might also have mentioned Fitzgerald whom he resembles in this respect as well as in many others, including his sense of the integral relation between the moral health of the artist and the quality of his art conceived as "style." "A really good style," said Mailer in his

Paris Review interview of 1964, as if in echo of a dozen similar testimonies by Fitzgerald, "comes only when a man has become as good as he can be. Style is character."

As late as the early sixties, fairly literate people — often critics and teachers — were still saying that though Mailer certainly had a novelist's gift he "couldn't write." He was in their minds a kind of James Jones who, with no appropriate arsenal of sophistication, had gone adventuring into frontier territories of the imagination and was never heard of again. "I can't read him any more," they would say; and it was at least evident that these people who made themselves responsible for keeping up with Bellow and Malamud, Styron and Barth — current writers favored with recognition by the critical establishment — *weren't* reading him, whether or not they *couldn't* read him. To them he was at once nuttier than D. H. Lawrence, dumber than Sinclair Lewis, artistically more unselective than Thomas Wolfe, these faults clumsily wrapped in a style as undistinguished as Dreiser's. Because they weren't reading him it wasn't possible to argue with any hope of success that his "beliefs" were the poetical vehicles of a metaphysician's speculative insights; that he was the only important novelist on the American scene who was also an authentic and sophisticated intellectual; that if he was temperamentally the inclusive artist, he was also deftly capable of the lean and compact virtuoso performance; and that as a "stylist" his brilliancy was matched by his variety and range. An example from *The Armies of the Night*:

There was an aesthetic economy to symbolic gestures — you must not repeat yourself. Arrested once, TV land would accept him (conceivably) as a man willing to stand up for his ideas; get busted twice on the same day, and they would view him as a freak-out panting for arrest. (Mailer's habit of living — no matter how unsuccessfully — with his image, was so ingrained by now, that like a dutiful spouse he was forever consulting his better half.)

The preceding is Mailer as incisive stylist, cutting an idea down to the gem of epigram at its center. The following is Mailer as

progenitive stylist, pushing out from the central root-and-trunk idea a branch-bud-and-leaf exfoliation of confirmatory images:

It is the wisdom of a man who senses death within him and gambles that he can cure it by risking his life. It is the therapy of the instinct, and who is so wise as to call it irrational? Before he went into the Navy, Kennedy had been ailing. Washed out of Freshman year at Princeton by a prolonged trough of yellow jaundice, sick for a year at Harvard, weak already in the back from an injury at football, his trials suggest the self-hatred of a man whose resentment and ambition are too large for his body. Not everyone can discharge their furies on an analyst's couch, for some angers can be relaxed only by winning power, some rages are sufficiently monumental to demand that one try to become a hero or else fall back into that death which is already within the cells. But if one succeeds, the energy aroused can be exceptional. . . . One thinks of that three-mile swim with the belt in his mouth and McMahon holding it behind him. There are pestilences which sit in the mouth and rot the teeth — in those five hours how much of the psyche must have been remade, for to give vent to the bite in one's jaws and yet use that rage to save a life: it is not so very many men who have the apocalyptic sense that heroism is the First Doctor. . . . With such a man in office the myth of the nation would again be engaged . . .

Mailer's style is a style of eddying gusts and pointed audible silences textured on a background of the musing, ruminating, wondering human voice. Voice is the medium of his style, wit and amplification its chief instruments of artistic control. Using dynamic interplay of the reciprocal rhetorics of incision and proliferation, Mailer's style intends through rhetorical implosion and explosion of the facts and patterns of common life, to force a new vision upon the reader, to disclose to him the submerged realities of his experience — to transform him, galvanize him, free him to become the vehicle of apocalypse. It is predictable that an imagination so metaphysically ambitious as Mailer's should generate fictions which, though open-ended and loosely shaped, contain a dense internal unity of interlocking analogies, and that that unity should be mirrored in a prose coordinately dense with analogizing metaphor.

Mailer's style of imagination is a *forcing* style: it exerts *force* upon reality; it seeks to *force* reality into the matrix of an idiosyncratic vision. This *urgency* is the key to Mailer's most prominent strengths: the relentless energy of desperation which makes *An American Dream* a single breathless action, and gathers the many moods and modes of *Advertisements* into a sharply unified portrait of the artist as a young man fighting the demons of crack-up; the monumentality of certain of his chief theme-bearing characters — John F. Kennedy and Herman Teppis, Sonny Liston and Deborah Kelly Rojack — who remain in the memory as vivid larger-than-life creatures of myth; and the fluency everywhere, from the close, sharp lash of the goading scatologist to the barrel-toned magniloquence of the bard.

But these strengths are shadowed by related weaknesses: a flatness, stockness, vagueness in characterization often, when the fictionist in the author inevitably capitulates to the didact; a tendency to flatulence and clotted heaviness of expression that threatens to choke the naturally vigorous life of the prose; and an occasional self-permissive garrulousness that can, alas, turn into tedium. One becomes bored, then finally deafened, by the sado-masochistic acid-head bebop and chowder mannerisms of D. J. Jethroe's nonstop answer to the question Why Are We in Vietnam? — though there are "good things" in this work, and tightened up it might have made a memorable short story or novella. Sergius O'Shaugnessy is unfortunately vague, and Marion Faye is flat; their central moral significance in *The Deer Park* is diminished to abstraction and formula by their failure to be as human as the roundly conceived moral cripples surrounding them in the populous world of Desert D'Or. (Collie Munshin is a pretty bloom of humanity by comparison.) And the ingenious dialogues on the metaphysics of death and excrement in *The Presidential Papers* and *Cannibals and Christians* are, when all is said and done, overextended and boring. And boring is, of course, one of the most undesirable things you can be in the Mailer canon of humane values. These qualities represent a temptation perhaps innate to Mailer's kind of sensibility. In *The Armies of the Night*,

for example, he is attracted by the idea of "a short novel about a young American leading a double life in college as a secret policeman." Such a novel might be somewhat less vulnerable to prefabricated literary patterning than *Vietnam* (father-son tensions, heterosexual-homosexual tensions, man-beast tensions, all framed in a "significant" Texas-Alaska polar symbology); but even so it would threaten to become an "idea for a novel novel," something quite "made up" and possibly *forced*.

Toward the end of *The Armies of the Night,* Mailer writes of his feelings upon his release from jail after the demonstrations in Washington: "yes, in this resumption of the open air after twenty-four hours, no more, there was a sweet clean edge to the core of the substance of things — *a monumentally abstract remark which may be saved by the concrete observation* that the air was good in his lungs . . . [my italics]." The bard, perhaps wearied by labor too large and prolonged, has mauled a small bright human fact with the dull brutality of abstraction; and "Mailer," throwing off the robes of office, rebukes his alter ego for this crime against nature.

Mailer once wrote a story called "The Paper House," one of his conventionally "realistic" stories of the early 1950's that he did not take very seriously a decade later. The story is all about how reality takes its vengeance upon the criminal abstractionist. The setting is Japan. An arrogant, boorish, and selfish G.I. named Hayes is unsparingly loved by Yuriko, a geisha uncommonly endowed with dignity as well as tenderness. By night he nourishes upon her love. By day he is the thorough cynic: "crap" is what he calls the unhappy story of her family's misfortunes, her indenturing to training and service, and her final and staunch pride in earning the status of "first-class geisha." Crap: she is a common whore. He subconsciously wants to marry her, the natural concomitant in him of her unqualified love. But instead he drunkenly jeers at her: she is a common whore, and he will return to the States without her. When she responds by claiming him with increased vigor he strikes and strips her, brutally humiliating her before her peers and their clients. Later, when he meekly returns,

she is as warm with him as ever, but sad and a bit withdrawn. What does this mean? She must go on a journey very soon, somewhat before his own departure for the States. Where? he persists. Why? What sort of journey? Finally he learns: because she, a first-class geisha, has been publicly dishonored by her lover, she will commit hari-kari. Crap! he cries in irritable disdain. He will speak no more of it. A whore is a whore! But through the days that follow, her familiar tender attentions are touched with silent grief. Though he does not deign to speak of her threat, inside he aches with dread. And on the appointed day he cannot hold himself back from going to her. He finds her dressed in white, "without ornament, and without makeup," pleased that he has come after all to say "Bye-bye." As she turns to go to her self-appointed justice, he catches her by the arm, crying, "You got to stop this. It's crap." "Crap-crap," says Yuriko in answer, giggling. And hidden all around, the other geishas echo, "Crap-crap." Hayes retreats, and the girls follow him, a massed march of laughing, bright-kimonoed angels of derision jeering the conquered bully through the town to the chorused tune of "Crap-crap, Crap-crap."

A memorably fine story in its own right (Mailer acknowledges indebtedness to Vance Bourjaily for the anecdote on which it is based), it is also a model of Mailer's vision of marriage (in the soul-dimension Hayes and Yuriko are already "married") as the ultimate battleground of the laws of strife that govern love and sexuality, and in turn all of life. Alternatively turned on its side, up-ended, and inverted. "The Paper House" becomes a paradigm of the love-as-soulmaking-or-soulbreaking-combat themes of *The Deer Park*, "The Time of Her Time," and *An American Dream*. But it can also be read as a paradigm of the larger operations of a yet more ultimate law. In sharp contrast to his tender and humane buddy who narrates the story, Hayes is terrified of empathy. His is the naturally totalitarian temperament, bellowing, pounding, *forcing* reality to the shape of his belief. But Yuriko, whose unreasoning love frightens him into his worst brutality, *is* reality. The dignity of her otherness will not bend; she will not, finally, be forced. Her suavely just humiliation of her lover is so satisfy-

ing because it is a *natural* justice. A perfect illustration of the
penalties which in the natural scheme of things are levied against
unrepentant abstractionists who sin, through violence or neglect,
against the actual.

This formula may provide one explanation of why it is that
some people "can't read" Mailer and why even those who can and
do read him find themselves at times, especially when reading
his fiction, fatigued, irritated, hankering after something which
the apocalyptic apparatus of his imagination quite purposely extracts and draws off from his material so that no dilution will
threaten the strong potion of his doctrine. Perhaps it is thanks to
the just and beneficent workings of Yuriko's law that Mailer cannot finally succeed in this effort. Perhaps this explains why his
best work, the work that moves as well as amazes, is his most "im-
pure" — as in *The Deer Park*, where the mere presence of Charles
Francis Eitel and Elena Esposito mocks, with the awesome poignant reality of their flawed selves and failed love, the unreality of
Sergius O'Shaugnessy and Marion Faye, those stiff and faceless
standardbearers of the author's abstract redemptive "truth."

While Mailer has steadfastly refused to be apologetic about his
journalism, he has equally steadfastly identified his highest goals
as a writer with some major achievement as a novelist. In *The
Armies of the Night* he shows himself quite openly if good-
humoredly annoyed by Robert Lowell's insistent praises of him
as our greatest "journalist" at the same time he envies Lowell's
quiet authority in the role of "poet." It is a fact, I think, that the
large and responsive audience Mailer had won at the close of the
sixties would tend to agree, no doubt to the writer's chagrin, that
his "best" work has been in nonfiction. In putting forth my own
concurrence I would want to make clear that while I view *Barbary Shore* and *Why Are We in Vietnam?* as inferior achievements (they are "abstract" in my sense of the word: they busy
themselves making points rather than peopling a world; and the
mannerisms of their prose, portentous in one case, ranting in the
other, are inadequate compensation for this impoverishment)
they nevertheless have interest and deserve respect in the total pic-

ture of Mailer's career as honorable attempts at experiment and innovation.

Granting the solid excellence — its truth of substance and feeling, as well as its art — of *The Naked and the Dead,* and the daring virtuosity of *An American Dream,* only *The Deer Park* remains in the running for honors as a "great" novel. Its depth and breadth of imaginative engagement with our time, its acute and inclusive sensing of our palsied and anxious life in mid-century America, through deft selection of setting and symbol and deft portraiture of a dozen varied secondary characters that are real as well as symptomatic, make it impressive. But as we move toward the core of this book — the affair between Elena and Eitel — surely we move from the impressive into the field of force of something like "greatness." Eitel, the hero-gentleman demeaned by history, is a complex character of almost tangible reality; he has all the fullness of being that Fitzgerald could not finally give to Dick Diver. Elena, the soiled broad and dumb waif of petty disasters, is rich with an inner gift of instinctive warmth and natural dignity worthy of Cleopatra; she is one of the few great woman characters in American fiction after James. The delicate, tender persistence of Mailer's articulation of the life of their affair, its growth, flowering, deterioration, and crippled resolution, is rare and magnificent. It is the *real* "armature" of the book, despite Mailer's efforts to give that power to his prophets of new consciousness, Marion Faye and Sergius O'Shaugnessy. Because Sergius, like Lovett in *Barbary Shore,* seems neither intelligent nor sensitive nor good enough, nor even *visible* enough, to attract the friendship and confidence of a man like Eitel, we do not believe in him. But we cannot quite console ourselves by saying, with Lawrence, "Never trust the author, trust the tale," because we are distracted and fatigued as we read by the badgering of Mailer's forcing style of imagination — and the book's armature slows, finally, and falters. *The Deer Park,* one can say (Mailer's exactly opposite account of its shortcomings notwithstanding), was a potentially great novel flawed by an authorial excess of misled good intentions. It is perhaps yet another validation of Yuriko's law that what remains persistently alive in one's memory of *The Deer Park* is Eitel and Elena, and the real world, intimate and at large, of which they were the vital center.

In the middle 1950's Mailer professed a credo that would still seem to hold for him in the 1970's:

I suppose that the virtue I should like most to achieve as a writer is to be genuinely disturbing . . . It is, I believe, the highest function a writer may serve, to see life (no matter by what means or form or experiment) as others do not see it, or only partially see it, and therefore open for the reader that literary experience which comes uniquely from the novel — the sense of having one's experience enlarged, one's perceptions deepened, and one's illusions about oneself rendered even more untenable. For me, this is the highest function of art, precisely that it is disturbing, that it does not let man rest, and therefore forces him so far as art may force anything to enlarge the horizons of his life.

It is clear that most of his work to date has been done in the light of this statement of principle, and it seems probable that it will continue to be, if only because it is the kind of principle that any serious novelist of whatever artistic or philosophic persuasion would be likely to subscribe to with dedication. But it could be argued that in his fiction, at least, Mailer has yet to write a book worthy of the strictest interpretation of his principle. If he eventually completes the multi-volume quasi-epic of neo-Joycean structure and Burroughs-cum-Tolstoian substance that he once promised, it probably will not be the novel, any more than his others have been, that fulfills the high aims of this credo. If he is to write a truly "great" novel, it will be the product of some new, subtler, and perhaps unimaginably humbler synthesis of the gifts for which he has now come to be appreciated. Perhaps he will learn something from his readers' obstinate tendency to prefer his nonfiction, where, with no sacrifice of his skills and all benefit to the power of his vision, he is mired in reality, hobbled to the facts of time, place, self, as to an indispensable spouse of flesh and blood who continually saves him from his other self that yearns toward wasteful flirtations with *Spiritus Mundi*. In any case, he will have to come to know truly, if in his own way, the "Thou" to which the "I" of Martin Buber's world is inexorably wedded, and he will have to find his own style of that "negative capability" which Keats identified as the root of true imagination.

Perhaps Mailer would dismiss such cavils as typical of the solemnly moribund mentality of official literary criticism. And yet he might be reminded that the newly respectful interest in his work, represented even by such exceptions as these, is the natural harvest, sought or not, of his maverick persistence in his calling — and for Mailer writing has always been, literally, a "calling" — despite the years of criticism's ignorant undervaluation of him. He has finally forced criticism, which once dismissed him as a sensationalist barbarian egomaniac who couldn't write, to eat its own words, salted and spiced with the true savor of his actual achievements. Criticism has been made to confess at last that Mailer is a symbolist and mythmaker, the alchemy of his imagination being capable of turning excrement, madness, and perversion into lambent revelations of the condition of man and God; that he is a true intellectual — acute, sophisticated, and dead serious in his probing criticisms of the life of his time; that he is an extraordinary prose stylist in the big-voiced American tradition of Melville and Faulkner; and that he is fortunately endowed, as most apocalyptics are not, with the easing human graces of wit and humor. Even such a book as *Advertisements for Myself*, which at the time of its publication so outraged and embarrassed the critics with its naked revelations of its author's wounds and vanities, has now come to seem, in the manner of Fitzgerald's "Crack-Up" essays, a nobly original undertaking of self-definition, moving in content and daring in execution. *Advertisements* represented the invention, furthermore, of a new form (let's call it, to borrow a contemporaneous term that has been misapplied elsewhere, the "nonfiction novel"), a form that has since served him especially well in *The Presidential Papers* and *The Armies of the Night*, and will no doubt continue to do so.

Mailer became what he now is, a leading writer of his time, by reacting with aggressive creativity to what he was not in the middle 1950's — a *recognized* leading writer. He took the fact of his situation and ran it imaginatively to a transforming myth. He literally created himself in the imaginations of his contemporaries, winning a domain where, before, he had been all but denied standing room. And the work that generated the myth and brought it to its fullness of life, from *Advertisements for Myself* to *The Armies of the Night*, was both masterful and unique.

But what came after, the magazine pieces and the books assembled from them, didn't seem the same. Mailer as imaginative master of the fact now seemed the fact's appendage. Where he had once ruled, and thrillingly, he now served, engagingly. A forthcoming championship boxing match, a space exploration, a national election — one knew that Mailer would interest himself in such events, and that soon one would be reading his published prose about his interesting himself in them. One had begun to know what to expect from Mailer because Mailer had succeeded in just the way he did succeed.

A partial exception to this rule, perhaps, was *The Prisoner of Sex* (1971), Mailer's counterattack against the attack of a new generation of women's rights intellectuals upon male "chauvinism," including Mailer's own neo-Lawrencean brand of phallic mysticism. But the exception lay in the disappointment, this time, in finding one's expectations confirmed. The ideology of women's liberation was something politically new and vital in modern life, and Mailer's response to it was not "existential." It was only charming, shrewd, and stylish, an extension of cocktail-party dialectics and effective public showmanship. Mailer's response to the women ("the ladies") indicated that he did not understand that they were serious, and that this was not to be just another coy move in the sex-game.

New books came forth from Norman Mailer in cheap disposable form (*St. George and the Godfather*, 1972, Mailer's account of the Nixon and McGovern candidacies for the presidency, was published only in a paper-cover edition), while large retrospective tomes (*The Long Patrol: Twenty-Five Years of Writing from the Work of Norman Mailer*, 1971) were issued in hard covers and at very high prices. An interpreter of symbols might see in this phenomenon a suggestion that Mailer's growth became arrested when he achieved "success," and that any following books were to be stuck on the achieved central monument as mere confirmatory fillips. This is, of course, a disagreeable interpretation for readers of Mailer who think of him as a uniquely gifted American writer of major stature. It might even be disagreeable for readers who just continue to enjoy his books without necessarily "thinking."

I hope that a reader of these words in some more or less distant future will be able to recall to himself that Mailer's next great period began, once the elections of 1972 were out of the way and the anguish of the Vietnam war was laid to rest, when Mr. Mailer, despite his own predilections and the monetary blandishments of publishers, decided *not* to write a book on the second Fraser-Ali championship fight.

SELECTED BIBLIOGRAPHIES

Selected Bibliographies

EDGAR ALLAN POE

Works

PRINCIPAL SEPARATE WORKS

Tamerlane and Other Poems, "by a Bostonian." Boston: Calvin F. S. Thomas, Printer, 1827.

Al Aaraaf, Tamerlane, and Minor Poems. Baltimore: Hatch and Dunning, 1829.

Poems, "Second Edition." New York: Elam Bliss, 1831.

The Narrative of Arthur Gordon Pym. New York: Harper, 1838.

Tales of the Grotesque and Arabesque. 2 vols. Philadelphia: Lea and Blanchard, 1840.

Tales. New York: Wiley and Putnam, 1845.

The Raven and Other Poems. New York: Wiley and Putnam, 1845.

Eureka: A Prose Poem. New York: Putnam, 1848.

COLLECTED AND SELECTED EDITIONS

The Works of the Late Edgar Allan Poe, with Memoir by Rufus Wilmot Griswold and "Notices of His Life and Genius" by N. P. Willis and J. R. Lowell. 4 vols. New York: J. S. Redfield, 1850–56.

The Works of E. A. Poe, edited by John H. Ingram. 4 vols. New York: W. J. Widdleton, 1876.

The Works of Edgar Allan Poe, edited by Richard H. Stoddard. 6 vols. New York: A. C. Armstrong, 1884.

The Works of Edgar Allan Poe, edited by Edmund C. Stedman and George E. Woodberry. 10 vols. Chicago: Stone and Kimball, 1894–95.

The Complete Works of Edgar Allan Poe (Virginia Edition), edited by James A. Harrison. 17 vols. New York: George D. Sproul, 1902. Also printed as the Monticello Edition in the same year.

The Complete Works of E. A. Poe, with Biography and Introduction by Nathan H. Dole. 10 vols. Akron, Ohio: Werner Co., 1908.

The Complete Poems of E. A. Poe, edited by J. H. Whitty. Boston: Houghton Mifflin, 1911.

The Poems of Edgar Allan Poe, edited by Killis Campbell. Boston: Ginn, 1917.

The Works of Edgar Allan Poe, with Biographical Introduction by Hervey Allen. New York: W. J. Black, 1927.

Selected Poems of E. A. Poe, edited by Thomas O. Mabbott. New York: Macmillan, 1928.

The Complete Poems and Stories of E. A. Poe, with Selections from His Critical Writings, edited by Arthur H. Quinn. 2 vols. New York: Knopf, 1946.

The Letters of Edgar Allan Poe, edited by John W. Ostrom. Cambridge, Mass.: Harvard University Press, 1948. Reprinted with Supplement, New York: Gordian Press, 1966.

Collected Works of Edgar Allan Poe, edited by Thomas O. Mabbott. Cambridge, Mass.: Harvard University Press, 1969–. Vol. I, *Poems,* 1969. Other volumes in preparation.

Bibliographies

Dameron, J. Lasley. *Edgar Allan Poe: A Checklist of Criticism, 1942–1960.* Charlottesville: Bibliographical Society of the University of Virginia, 1966.

Heartman, Charles F., and James R. Canny. *A Bibliography of First Printings of the Writings of Edgar Allan Poe.* Hattiesburg, Miss.: The Book Farm, 1943.

Hubbell, Jay B. "Poe" in *Eight American Authors: A Review of Research and Criticism,* edited by James Woodress. Revised edition. New York: Norton, 1971.

Robbins, J. Albert. *The Merrill Checklist of Edgar Allan Poe.* Columbus, Ohio: C. E. Merrill, 1969.

Robertson, John W. *Bibliography of the Writings of Edgar Allan Poe.* 2 vols. San Francisco, 1934.

Note: A periodical, *Poe Studies* (formerly *Poe Newsletter*), begun in 1968, publishes at least twice annually articles, notes, and exhaustive bibliographies on Poe.

Concordance

Booth, Bradford, and Claude E. Jones. *A Concordance of the Poetical Works of Edgar Allan Poe.* Baltimore: Johns Hopkins Press, 1941.

Critical and Biographical Studies

Alexander, Jean. *Affidavits of Genius: E. A. Poe and the French Critics, 1874–1924*. Port Washington, N.Y.: Kennicat Press, 1971.

Allen, Hervey. *Israfel: The Life and Times of Edgar Allan Poe*. 2 vols. New York: Doran, 1926.

Allen, Michael. *Poe and the British Magazine Tradition*. Cambridge, Mass.: Harvard University Press, 1969.

Bachelard, Gaston. *L'Eau et les rêves*. Paris: Corti, 1942.

———. *L'Air et les songes*. Paris: Corti, 1943.

Baudelaire, Charles. *Baudelaire on Poe: Critical Papers*, translated by Lois and Francis E. Hyslop, Jr. State College, Pa.: Bald College Press, 1952.

Benton, Richard P. *New Approaches to Poe: A Symposium*. Hartford, Conn.: Transcendentalist Books, 1970.

Bittner, William. *Poe, a Biography*. Boston: Little, Brown, 1962.

Bonaparte, Marie. *The Life and Works of Edgar Allan Poe,* translated by John Rodker. London: Imago, 1949.

Broussard, Louis. *The Measure of Poe*. Norman: University of Oklahoma Press, 1969.

Buranelli, Vincent. *Edgar Allan Poe*. New York: Twayne, 1961.

Campbell, Killis. *The Mind of Poe and Other Studies*. Cambridge, Mass.: Harvard University Press, 1933.

Carlson, Eric W., editor. *The Recognition of Edgar Allan Poe*. Ann Arbor: University of Michigan Press, 1966. (An anthology of Poe criticism.)

Cobb, Palmer. *The Influence of E. T. A. Hoffmann on the Tales of E. A. Poe*. Chapel Hill: North Carolina University Press, 1908.

Davidson, Edward H. *Poe: A Critical Study*. Cambridge, Mass.: Harvard University Press, 1957.

Eliot, T. S. "From Poe to Valéry," *Hudson Review*, 2:327–43 (August 1949).

Fagin, N. Bryllion. *The Histrionic Mr. Poe*. Baltimore: Johns Hopkins Press, 1949.

Fiedler, Leslie A. *Love and Death in the American Novel*. New York: Criterion Books, 1960.

Foerster, Norman, *American Criticism: A Study in Literary Theory from Poe to the Present Day*. New York: Houghton Mifflin, 1928.

Hoffman, Daniel. *Poe Poe Poe Poe Poe Poe Poe*. New York: Doubleday, 1972.

Huxley, Aldous. "Vulgarity in Literature," in *Music at Night*. London: Chatto and Windus, 1930.

Jacobs, Robert D. *Poe: Journalist and Critic*. Baton Rouge: Louisiana State University Press, 1969.

Krutch, Joseph Wood. *Edgar Allan Poe: A Study in Genius*. New York: Knopf, 1926.

Lawrence, D. H. *Studies in Classic American Literature*. London: Thomas Seltzer, 1923.

Moss, Sidney P. *Poe's Major Crisis: His Libel Suit and New York's Literary World*. Durham, N.C.: Duke University Press, 1970.

Parks, Edd W. *Edgar Allan Poe as Literary Critic*. Athens: University of Georgia Press, 1964.

Pollin, Burton R. *Dictionary of Names and Titles in Poe's Collected Works.*
New York: Da Capo, 1968.

_____. *Discoveries in Poe.* Notre Dame, Ind.: University of Notre Dame
Press, 1970.

Quinn, Arthur Hobson, *Edgar Allan Poe: A Critical Biography.* New York:
Appleton-Century, 1941.

Quinn, Patrick F. *The French Face of Edgar Poe.* Carbondale: Southern Illinois University Press, 1957.

_____. *Poe and France: The Last Twenty Years.* Baltimore: E. A. Poe So-
ciety, 1970.

Rans, Geoffrey. *Edgar Allan Poe.* Edinburgh and London: Oliver and Boyd,
1965.

Regan, Robert, editor. *Poe: A Collection of Critical Essays.* Englewood
Cliffs, N.J.: Prentice-Hall, 1967.

Shanks, Edward. *Edgar Allan Poe.* London: Macmillan, 1937.

Stovall, Floyd. *Edgar Poe the Poet: Essays New and Old on the Man and
His Work.* Charlottesville: University Press of Virginia, 1969.

Tate, Allen. "The Angelic Imagination: Poe and the Power of Words," *Kenyon Review,* 14:455–75 (Summer 1952).

_____. "Our Cousin, Mr. Poe," in *Collected Essays.* Denver: Swallow, 1959.

Wagenknecht, Edward. *Edgar Allan Poe: The Man behind the Legend.*
New York: Oxford University Press, 1963.

Winters, Yvor. "Edgar Allan Poe: A Crisis in the History of American
Obscurantism," in *Maule's Curse.* New York: New Directions, 1938.

Woodberry, George E. *Edgar Allan Poe.* Boston, 1885.

_____. *The Life of Edgar Allan Poe, Personal and Literary, with His Chief
Correspondence with Men of Letters.* 2 vols. Boston, 1909.

Woodson, Thomas, ed. *Twentieth Century Interpretations of "The Fall of
the House of Usher."* Englewood Cliffs, N.J.: Prentice-Hall, 1969.

GEORGE SANTAYANA

Principal Works

Lotze's System of Philosophy (Harvard University doctoral dissertation, 1889),
edited with an introduction by Paul Grimley Kuntz. Bloomington: Indiana
University Press, 1971.

The Sense of Beauty: Being the Outlines of Aesthetic Theory. New York:
Scribner's, 1896.

Interpretations of Poetry and Religion. New York: Scribner's, 1900.

The Life of Reason, or the Phases of Human Progress: Vol. I, *Reason in Common Sense*; Vol. II, *Reason in Society*; Vol. III, *Reason in Religion*; Vol. IV,
Reason in Art; Vol. V, *Reason in Science.* New York: Scribner's 1905–6. One-
volume edition revised and abridged by Santayana and Daniel Cory, 1954.

Three Philosophical Poets: Lucretius, Dante, and Goethe. Cambridge, Mass.:
Harvard University Press, 1910.

Character and Opinion in the United States, with Reminiscences of William James and Josiah Royce and Academic Life in America. New York: Scribner's, 1920.

Soliloquies in England and Later Soliloquies. New York: Scribner's, 1922.

Scepticism and Animal Faith: Introduction to a System of Philosophy. New York: Scribner's, 1923.

Poems, selected by the author and revised. New York: Scribner's, 1923. (Contains a remarkable preface by Santayana.)

Dialogues in Limbo. New York: Scribner's, 1926. New and enlarged edition, 1948.

The Realms of Being: Book First, *The Realm of Essence,* 1927; Book Second, *The Realm of Matter,* 1930; Book Third, *The Realm of Truth,* 1938; Book Fourth, *The Realm of Spirit,* 1940. New York: Scribner's. One-volume edition, 1942.

The Last Puritan: A Memoir in the Form of a Novel. New York: Scribner's, 1936.

The Philosophy of Santayana, selections edited, with an introductory essay; by Irwin Edman. New York: Modern Library, 1936. Enlarged edition, Scribner's, 1953. (Contains an autobiographical essay, selected sonnets, book reviews, and occasional pieces, besides selections from the philosophical works.)

The Idea of Christ in the Gospels: Or God in Man, A Critical Essay. New York: Scribner's, 1946.

Dominations and Powers: Reflections on Liberty, Society and Government. New York: Scribner's, 1951.

Essays in Literary Criticism of George Santayana, selections edited with an introduction by Irving Singer. New York: Scribner's, 1956.

The Genteel Tradition: Nine Essays by George Santayana, edited with an introduction by Douglas L. Wilson. Cambridge, Mass.: Harvard University Press, 1967. (Contains "The Genteel Tradition in American Philosophy," "The Genteel Tradition at Bay," and the poem "Young Sammy's First Wild Oats.")

Selected Critical Writings of George Santayana, edited by Norman Henfrey. 2 vols. New York: Cambridge University Press, 1968.

Autobiography and Letters

Persons and Places: Vol. I, *The Background of My Life,* 1944; Vol. II, *The Middle Span,* 1945; Vol. III, *My Host the World,* 1953. New York: Scribner's.

The Letters of George Santayana, edited with an introduction and commentary by Daniel Cory. New York: Scribner's, 1955.

Critical and Biographical Studies

Arnett, Willard E. *George Santayana.* Great American Thinkers Series. New York: Washington Square Press, 1968.

Butler, Richard. *The Life and World of George Santayana.* Chicago: Regnery, 1960.

Cory, Daniel. *Santayana The Late Years: A Portrait with Letters.* New York: Braziller, 1963.

Howgate, George W. *George Santayana.* Philadelphia: University of Pennsylvania Press, 1938.

Schilpp, Paul A., ed. *The Philosophy of George Santayana.* 2nd edition. La Salle, Ill.: Open Court, 1951. (Essays by a number of critics including Bertrand Russell and John Dewey, with an introduction and replies by Santayana; bibliography.)

STEPHEN CRANE

Works

NOVELS

Maggie: A Girl of the Streets (A Story of New York), "by Johnston Smith" (pseud.). N.p. [1893]. Revised edition, *Maggie: A Girl of the Streets.* New York: Appleton, 1896. There have been three recent reprints of note: one edited by Joseph Katz (Gainesville, Fla.: Scholars' Facsimiles and Reprints, 1966); another by Maurice Bassan (*Stephen Crane's Maggie, Text and Context,* Belmont, Calif.: Wadsworth Publication, 1966); and the third by Donald Pizer (San Francisco: Chandler, 1968).

The Red Badge of Courage. New York: Appleton, 1895.

George's Mother. New York and London: Edward Arnold, 1896.

The Third Violet. New York: Appleton, 1897.

Active Service. New York: Frederick A. Stokes, 1899.

The O'Ruddy. New York: Frederick A. Stokes, 1903.

The Complete Novels of Stephen Crane, edited by Thomas A. Gullason. New York: Doubleday, 1967.

SHORT STORIES AND SKETCHES

The Little Regiment and Other Episodes of the American Civil War. New York: Appleton, 1896.

The Open Boat and Other Stories. New York: Doubleday and McClure, 1898.

The Monster and Other Stories. New York: Harper, 1899. (Contains only "The Monster," "The Blue Hotel," and "His New Mittens.")

Whilomville Stories. New York and London: Harper, 1900.

Wounds in the Rain. New York: Frederick A. Stokes, 1900.

Great Battles of the World. Philadelphia: Lippincott, 1901.

The Monster. London: Harper, 1901. (Contains "The Monster," "The Blue Hotel," "His New Mittens," "Twelve O'Clock," "Moonlight on the Snow," "Manacled," and "An Illusion in Red and White.")

Last Words. London: Digby, Long, 1902.

Men, Women and Boats, edited with an introduction by Vincent Starrett. New York: Boni and Liveright, 1917. (Contains seventeen stories and sketches.)

A Battle in Greece. Mount Vernon, N.Y.: Peter Pauper Press, 1936. (Contains a reprint of the battle sketch which appeared in the *New York Journal* of June 13, 1897.)

The Sullivan County Sketches, edited by Melvin Schoberlin. Syracuse, N.Y.: Syracuse University Press, 1949.

The Complete Short Stories and Sketches of Stephen Crane, edited by Thomas A. Gullason. New York: Doubleday, 1963.

The New York City Sketches of Stephen Crane and Related Pieces, edited by R. W. Stallman and E. R. Hagemann. New York: New York University Press, 1966.

Stephen Crane: Sullivan County Tales and Sketches, edited by R. W. Stallman. Ames: Iowa State University Press, 1968.

WAR DISPATCHES

The War Dispatches of Stephen Crane, edited by R. W. Stallman and E. R. Hagemann. New York: New York University Press, 1964.

POETRY AND PLAYS

The Black Riders and Other Lines. Boston: Copeland and Day, 1895.

A Souvenir and a Medley. East Aurora, N.Y.: Roycroft Printing Shop, 1896. (Contains seven poems, as well as a sketch entitled "A Great Mistake" and a fifteen-line piece printed in capitals, "A Prologue," which reads like stage directions.)

War Is Kind. New York: Frederick A. Stokes, 1899.

The Collected Poems of Stephen Crane, edited by Wilson Follett. New York: Knopf, 1930.

The Poems of Stephen Crane, a critical edition by Joseph Katz. New York: Cooper Square Publishers, 1966.

At Clancy's Wake, in *Last Words.* London: Digby, Long, 1902.

The Blood of the Martyr. Mount Vernon, N.Y.: Peter Pauper Press, [1940]. (A play originally printed in the Sunday magazine of the *New York Press* on April 3, 1898.)

Drama in Cuba, in *The War Dispatches of Stephen Crane,* edited by R. W. Stallman and E. R. Hagemann. New York: New York University Press, 1964.

COLLECTED EDITIONS

The Work of Stephen Crane, edited by Wilson Follett. 12 vols. New York: Knopf, 1925–27. Recently reprinted in 6 vols., New York: Russell and Russell, 1963.

Stephen Crane: An Omnibus, edited by R. W. Stallman. New York: Knopf, 1952.

Stephen Crane: Uncollected Writings, edited with an introduction by Olov W. Fryckstedt. Uppsala: Almqvist and Wiksell, 1963.

The Works of Stephen Crane, edited by Fredson Bowers. 10 vols. Charlottesville: University Press of Virginia, 1969–. Vol. I, *Bowery Tales,* 1969. Vol. IV, *The O'Ruddy,* 1971. Vol. V, *Tales of Adventure,* 1970. Vol. VI, *Tales of War,* 1970. Vol. VII, *Tales of Whilomville,* 1969. Vol. VIII, *Tales, Sketches, and Reports,* 1973. Vol. IX, *Reports of War,* 1971. Others in preparation.

LETTERS AND NOTEBOOK

Stephen Crane: Letters, edited by R. W. Stallman and Lillian Gilkes. New York: New York University Press, 1960.

The Notebook of Stephen Crane, edited by Donald J. Greiner and Ellen B. Greiner. Charlottesville: University Press of Virginia, 1969.

Bibliographies

Since 1963 Syracuse University has issued an annual Crane bibliography in *Thoth.*

Gross, Theodore L., and Stanley Wertheim. *Hawthorne, Melville, Stephen Crane: A Critical Bibliography.* New York: Free Press, 1971.

Stallman, R. W. *Stephen Crane: A Critical Bibliography.* Ames: Iowa State University Press, 1972.

Williams, Ames W., and Vincent Starrett. *Stephen Crane: A Bibliography.* Glendale, Calif.: John Valentine, 1948.

Biographies

Beer, Thomas. *Stephen Crane.* New York: Knopf, 1923.

Berryman, John. *Stephen Crane.* New York: William Sloane Associates, 1950. Reprinted in 1962 as a Meridian paperback with an additional preface.

Gilkes, Lillian. *Cora Crane.* Bloomington: Indiana University Press, 1960. (Although centered on Cora, this contains much information on the life of the couple in England.)

Raymond, Thomas L. *Stephen Crane.* Newark, N.J.: Carteret Book Club, 1923.

Stallman, R. W. *Stephen Crane.* New York: Braziller, 1968.

Critical Studies

Bassan, Maurice. "Crane, Townsend, and Realism of a Good Kind," *Proceedings of the New Jersey Historical Society,* 82:128–35 (April 1964).

Berryman, John. "The Red Badge of Courage," in *The American Novel,* edited by Wallace Stegner. New York: Basic Books, 1965.

Berthoff, Warner. *The Ferment of Realism: American Literature 1884–1919.* New York: Free Press, 1965.

Cady, Edwin H. *Stephen Crane.* New York: Twayne, 1962.

Colvert, James B. "The Origins of Stephen Crane's Literary Creed," *University of Texas Studies in English,* 34:179–88 (1955).

Ellison, Ralph. Introduction to *The Red Badge of Courage.* New York: Dell, 1960. Reprinted in *Shadow and Act.* New York: Random House, 1964.

Geismar, Maxwell. *Rebels and Ancestors.* Boston: Houghton Mifflin, 1953.

Gibson, Donald B. *The Fiction of Stephen Crane.* Carbondale: Southern Illinois University Press, 1968.

Gordan, John D. *"The Ghost* at Brede Place," *Bulletin of the New York Public Library,* 56:591–96 (December 1952).

Greenfield, Stanley B. "The Unmistakable Stephen Crane," *PMLA,* 73:562–72 (December 1958).

Gullason, Thomas. "Stephen Crane's Private War on Yellow Journalism," *Huntington Library Quarterly,* 22:200–8 (May 1959).

———, ed. *Stephen Crane's Career: Perspectives and Evaluations.* New York: New York University Press, 1972.

Hoffman, D. G. *The Poetry of Stephen Crane.* New York: Columbia University Press, 1957.

———. "Stephen Crane's Last Novel," *Bulletin of the New York Public Library,* 64:337–43 (June 1960).

Katz, Joseph. " 'The Blue Battalions' and the Uses of Experience," *Studia Neophilogica,* 38:107–16 (1966).

———, ed. *Stephen Crane Newsletter,* Fall 1966 to date.

Kazin, Alfred. "American Fin de Siècle," in *On Native Grounds.* New York: Reynal and Hitchcock, 1942.

La France, Marston. *A Reading of Stephen Crane.* London: Oxford University Press, 1971.

Lytle, Andrew. " 'The Open Boat': A Pagan Tale," in *The Hero with the Private Parts.* Baton Rouge: Louisiana State University Press, 1966.

Martin, Jay. *Harvests of Change: American Literature, 1865–1914.* Englewood Cliffs, N.J.: Prentice-Hall, 1967.

Modern Fiction Studies, 5:199–291 (Autumn 1959). (Essays on Crane by Thomas A. Gullason, Robert F. Gleckner, Peter Buitenhuis, James B. Colvert, R. W. Stallman, Hugh Maclean, Eric Solomon, James T. Cox; also contains a good selective bibliography.)

Nelson, Harland S. "Stephen Crane's Achievement as a Poet," *University of Texas Studies in Literature and Language,* 4:564–82 (Winter 1963).

Pizer, Donald. "Stephen Crane," in *Fifteen American Authors before 1900,* edited by Robert A. Rees and Earl N. Harbert. Madison: University of Wisconsin Press, 1971.

Ross, Lillian. *Picture.* London: Penguin Books, 1962. Reprinted from the *New Yorker,* May–June 1952. (An account of the filming of *The Red Badge of Courage* for MGM under the direction of John Huston.)

Schneider, Robert W. *Five Novelists of the Progressive Era.* New York: Columbia University Press, 1965.

Solomon, Eric. *Stephen Crane: From Parody to Realism.* Cambridge, Mass.: Harvard University Press, 1966.

Vasilievskaya, O. B. *The Work of Stephen Crane.* Moscow: Nayka Editions, 1967. (A critical study in Russian.)

Walcutt, Charles Child. *American Literary Naturalism, a Divided Stream.* Minneapolis: University of Minnesota Press, 1956.

Weisenberger, Bernard. "The Red Badge of Courage," in *Twelve Original Essays on Great American Novels,* edited by Charles Shapiro. Detroit: Wayne State University Press, 1958.

Weiss, Daniel. "The Red Badge of Courage," *Psychoanalytic Review,* 52:32–52 (Summer 1965), 52:130–54 (Fall 1965).

Westbrook, Max. "Stephen Crane's Poetry: Perspective and Arrogance," *Bucknell Review,* 11:23–34 (December 1963).

Ziff, Larzer. *The American 1890s.* New York: Viking, 1966.

GERTRUDE STEIN

Principal Works

Three Lives. New York: Grafton Press, 1909.

Tender Buttons. New York: Claire Marie, 1914.

Geography and Plays. Boston: The Four Seas, 1922.

The Making of Americans. Paris: Contact Editions, 1925. Abridged edition, New York: Harcourt, Brace, 1934.

Composition as Explanation. London: Hogarth, 1926.

Useful Knowledge. New York: Payson and Clarke, 1928.

How to Write. Paris: Plain Edition, 1931.

The Autobiography of Alice B. Toklas. New York: Harcourt, Brace, 1933.

Portraits and Prayers. New York: Random House, 1934.

Lectures in America. New York: Random House, 1935.

Narration. Chicago: University of Chicago Press, 1935.

The Geographical History of America. New York: Random House, 1936.

Everybody's Autobiography. New York: Random House, 1937.

Picasso. New York: Scribner's, 1939.

Paris France. New York: Scribner's, 1940.

What Are Masterpieces. Los Angeles: Conference Press, 1940.

Ida, a Novel. New York: Random House, 1941.

Wars I Have Seen. New York: Random House, 1944.

Brewsie and Willie. New York: Random House, 1946.

Four in America. New Haven: Yale University Press, 1947.

Last Operas and Plays. New York: Rinehart, 1949.

Things as They Are. Pawlet, Vt.: Banyan, 1951.

Two: Gertrude Stein and Her Brother. New Haven: Yale University Press, 1951.

Mrs. Reynolds. New Haven: Yale University Press, 1952.

Bee Time Vine. New Haven: Yale University Press, 1953.

As Fine as Melanctha. New Haven: Yale University Press, 1954.

Painted Lace. New Haven: Yale University Press, 1955.

Stanzas in Meditation. New Haven: Yale University Press, 1956.

Alphabets and Birthdays. New Haven: Yale University Press, 1957.

A Novel of Thank You. New Haven: Yale University Press, 1958.

Bibliographies

Haas, Robert B., and Donald C. Gallup. *A Catalogue of the Published and Unpublished Writings of Gertrude Stein*. New Haven: Yale University Library, 1941.

Sawyer, Julian. *Gertrude Stein: A Bibliography*. New York: Arrow Editions, 1940.

Critical and Biographical Studies

Auden, W. H. "All about Ida," *Saturday Review of Literature*, 23:8 (February 22, 1941).

Baldanza, Frank. "Faulkner and Stein: A Study in Stylistic Intransigence," *Georgia Review*, 13:274–86 (Fall 1959).

Beaver, Harold. "A Figure in the Carpet: Irony and the American Novel," *Essays and Studies*, 15:101–14 (1962).

Bloom, E. F. "Three Steins: A Very Personal Recital," *Texas Quarterly*, 13:14–22 (Summer 1970).

Bridgman, Richard. *Gertrude Stein in Pieces*. New York: Oxford University Press, 1970.

Brinnin, John Malcolm. *The Third Rose: Gertrude Stein and Her World*. Boston: Atlantic, Little, Brown, 1959.

Burke, Kenneth. "Engineering with Words," *Dial*, 74:408–12 (April 1923).

Corke, Hilary. "Reflections on a Great Stone Face: The Achievement of Gertrude Stein," *Kenyon Review*, 23:367–89 (Summer 1961).

Dupee, F. W. "Gertrude Stein," *Commentary*, 33:519–23 (June 1962).

Eagleson, Harvey. "Gertrude Stein: Method in Madness," *Sewanee Review*, 44:164–77 (1936).

Gass, W. H. "Gertrude Stein: Her Escape from Protective Language," *Accent*, 18:233–44 (Autumn 1958).

Haines, George, IV. "Forms of Imaginative Prose: 1900–1940," *Southern Review*, 7:755 (Spring 1942).

———. "Gertrude Stein and Composition," *Sewanee Review*, 57:411–24 (Summer 1959).

Hoffman, Michael J. *The Development of Abstractionism in the Writings of Gertrude Stein*. Philadelphia: University of Pennsylvania Press, 1965.

Kazin, Alfred. "The Mystery of Gertrude Stein," in *Contemporaries*. Boston: Little, Brown, 1962.

Miller, Rosamond S. *Gertrude Stein: Form and Intelligibility*. New York: Exposition Press, 1949.

Moore, Marianne. "The Spare American Emotion," *Dial*, 80:153–56 (February 1926).

Porter, Katherine A. "Gertrude Stein: Three Views," in *The Days Before*. New York: Harcourt, Brace, 1952.

Purdy, Strother B. "Gertrude Stein at Marienbad," *PMLA*, 85:1096–105 (October 1970).

Rago, Henry. "Gertrude Stein," *Poetry*, 69:93–97 (November 1946).

Reid, B. L. *Art by Subtraction: A Dissenting Opinion of Gertrude Stein.* Norman: University of Oklahoma Press, 1958.

Riding, Laura. "The New Barbarism and Gertrude Stein," *transition*, 3:153–68 (June 1927).

Rogers, W. G. *When This You See Remember Me.* New York: Rinehart, 1948.

Skinner, B. F. "Has Gertrude Stein a Secret?" *Atlantic Monthly*, 153:50 (January 1934).

Sprigge, Elizabeth. *Gertrude Stein: Her Life and Her Work.* New York: Harper, 1957.

Stein, Leo. *Journey into the Self,* edited by Edmund Fuller. New York: Crown, 1950.

Stewart, Allegra. *Gertrude Stein and the Present.* Cambridge, Mass.: Harvard University Press, 1967.

Sutherland, Donald. *Gertrude Stein: A Biography of Her Work.* New Haven: Yale University Press, 1951.

Toklas, Alice B. *What Is Remembered.* New York: Holt, Rinehart, 1963.

Troy, William. "A Note on Gertrude Stein," *Nation*, 137:274–75 (September 6, 1933).

Weinstein, Norman. *Gertrude Stein and the Literature of the Modern Consciousness.* New York: Ungar, 1970.

Wilson, Edmund. "Brewsie and Willie," *New Yorker*, 22:192 (June 15, 1946).
_____. "Gertrude Stein," in *Axel's Castle.* New York: Scribner's, 1931.

Wright, George T. "Gertrude Stein and Her Ethic of Self-Containment," *Tennessee Studies in Literature*, 8:17–23 (1963).

VLADIMIR NABOKOV

Works

Note: In the essay above, the dates in parentheses after titles are those of first publication in the language in which the work was originally composed.

NOVELS AND COLLECTED SHORT STORIES

Mary (Mashen'ka). Berlin: "Slovo," 1926. English translation, New York: McGraw-Hill, 1970.

King, Queen, Knave (Korol', Dama, Valet). Berlin: "Slovo," 1928. English translation, New York: McGraw-Hill, 1968.

The Defense (Zashchita Luzhina). Berlin: "Slovo," 1930. English translation, New York: Putnam, 1964.

The Eye (Soglyadatay). Paris: Contemporary Annals, No. 44, 1930. English translation, New York: Phaedra, 1965.

Glory (Podvig). Paris: Contemporary Annals, Nos. 45–48, 1932. English translation, New York: McGraw-Hill, 1971.

Camera Obscura (Kamera Obskura). Paris: Contemporary Annals, Nos. 49–52, 1932–33. English translation, London: John Long, 1936; American edition with author's alterations and retitled *Laughter in the Dark*, Indianapolis: Bobbs-Merrill, 1938.

Despair (Otchayanie). Berlin: Petropolis, 1936. English translation, New York: Putnam, 1966.

Invitation to a Beheading (Priglashenie na Kazn'). Paris: Don Knigi, 1938. English translation, New York: Putnam, 1959.

The Gift (Dar). Paris: Contemporary Annals, Nos. 63–67, 1937–38 (without the fourth chapter). New York: Chekhov Publishing House, 1952 (complete). English translation, New York: Putnam, 1963.

The Real Life of Sebastian Knight. Norfolk, Conn.: New Directions, 1941.

Bend Sinister. New York: Henry Holt, 1947.

Lolita. Paris: Olympia Press, 1955. Russian translation by the author, New York: Phaedra, 1967.

Pnin. New York: Doubleday, 1957.

Nabokov's Dozen. New York: Doubleday, 1958. (Thirteen short stories.)

Pale Fire. New York: Putnam, 1962.

Nabokov's Quartet. New York: Phaedra, 1966. (Four long short stories.)

Ada, or Ardor: A Family Chronicle. New York: McGraw-Hill, 1969.

Transparent Things. New York: McGraw-Hill, 1972.

MEMOIRS

Conclusive Evidence. London: Victor Gollancz, 1951; New York: Harper, 1951. Subsequently retitled in American reprintings *Speak, Memory*. Revised and expanded edition under latter title, New York: Putnam, 1966.

Drugiye Berega [Other Shores]. New York: Chekhov Publishing House, 1954.

VERSES

Poems. New York: Doubleday, 1959.

Poems and Problems. New York: McGraw-Hill, 1970.

TRANSLATIONS

Three Russian Poets: Translations of Pushkin, Lermontov and Tiutchev. Norfolk, Conn.: New Directions, 1944.

The Song of Igor's Campaign. New York: Random House, 1960.

Eugene Onegin, by Aleksandr Pushkin. 4 vols. New York: Pantheon, 1964.

CRITICISM

Nikolai Gogol. Norfolk, Conn.: New Directions, 1944.

Bibliographies

Field, Andrew. "In Place of a Bibliography" and "Concluding Remarks," in *Nabokov: His Life in Art*. Boston: Little, Brown, 1967.

Zimmer, Dieter E. *Vladimir Nabokov: Bibliographie des Gesamtwerks*. Hamburg: Rowohlt, 1963.

Critical and Biographical Studies

Appel, Alfred, and Charles Newman, editors. *Nabokov: Criticism, Reminiscences, Tributes.* Evanston, Ill.: Northwestern University Press, 1970.

Dembo, L. S., ed. *Nabokov the Man and His Works: Studies.* Madison: University of Wisconsin Press, 1967.

Dupee, F. W. "The Coming of Nabokov," in *"The King of the Cats" and Other Remarks on Writers and Writing.* New York: Farrar, Straus and Giroux, 1965.

Field, Andrew. *Nabokov: His Life in Art.* Boston: Little, Brown, 1967.

Proffer, Karl. *Keys to Lolita.* Bloomington: Indiana University Press, 1968.

Rowe, William Woodin. *Nabokov's Deceptive World.* New York: New York University Press, 1971.

Smith, Peter Duval. "Vladimir Nabokov on His Life and Work," *Listener,* 68:856–58 (November 22, 1962). (Text of broadcast interview.)

Stegner, Page. *Escape into Aesthetics: The Art of Vladimir Nabokov.* New York: Dial, 1966.

ROBERT PENN WARREN

Principal Works

POETRY

Thirty-Six Poems. New York: Alcestis Press, 1935.

Eleven Poems on the Same Theme. Norfolk, Conn.: New Directions, 1942.

Selected Poems, 1923–1943. New York: Harcourt, Brace, 1944.

Brother to Dragons: A Tale in Verse and Voices. New York: Random House, 1953.

Promises: Poems 1954–1956. New York: Random House, 1957.

You, Emperors, and Others: Poems 1957–1960. New York: Random House, 1960.

Selected Poems: New and Old, 1923–1966. New York: Random House, 1966.

Incarnations: Poems 1966–1968. New York: Random House, 1968.

Audobon: A Vision. New York: Random House, 1969.

NOVELS AND SHORT STORIES

Night Rider. Boston: Houghton Mifflin, 1939.

At Heaven's Gate. New York: Harcourt, Brace, 1943.

All the King's Men. New York: Harcourt, Brace, 1946.

Blackberry Winter. Cummington, Mass.: Cummington Press, 1946.

The Circus in the Attic and Other Stories. New York: Harcourt, Brace, 1948.

World Enough and Time: A Romantic Novel. New York: Random House, 1950.

Band of Angels. New York: Random House, 1955.

The Cave. New York: Random House, 1959.

Wilderness. New York: Random House, 1961.

Flood. New York: Random House, 1964.
Meet Me in the Green Glen. New York: Random House, 1971.

PLAYS

"Proud Flesh." Unpublished, 1939. (First performed, 1946.)
"All the King's Men." Unpublished, 1947.
All the King's Men. New York: Random House, 1960.

NONFICTION

John Brown: The Making of a Martyr. New York: Payson and Clarke, 1929.
"The Briar Patch," in *I'll Take My Stand,* by Twelve Southerners. New York: Harper, 1930.
Understanding Poetry, edited by Cleanth Brooks and R. P. Warren. 1st edition, New York: Holt, 1938; 2nd edition, 1951.
Understanding Fiction, edited by Cleanth Brooks and R. P. Warren. 1st edition, New York: Appleton-Century-Crofts, 1943; 2nd edition, 1959; 3rd edition, 1960.
Segregation: The Inner Conflict in the South. New York: Random House, 1956.
Selected Essays. New York: Random House, 1958.
Remember the Alamo! (Landmark children's book.) New York: Random House, 1958.
The Gods of Mount Olympus. (Legacy children's book.) New York: Random House, 1959.
The Legacy of the Civil War: Meditations on the Centennial. New York: Random House, 1961.
Who Speaks for the Negro? New York: Random House, 1965.
Homage to Theodore Dreiser, August 27, 1871–December 28, 1945, on the Centennial of His Birth. New York: Random House, 1971.
John Greenleaf Whittier's Poetry: An Appraisal and a Selection. Minneapolis: University of Minnesota Press, 1971.

Bibliographies

Casper, Leonard. "The Works of Robert Penn Warren: A Chronological Checklist," in *Robert Penn Warren: The Dark and Bloody Ground.* Seattle: University of Washington Press, 1960.
Huff, Mary N., editor. *Robert Penn Warren: A Bibliography.* New York: D. Lewis, 1968.

Critical Studies

"All the King's Men: A Symposium," Folio, vol. 15 (May 1950).
Bentley, Eric. "The Meaning of Robert Penn Warren's Novels," *Kenyon Review,* 10:407–24 (Summer 1948).
Bohner, Charles H. *Robert Penn Warren.* New York: Twayne, 1964.
Bradbury, John M. *The Fugitives: A Critical Account.* Chapel Hill: University of North Carolina Press, 1958.

Brooks, Cleanth. *The Hidden God.* New Haven: Yale University Press, 1963.

Casper, Leonard. *Robert Penn Warren: The Dark and Bloody Ground.* Seattle: University of Washington Press, 1960.

Cowan, Louise. *The Fugitive Group: A Literary History.* Baton Rouge: Louisiana State University Press, 1959.

Cowley, Malcolm, editor. *Writers at Work: The Paris Review Interviews* (first series). New York: Viking, 1958.

Fiedler, Leslie A. "On Two Frontiers," *Partisan Review,* 17:739–43 (September–October 1950).

Flint, F. Cudworth. "Mr. Warren and the Reviewers," *Sewanee Review,* 64:632–45 (Autumn 1956).

Ford, Newell F. "Kenneth Burke and Robert Penn Warren: Criticism by Obsessive Metaphor," *Journal of English and Germanic Philology,* 53:172–77 (April 1954).

Frank, Joseph. "Romanticism and Reality in Robert Penn Warren," *Hudson Review,* 4:248–58 (Summer 1951).

Frohock, W. M. "Mr. Warren's Albatross," *Southwest Review,* 36:48–59 (Winter 1951).

Goldfarb, Russell M. "Robert P. Warren's Tollivers and George Eliot's Tollivers," *University Review* (Kansas City), 36:209–13 (March 1970).

———. "Warren's Tollivers and Eliot's Tullivers II," *University Review* (Kansas City), 36:275–79 (June 1970).

Heseltine, H. P. "The Deep, Twisting Strain of Life: The Novels of Robert Penn Warren," *Melbourne Critical Review,* 5:76–89 (1962).

Hynes, Sam. "Robert Penn Warren: The Symbolic Journey," *University of Kansas City Review,* 17:279–85 (Summer 1951).

Isherwood, Christopher. "Tragic Liberal," *New Republic,* 99:108 (May 31, 1939).

Kazin, Alfred. *Contemporaries.* Boston: Little, Brown, 1962.

Langman, F. H. "The Compelled Imagination: Robert Penn Warren's Conception of the Philosophical Novelist," *Southern Review* (Adelaide), 4:192–202 (1971).

Létargeez, J. "Robert Penn Warren's Views of History," *Revue des langues vivantes,* 22:533–43 (1956).

Longley, John L., Jr., editor. *Robert Penn Warren: A Collection of Critical Essays.* New York: New York University Press, 1965.

Lowell, Robert. "Prose Genius in Verse," *Kenyon Review,* 15:619–25 (Autumn 1953).

Matthiessen, F. O. "American Poetry Now," *Kenyon Review,* 6:683–96 (Autumn 1944).

Meckier, Jerome. "Burden's Complaint: The Disintegrated Personality as Theme and Style in Robert Penn Warren's *All the King's Men,*" *Studies in the Novel,* 2:7–21 (Spring 1970).

Mizener, Arthur. "Amphibium in Old Kentucky," *Kenyon Review,* 12:697–701 (Autumn 1950).

Mohrt, Michel. *Le nouveau roman américain.* Paris: Gallimard, 1955.

O'Connor, William Van. "Robert Penn Warren's Short Fiction," *Western Review*, 12:251–53 (Summer 1948).

Rock, Virginia. "The Fugitive-Agrarians in Response to Social Change," *Southern Humanities Review*, 1:170–81 (Summer 1967).

Rubin, Louis D., Jr. "All the King's Meanings," *Georgia Review*, 8:422–34 (Winter 1954).

Sale, Richard B. "An Interview in New Haven with Robert Penn Warren," *Studies in the Novel*, 2:325–54 (Fall 1970).

Shepherd, Allen. "Robert Penn Warren as a Philosophical Novelist," *Western Humanities Review*, 24:157–68 (September 1970).

Sochatoff, Fred, editor. *All the King's Men: A Symposium*. Pittsburgh: Carnegie Press, 1957.

Stewart, John L. *Burden of Time, the Fugitives and Agrarians*. Princeton, N.J.: Princeton University Press, 1965.

Strugnell, John R. "Robert Penn Warren and the Uses of the Past," *Review of English Literature*, 4:93–102 (October 1963).

Tate, Allen. "*The Fugitive*, 1922–1925," *Princeton University Library Chronicle*, 3:75–84 (April 1942).

Tyler, Parker. "Novel into Film: *All the King's Men*," *Kenyon Review*, 12:369–76 (Spring 1950).

Virtanen, Reino. "Camus' *Le Malentendu* and Some Analogues," *Comparative Literature*, 10:232–40 (Summer 1958).

Warren, Robert Penn. "*All the King's Men*: The Matrix of Experience," *Yale Review*, 53:161–67 (Winter 1964).

Whittington, Curtis. "The 'Burden' of Narration: Democratic Perspective and First-Person Point of View in the American Novel," *Southern Humanities Review*, 2:236–45 (Spring 1968).

Wilson, Angus. "The Fires of Violence," *Encounter*, 4:75–78 (May 1955).

NORMAN MAILER

Works

NOVELS AND COLLECTIONS OF SHORT STORIES

The Naked and the Dead. New York: Holt, Rinehart, and Winston, 1948.
Barbary Shore. New York: Holt, Rinehart, and Winston, 1951.
The Deer Park. New York: Putnam, 1955; Dial, 1967.
An American Dream. New York: Dial, 1965.
The Short Fiction of Norman Mailer. New York: Dell (paperback), 1967.
Why Are We in Vietnam? New York: Putnam, 1967.

OTHER PROSE

The White Negro. San Francisco: City Lights Book Shop, 1958.
Advertisements for Myself. New York: Putnam, 1959.
The Presidential Papers. New York: Putnam, 1963.
Cannibals and Christians. New York: Dial, 1966.

The Armies of the Night. New York: New American Library, 1968.

The Bullfight, a Photographic Narrative with Text by Norman Mailer. New York: CBS Legacy Collection Book, distributed by Macmillan, 1967.

The Idol and the Octopus: Political Writings by Norman Mailer on the Johnson and Kennedy Administrations. New York: Dell, 1968.

Miami and the Siege of Chicago: An Informal History of the Republican and Democratic Conventions of 1968. New York: World, 1968.

Of a Fire on the Moon. Boston: Little, Brown, 1970.

The Prisoner of Sex. Boston: Little, Brown, 1971.

Maidstone, a Mystery. New York: Signet (paperback), 1971.

The Long Patrol: Twenty-Five Years of Writing from the Work of Norman Mailer, edited by Robert F. Lucid. New York: World, 1971.

Existential Errands. Boston: Little, Brown, 1972.

St. George and the Godfather. New York: Signet (paperback), 1972.

PLAY

The Deer Park. New York: Dial, 1967.

POEMS

Deaths for the Ladies, and Other Disasters. New York: Putnam, 1962.

Bibliography

Sokoloff, B. A. *A Comprehensive Bibliography of Norman Mailer.* Limited edition. Darby, Pa.: Darby Books, 1970.

Critical and Biographical Material

Aldridge, John W. *Time to Murder and Create.* New York: McKay, 1966.

——. "From Vietnam to Obscenity," *Harper's,* 236:91–97 (February 1968). Reprinted in Lucid, pp. 180–92.

Alter, Robert. "The Real and Imaginary Worlds of Norman Mailer," *Midstream,* 15:24–35 (January 1969).

Baldwin, James. "The Black Boy Looks at the White Boy," *Esquire,* 55:102–6 (May 1961). Reprinted in Lucid, pp. 218–237; in Braudy, pp. 66–81.

Bersani, Leo. "Interpretation of Dreams," *Partisan Review,* 32:603–8. Reprinted in Lucid, pp. 171–79; in Braudy, pp. 120–26.

Blotner, Joseph. *The Political Novel in America.* Austin and London: University of Texas Press, 1966.

Braudy, Leo, editor. *Norman Mailer, a Collection of Critical Essays.* Englewood Cliffs, N.J.: Prentice-Hall, 1972.

Breit, Harvey. *The Writer Observed.* Cleveland and New York: World, 1956.

Brown, C. H. "Rise of New Journalism," *Current,* 141:31–38 (June 1972).

Burgess, Anthony. "The Postwar American Novel: A View from the Periphery," *American-German Review,* 35:150–56 (Winter 1965–66).

Carroll, Paul. "An Interview with Norman Mailer," *Playboy,* 15:69–84. Reprinted in Lucid, pp. 259–95.

Corrington, J. W. "An American Dream," *Chicago Review*, 18:58–66 (Summer 1965).

Cowan, Michael. "The Americanness of Norman Mailer," in *Norman Mailer, a Collection of Critical Essays*, edited by Leo Braudy. New York: Prentice-Hall, 1972.

Dienstfrey, Harris. "Norman Mailer," in *On Contemporary Literature*, edited by Richard Kostelanetz. New York: Avon, 1964.

Eisinger, Chester E. *Fiction of the Fifties*. Chicago: University of Chicago Press, 1963.

Elliott, George P. "Destroyers, Defilers, and Confusers of Men," *Atlantic Monthly*, 222:74–80 (December 1968).

Flaherty, Joe. *Managing Mailer*. New York: Coward-McCann, 1970.

Foster, Richard. "Mailer and the Fitzgerald Tradition," *Novel*, 1:219–30 (Spring 1968). Reprinted in Braudy, pp. 127–42.

Glicksberg, Charles I. "Norman Mailer: The Angry Young Novelist in America," *Wisconsin Studies in Contemporary Literature*, 1:25–34 (Winter 1960).

Gordon, Andrew. "*The Naked and the Dead:* The Triumph of Impotence," *Literature and Psychology*, 19:3–13 (1969).

Green, Martin. "Amis and Mailer: The Faustian Contract," *Month*, 3:45–48, 52 (February 1971).

Greer, Germaine. "My Mailer Problem," *Esquire*, 76:90–93, 214, 216 (September 1971).

Harper, Howard M., Jr. *Desperate Faith*. Chapel Hill: University of North Carolina Press, 1967.

Hassan, Ihab. "The Novel of Outrage: A Minority Voice in Postwar American Fiction," *American-German Review*, 34:239–53 (Spring 1965).

Hoffman, Frederick J. "Norman Mailer and the Heart of the Ego: Some Observations on Recent American Literature," *Wisconsin Studies in Contemporary Literature*, 1:5–12 (Fall 1960).

Kaufmann, Donald L. *Norman Mailer: The Countdown*. Carbondale: Southern Illinois University Press, 1969.

Kazin, Alfred. *Contemporaries*. Boston: Little, Brown, 1962. Reprinted as "How Good Is Norman Mailer?" in Lucid, pp. 89–94.

Leeds, Barry H. *The Structured Vision of Norman Mailer*. New York: New York University Press, 1969.

Lodge, David. "The Novelist at the Crossroads," *Critical Quarterly*, 11:105–32 (Summer 1969).

Lucid, Robert F., editor. *Norman Mailer: The Man and His Work*. Boston: Little, Brown, 1971.

Ludwig, Jack. *Recent American Novelists*. Minneapolis: University of Minnesota Press, 1962.

Macdonald, Dwight. "Our Far-Flung Correspondents: Massachusetts vs. Mailer," *New Yorker*, 36:154–66 (October 8, 1960).

Marcus, Steven. "An Interview with Norman Mailer," *Paris Review*, 8:28–58 (Winter-Spring 1964). Reprinted in Braudy, pp. 21–41; in *Writers at Work: The Paris Review Interviews* (third series), with an introduction by Alfred Kazin. New York: Viking, 1967.

Manso, Peter, editor. *Running against the Machine: The Mailer-Breslin Campaign*. Garden City, N.Y.: Doubleday, 1969.

Martien, Norman. "Norman Mailer at Graduate School: One Man's Effort," *New American Review*, 1:233–41 (September 1967). Reprinted in Lucid, pp. 245–55.

Millet, Kate. *Sexual Politics*. Garden City, N.Y.: Doubleday, 1970.

Millgate, Michael. *American Social Fiction: James to Cozzens*. Edinburgh and London: Oliver and Boyd, 1964.

Newman, Paul B. "Mailer: The Jew as Existentialist," *North American Review*, 2:48–55 (July 1965).

Peter, John. "The Self-Effacement of the Novelist," *Malahat Review*, no. 8:119–28 (October 1968).

Podhoretz, Norman. "Norman Mailer: The Embattled Vision," *Partisan Review*, 26:371–91 (Summer 1959). Reprinted in Lucid, pp. 60–85.

Poirier, Richard. *Norman Mailer*. New York: Viking, 1972.

Schrader, George A. "Norman Mailer and the Despair of Defiance," *Yale Review*, 51:267–80 (Winter 1962).

Schulz, Max F. "Mailer's Divine Comedy," *Contemporary Literature*, 9:36–57 (Winter 1968).

Sheed, Wilfrid. "Genius or Nothing: A View of Norman Mailer," *Encounter*, 36:66–71 (June 1971).

Solotaroff, Robert. "Down Mailer's Way," *Chicago Review*, 19:11–25 (June 1967).

Tanner, Tony. "The American Novelist as Entropologist," *London Magazine*, 10:5–18 (October 1970).

———. "On the Parapet: A Study of the Novels of Norman Mailer," *Critical Quarterly*, 12:153–76 (Summer 1970).

Toback, James. "Norman Mailer Today," *Commentary*, 44:68–76 (October 1967).

Trilling, Diana. "The Radical Moralism of Norman Mailer," in *The Creative Present*, edited by Nona Balakian and Charles Simmons. Garden City, N.Y.: Doubleday, 1963. Reprinted in Lucid, pp. 108–36; in Braudy, pp. 42–65.

Volpe, Edmund L. "James Jones — Norman Mailer," in *Contemporary American Novelists*, edited by Harry T. Moore. Carbondale: Southern Illinois University Press, 1964.

Wagenheim, Allen J. "Square's Progress: *An American Dream*," *Critique*, 10:45–68 (Winter 1968).

Waldmeir, Joseph L. "Only an Occasional Rutabaga: American Fiction since 1945," *Modern Fiction Studies*, 15:467–81 (1969–70).

Weber, Brom. "A Fear of Dying: Norman Mailer's *An American Dream*," *Hollins Critic*, 2:1–6 (1965).

Willingham, Calder. "The Way It Isn't Done," *Esquire*, 60:306–8 (December 1963). Reprinted in Lucid, pp. 238–44.

Witt, Grace. "The Bad Man as Hipster: Norman Mailer's Use of Frontier Metaphor," *Western American Literature*, 4:203–71 (Fall 1969).

Wood, Margery. "Norman Mailer and Nathalie Sarraute: A Comparison of Existentialist Novels," *Minnesota Review*, 6:67–72 (Spring 1966).

ABOUT THE AUTHORS

About The Authors

ROGER ASSELINEAU is a professor of American literature at the Sorbonne, Paris, and a co-editor of *Etudes Anglaises*. Among his books are *The Literary Reputation of Mark Twain* and *The Evolution of Walt Whitman*.

NEWTON P. STALLKNECHT, professor of comparative literature and criticism at Indiana University and director emeritus of its School of Letters, has written, edited, or co-authored books in comparative literature and the history of philosophy as well as studies in literary criticism.

JEAN CAZEMAJOU is a professor of English at the University of Bordeaux (France). His articles have appeared in *Etudes Anglaises* and other French literary magazines. Among his books is *Stephen Crane écrivain journaliste*.

FREDERICK J. HOFFMAN, who taught at the University of Wisconsin, Milwaukee, was the author, co-author, or editor of a number of books. Among them are *Freudianism and the Literary Mind, The Modern Novel in America,* and *The Twenties*.

JULIAN MOYNAHAN, professor of English at Rutgers University, is the author of three novels as well as a critical study of D. H. Lawrence entitled *The Deed of Life*.

PAUL WEST, professor of English and comparative literature at Pennsylvania State University, has published eight novels, most recently *Caliban's Filibuster* and *Bela Lugosi's White Christmas,* as well as volumes of autobiography and criticism.

RICHARD FOSTER is a professor of English at Macalester College. He has written *The New Romantics,* edited *Six American Novelists of the Nineteenth Century* and *The Novels of Elizabeth Stoddard,* and co-edited *Modern Criticism: Theory and Practice.*

INDEX

Index